PLEASE
NO TIPS ALLOWED

Phone : 43737-41237
Grams : "PRAMMA"

10, Cantonment,
AMRITSAR.

Mrs. T. Bhandari/Miss R. Bhandari

15
VISAS

14
VISAS

المملكة الأردنية الهاشمية
THE HASHEMITE KINGDOM OF THE JORDAN
Emergency Visa
Valid for a Single
Entry Only
No.

Mr S J DRING
BRITISH PASSPORT

Mohd. Gul & Niematullah
RUBBER SCREP MERCHANT

ON THE ROAD AGAIN

For
DOT,
who made my journey complete
and
MY PARENTS,
who let me make it in the first place

ON THE ROAD AGAIN

THIRTY YEARS ON THE
TRAVELLER'S TRAIL TO INDIA

SIMON DRING

BBC BOOKS

ACKNOWLEDGEMENTS

It is impossible to thank individually all those who encouraged me and helped me with my last journey - all the people back in Britain and those I met along the road to India. But without the following, I certainly could not have made the journey, the BBC TV/ Discovery Channel series or written the book: Alison Thomas, Chris Barlas, Susan Laurie, Carol Haslam, Chris O'Hare, Helen Stroud, Christian Holland, Joy Hatwood, Ross Devenish, Rangam Mitra, Nick Comer-Calder, Michael Atwell, Kim Peat, Ron Orders, Sean Carswell, Dan Laurie, Michelle Smith, Bernie Duffy, Julian Sabath, Lisa Harney, Jacqui Timberlake, Adam Peacock, Anne Koch, Judith Melby, Peter Rawlinson, Charlie Hopkinson, Warren Burton, Richard Rosenberg, Reno Antoniades, Marc Berlin, Suzanne Webber, Charlotte Lochhead, Esther Jagger, Jane Coney, David Cottingham, my daughter Tanya and, always, Dot Feast.

This book is published to accompany the television series
On the Road Again which was first broadcast in Autumn 1995.
The series was produced by Convergence Productions Ltd for
BBC TV and The Discovery Channel
Executive Producer: Carol Haslam
Producer: Christopher O'Hare
Directors: Ron Orders and Simon Dring

Published by BBC Books, an imprint of BBC Worldwide Publishing,
BBC Worldwide Limited, Woodlands, 80 Wood Lane, London W12 OTT
First published 1995
© Simon Dring 1995
The moral right of the author has been asserted
ISBN 0 563 37172 2

**Photographs by Adam Peacock, Ron Orders, Sean Carswell,
Daniel Laurie and Simon Dring**

Maps by David Brown
Studio photography by Paul Bricknell
Photograph page 39 J. Allan Cash

Set in Gill Sans and Caslon by BBC Books
Printed in Great Britain by Cambus Litho Ltd, East Kilbride
Bound in Great Britain by Hunter & Foulis Ltd, Edinburgh
Colour separations by Radstock Reproductions Ltd, Midsomer Norton
Jacket printed by Lawrence Allen Ltd, Weston-super-Mare

**Title page: The Golden Temple, Amritsar, India
Pages 6 and 7: Making tracks across the desert beneath the
towering cliffs of Wadi Rum, Jordan**

CONTENTS

INTRODUCTION

'Oh I could fly, I'd fly with thee!
We'd make with joyful wing,
Our annual visit o'er the globe,
Companions of the Spring.'
Michael Bruce (1746-67) 'Ode to the Cuckoo'

On the Road Again is a road movie for the nineties - a story about people getting up and giving something a go, waking up one morning and throwing open all those doors before it's too late. Just imagine: it's another one of those grey, overcast Saturdays, nearly Monday already. It's got to be better than this! Sure, things are supposed to be on the turn, but somehow life doesn't seem to have much of a spark. The news is still full of stories about rising unemployment, rising crime - but not much about rising expectations, except in a political system and an economy that most people really don't have faith in any more. A recent survey said that 50 per cent of the population would up sticks and go abroad if they had the chance. Not forever, of course, but just to have a look, just to know there are a few options left and to have a bit of fun. It's all about taking a risk now and then - and yes, flinging your window open, sticking your head out and shouting, at least once in your lifetime: 'I don't give a damn!'

So why not? How about overland to India for starters? I'm not suggesting you make straight for Dover one morning instead of going to the office (well, maybe I am), but with a bit of planning it's possible - with almost any kind of vehicle. You could even take a bus - or get on your bike. It doesn't take long to get it together - and it's far cheaper than you could ever imagine. Try 50p for a good meal in Turkey and 1p a gallon for petrol in Iran. Or £1.80 a night for a reasonable hotel in India.

It's the classic journey, too. If you only ever make one trip in your life, then let it be this one. It's a voyage through some of the great European and Asian civilizations that formed our world, following in the footsteps of travellers like Marco Polo and the traders who carved out the Silk

Road between China and Europe more than seven hundred years ago. Just imagine: turn left at Calais and keep going. There's an overwhelming sense of freedom when you finally take to the road. You're out on your own now with nowhere to go except forward - and you can forget everything else. There's nobody around to criticize or complain. The horizon is there, not to stare at, but to cross. The black-top highway burns hot from the sun, but the breeze blows cool off emerald-blue seas as you follow the coastline of northern Greece towards Turkey. Istanbul rises out of a shimmering heat haze, a sprawling skyline of mosques and minarets: the gateway to Asia. And eastward, across the vast plains of central Anatolia that lead down through the mountains and sweet-smelling pine forests of southern Turkey, towards Syria and the labyrinthine bazaars of Aleppo and Damascus.... Keep dreaming!

The journey ahead is like a river that runs across the world, a slow-moving stream that weaves and blends the threads and textures of East and West; the colours and cloths; the music and languages; the smells and tastes of all our civilizations. This journey follows a route almost as old as time itself, 'humanity's greatest highway'. For some four thousand years the vast expanse of desert, mountain and plain that lies between Europe and Asia has been the stage for many journeys, through many dreams: for combat and conquest, adventure and commerce, daring and discovery.

Few people realize just how much of our heritage - our knowledge and our learning - comes from the East: from China and India and the great Mongol and Persian Empires. How many of us know that the science of mathematics had its origins in the Middle East and India? That the art of printing and

After you, too, Jean Bowie Shor, an American adventurer who 'gave it a go' in the 1950s

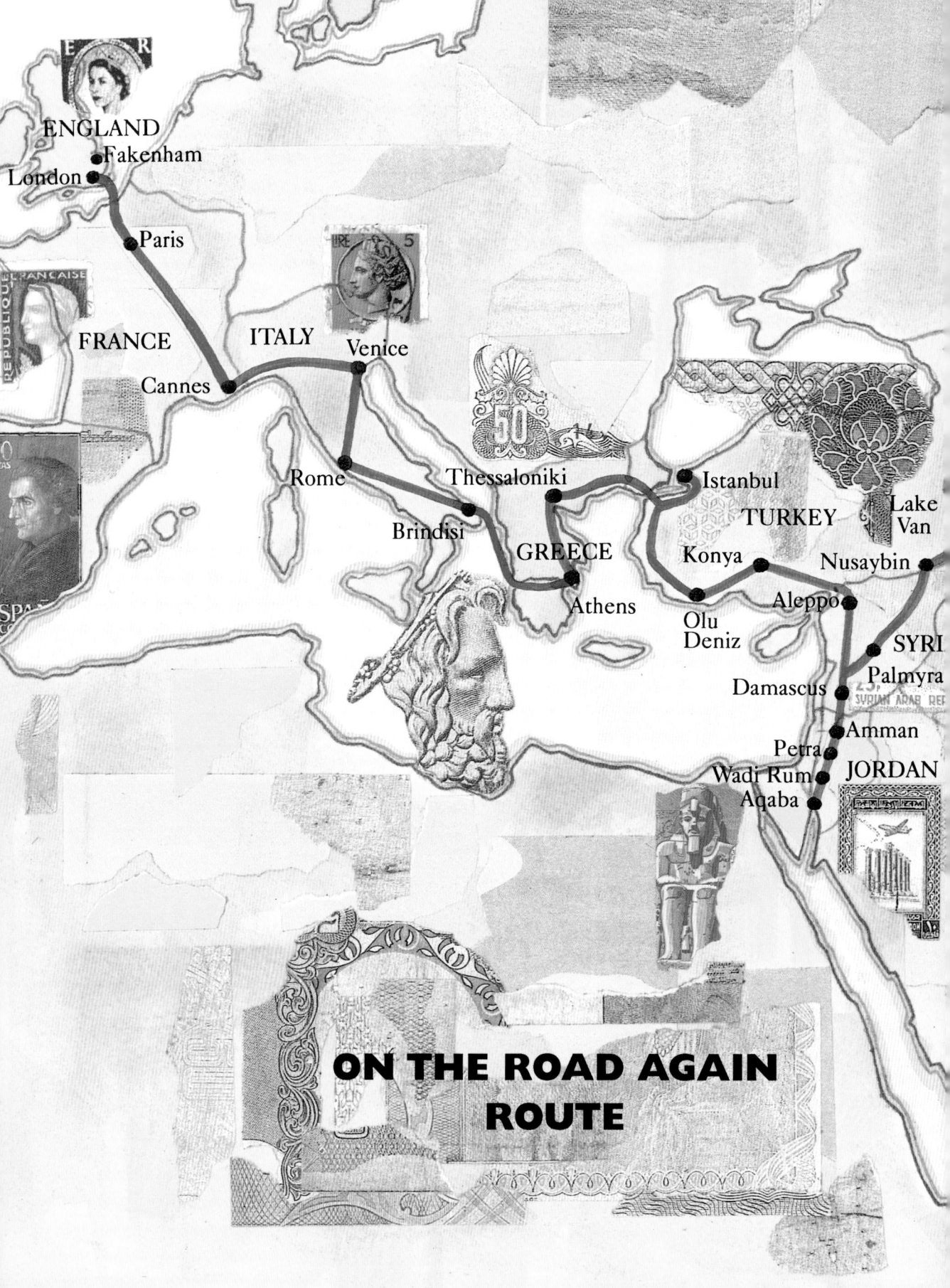

ON THE ROAD AGAIN
ROUTE

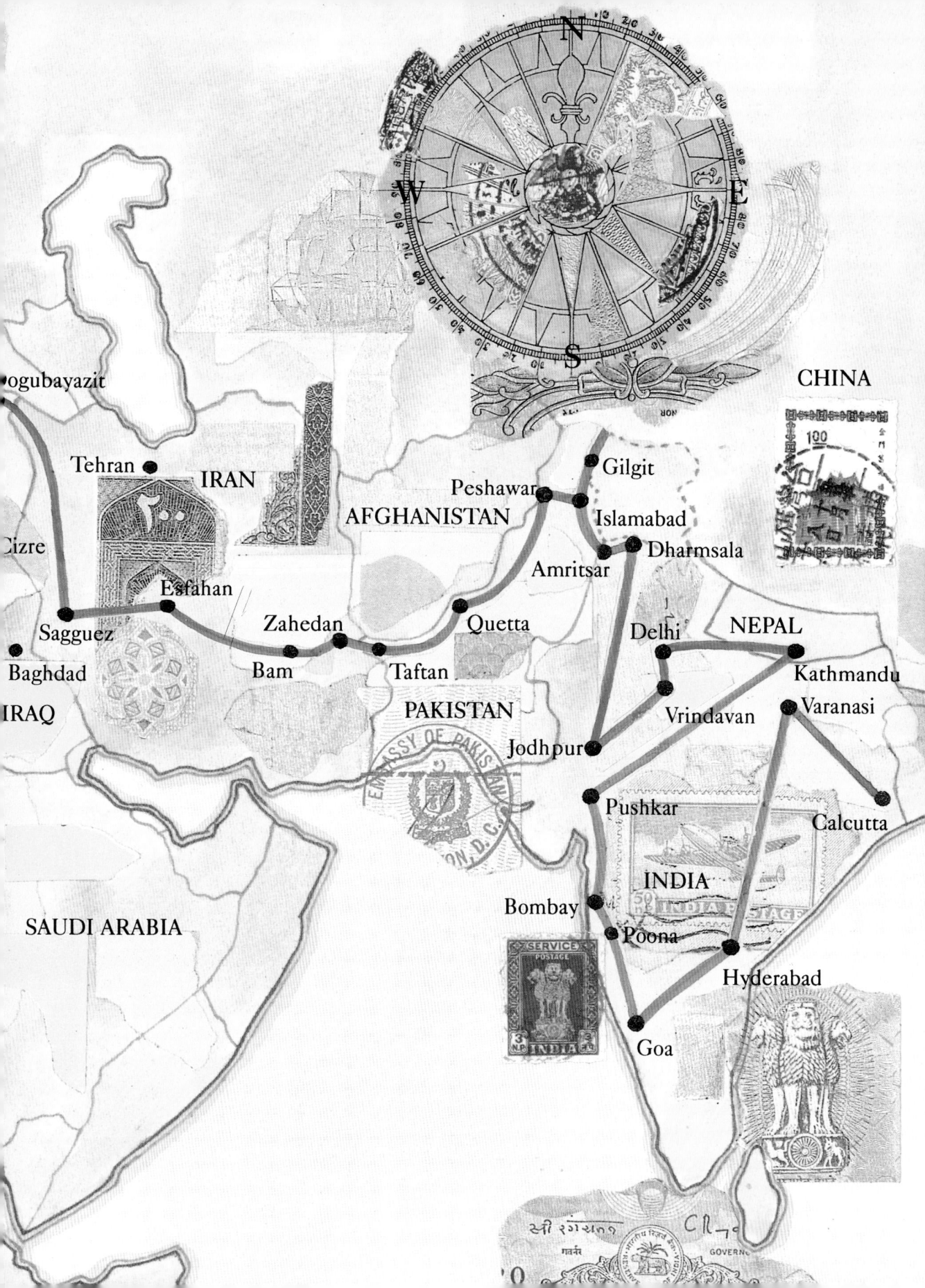

papermaking is an import from China? That so many of our recipes and foodstuffs are Asian? Folklore has it that even pasta first came from China. And forget about America pioneering the fast food business: you could get takeaway meatballs and banana fritters in India way back before the first public cookshop in London started selling roast finches in the twelfth century.

Marco Polo wrote in awe of the civilizations he encountered on his journey East: of ancient cities rising from the sands; of nomad kings in silken robes on gold-encrusted thrones; of lands far richer and more noble than any in the West. Still only seventeen, he wrote as though he was the first ever to travel such a road or to see such things. Since then it has been a journey rediscovered by successive generations - all thinking they were among the first to walk this way, each discovering something new to marvel at or fear. In the nineteenth century and even as late as the 1950s, Western explorers were writing of much the same kind of delights and difficulties along the road East. The hippies of the 1960s and 1970s were in many ways no different: another generation of travellers looking for change, choice and opportunity. They were latter-day nomads, backpacked and on foot, the symbol of a restless youth in search of a new world.

Today, even though the caravan trails have long since been obscured by road and rail, the sense of place, time and direction of the trade routes remains: spices and silks, precious stones, gold, silver and art are still being bought and sold in the markets of Europe and the East. Try Camden Market in London on a weekend; or Anjuna Beach in Goa on a Wednesday. Except for the palm trees, they could be the same place.

The nineties have seen a dramatic rebirth of that old nomadic sixties urge. Many thousands of people - young and old, from all over the world - now make their way eastward by truck and by bus, in a motley collection of cars and vans, as well as by bike and on foot. So what are the travellers of the nineties looking for, and are they finding it? Are their dreams and experiences the same ones that their parents were in search of in the sixties, or that even Marco Polo might have longed for in the

thirteenth century? How much has life on the road changed, and what is left of its history? And how much have the travellers themselves affected the countries and the cultures of the people through whose lives they have passed?

These are just some of the questions I have sought to answer during my journeys out to the East in the early 1990s, and which I have talked about in this book and in the BBC TV and the Discovery Channel series. *On the Road Again* is the story of those journeys as well as the first one I made, back in the summer of 1962 when I was still only sixteen. But mainly it is the story of the people I met along the way in 1992 and 1994, following in the footsteps of all those still finding a new magic and creating a new myth for their times along the road to India.

In truth we are all wanderers with hungry, sometimes hardened hearts, longing to be amazed and inspired and to discover new things about ourselves and the world we live in.

Simon Dring
London 1995

CHAPTER I

Chasing the Cuckoo

Leaving home for the first time

I was always running away from home. Not that I ever took the decision lightly. I mean, I was only sixteen when I finally made it - and had nothing more to sell than my mother's old shopping bike, two coronation commemorative coins and one of those wind-up tanks that blow talcum powder out of their gun. And how much can you save on £1 a week pocket money? Still, what's life without a few risks!

The idea started to take root when I was six going on seven, my imagination fired by all those bathtime stories of Peter Pan, Jack and the Beanstalk and my favourite, Ali Baba and his Forty Thieves. I'd sit there in the tub listening to Father tell that story for what always seemed like the first time, my white, skinny legs pulled up under my chin; the steaming, soapy hot water lapping at my navel; my blue and yellow plastic boats and ducks drifting unnoticed towards the tap end. If I shut my eyes, screwed them up really tight, I could see myself, white robes flapping in the wind, riding off into some huge, blood-red shimmering sunset, my gang of turbaned brigands, heads down, driving their horses across the sands of a wild and dangerous desert.

And then, for my daytime dreaming, hidden beneath the shiny green, leafy overhang of the laurel fence at the top of my parents' Norfolk garden, there was my make-believe friend Watcher. He was the keeper of my secrets and the voice that answered all my questions. I can remember the dry, dusty smell of the earth, the tiny stones digging into my bare knees as I crawled along the bottom of the old wooden fence and under the bushes into the safe, hideaway gloom where Watcher lived.

Watcher also looked after all the things I'd started to put aside for my great escape: the slide-top wooden pencil box with my initials carved on the lid and scribbled in with blue ink; three chewed pencils minus their rubbers; a dog-eared green exercise book; the 1952 Rupert Bear album; and, my most treasured possession, the cuckoo's feather I had found on the lawn by the yew tree. Now, if that hadn't been a sign?

I knew that one morning in early April - every April - I'd be woken by the haunting sound of the first cuckoo, that faraway, echoing call to spring. Pushing back the covers from the warmth of bed, I'd run down the stairs, out of the door, across the meadow and along the path by the river to the woods where I thought I would be

able to see the cuckoo sing. But I could never find her and I knew that by July she would have flown away again, to the other side of the world. I used to discuss all this very seriously with Watcher, the talk always revolving around the question 'What if...?' How would my parents react if I really did run off after the cuckoo? And would I still go to heaven?

I suppose all this restlessness, all this questioning, was to do with a vague but persistent thought in my head that there had to be something more out there than I was being told, both at home and at school. I used to sit in the presence of Watcher believing I was really learning something, solemnly nodding and agreeing, never arguing, living the exciting and the exotic and having adventures that sometimes terrified me in their daring. Watcher made it all seem so different. He was a friend of great loyalty and imagination - and he too believed in chasing cuckoos! He made it all right for me to want to go to all these far and distant lands - nothing like the ones my primary school teacher used to talk about, but remote, mist-shrouded Shangri-Las, lost mountain kingdoms where I'm sure cuckoos went in summer and somehow everything was possible.

Sometimes Aunt Marjorie, my mother's wonderfully wrinkled spinster sister, would take over bathtime, perched in her prickly red wool suits on the wooden lid of the loo, and, in her smoky voice, tell me that all those forbidden things could be mine if only I wanted them enough. 'There was this *man*,' she said once, leaning forward conspiratorially and pinching my cheek, 'but I never even kissed him.' For a brief moment her thickly powdered face and lipsticked mouth seemed frozen in sadness. From her description this 'man' sounded a bit like my dad's brother, Uncle Dick - he even had the same name; so I couldn't imagine why she hadn't kissed him. Come to think of it, she didn't even look shocked when I suggested it might be him. Instead she just said she'd always regretted not allowing herself to go with her dreams. What better, I thought, than chasing a few for her. Anyway, I loved the way she let me stay in the bath longer than anybody else. She'd probably have allowed me to run away, too, if I had asked.

My first attempt was a test, really, trying to find out the answer to the main 'What if...?' question. The suitcase had been packed the night before. No bigger than a sandwich box, it

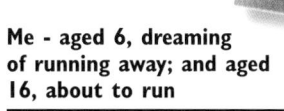

Me - aged 6, dreaming of running away; and aged 16, about to run

was a small battered brown cardboard thing with a single metal catch on the front and a couple of slightly faded Mickey Mouse and Goofy stickers. It was just before lunch when I made the break, slinking into the kitchen - case in hand - announcing tearfully, with my face buried in my mother's tweed skirt, that I was fed up and going to leave home. Then, suitably petulant, I ran into the hall, stretched up to open the huge wooden front door and slammed it again as hard as I could before darting into the dining room and hiding behind the old dark brown leather office chair in the corner.

The answer was shocking: my parents carried on as though nothing had happened, just eating their lunch, talking loudly about 'What a shame it is that he's gone' - but not crying or anything! Just eating their lunch, for heaven's sake! I could even hear the last of the shepherd's pie being scooped out of the dish. I could smell it. They didn't seem to care at all. And they didn't even blink when I finally slunk out from behind the chair and demanded that at least they save me some apple crumble. I never told them this, but that was the day I decided I really would run away. I thought I had found the answer to my question. And I didn't like it!

It was ten years later; one of those blustery, cloud-scudding, bright blue early July days when the greens, golds and yellows, the overgrown, multi-coloured hedgerow wildness of the Norfolk countryside sparkled with what felt like the last rains of spring and smelt like the first flowers of summer. I could only stare out through the car window at the fields of my childhood passing by and try to ignore the gentle swallowing of my mother holding back her tears. My father was staring stoically at the road ahead, his pipe clamped unlit between his teeth. Still

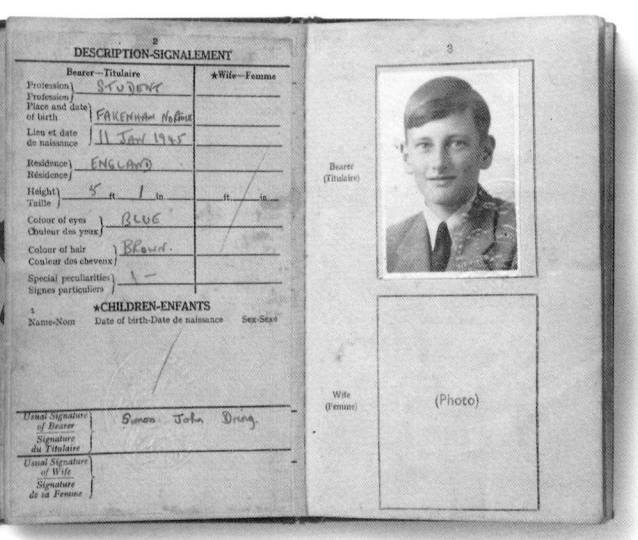

that was typical of him. The new pale green Austin A40 with its leather seats and wooden dash was his pride and joy. He gave it everything he had once he got behind the wheel.

I could feel the second-hand army rucksack beside me on the back seat, its buckles and metal clips pressing into my side. I leant into it, and imagined its weight pulling on my shoulders. I could smell it too. That old, slightly musty canvas smell. So this was it. After all this time, I really was about to leave: forbidden to date or smoke before I was sixteen, 1962 was to be the year of my liberation. They were letting me go and pick grapes in the South of France! By myself!

I know I only had two 'O' Levels and had been

expelled from boarding school at Woodbridge for midnight skinny dipping with a girlfriend in the River Ouse, but Father had been a bit heavy-handed about keeping me on (his idea of) the straight and narrow. That's what finally pushed me out of the door - not anger at him or at my mother, just the need to have a few options and to know a bit more about life, my life.

For a start he had stopped me seeing Vivian. She was my morning vision - every morning - on the bus to the King's Lynn Tech. Short and sweet, with flashing green eyes and enough hair for three people. Wonderfully Rubensesque, like one of the models out of *Nymph and Naiad*, a book of air-brushed, lily-white 'nude' photographs of forties beauties that my father kept hidden in his desk. I knew I was about to fall sensationally in love with Vivian and that, if I was really patient, she might well agree to go out with me - and even let me kiss, really kiss, that full, incredibly kissable country-girl mouth. I hadn't yet got much further than a hand-hold and a quick brush of lips with most of my previous girlfriends. But she wore leather mini-skirts and dyed her hair blonde, and according to my father that wouldn't look too good walking down Fakenham High Street on my arm, mainly, I suspect, because he worked in Barclay's Bank and was on the local council.

Mum and Dad, on the day he got his MBE, in 1962

Then, for much the same small-town snobbish reason, he banned me from Fakenham's only den of vice, the coffee bar, because they had a juke-box and allowed smoking. The points in favour of my going away were mounting steadily! Did I really want to spend my time listening to parental lectures about everything I should or should not be doing for the rest of my life? At least that was my frustrated, restless teenage reaction to what were probably no more than normal, affectionate concerns.

Even so, the romantic idea of my leaving home was really stirred by visions of a global walkabout in search of my manhood - and cheap cigarettes; of shared moments on long and winding roads with flaxen-haired girls; and the shape of some amazing future somewhere out there over the horizon. In truth it was all very innocent, and I had only the vaguest idea where I was going and what I was doing, or how I was even going to get there. Whatever, it all just seemed the right thing to do and the right time to do it. I can only imagine that my parents would have thought this to be the end of their dream of my becoming a banker and the start of what could only be a terrible, wasted life for me. So to make it easier I told them that it was just going to be a month picking grapes in the South of France before coming back to the Tech and cramming for my 'A' levels. That's why my mother packed twenty-two shirts (mostly those awful grey scratchy things from school) in my rucksack - enough so I wouldn't have to wash any before I returned. And now they were driving me to

King's Lynn, to leave me on what my father called 'the proper road to London'.

I think they both sensed that something was up, that maybe I was planning not to come back at all, but clearly nobody wanted to say anything to suggest this might be the case. And then we were there. Goodbyes are never easy, but best said quickly. It seemed like an eternity standing by the side of the road, all the looks, hugs and mumbled words, before my father and mother got back into the car, reversed on to the verge and set off home.

I will always remember the moment I turned to head off down that road south towards London and the Channel coast, the moment of my leaving: it was the first, and maybe the last feeling of true freedom I've ever known. The road in front of me glistened, running smooth and fast into the distance. Even though I heard the sound of my parents' car drifting away behind me I didn't want to look back. I didn't have to - that image, too, would stay in my mind forever: Mum- and Dad-hands waving out of the windows of the little green car, my mother turning in her seat, eyes brimming with tears, trying to watch me until I was finally gone.

I couldn't help smiling. It was like my whole life was opening up before me. Then I swung my pack on to my back and just started walking. It was to be four years and quite a few stories later before we saw each other again. By that time I would be a fully fledged war correspondent hot from the battlefields of Vietnam.

Me on the frontline in Vietnam 1965

I had left home with an overwhelming sense of curiosity - not only about what the world had to offer, but also about myself. Nothing had been planned; I just had a sense that things would probably work themselves out. Being so totally unworldly, so innocent and naive was probably the best thing I could have been for my survival.

In the summer of 1962 it was all beatniks and black furry sweaters - and in London the word was out that the grass was greener (and certainly cheaper) at Chez Popoff's in Paris; that Fats Domino was to headline at the Antibes Jazz Festival in the South of France; that if one could then get across Yugoslavia in one piece, the price for a pint of blood in Greece was at an all-time high. Istanbul was definitely the end of the road. At least that's what I thought.

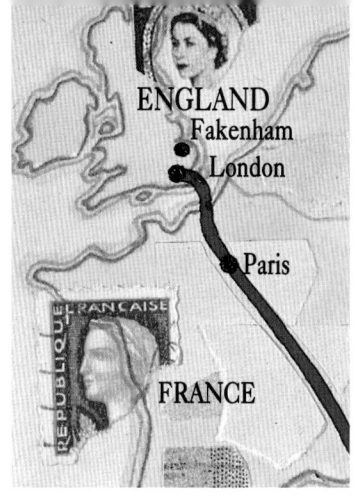

CHAPTER 2

On the Road Again

The genesis of an idea

I had been lying in the shade of a small clump of rocks for two days with no food and only half a canteen of water. I couldn't go any further. I was too tired and it was too hot. I tried walking at night, but it was 300 kilometres to Zahedan, the next town. The desert seemed endless. Getting a lift was not going to be easy. The road south was just a trail and there had been no traffic since a truck appeared over the horizon and drove past, its lights out, just before midnight. Three months after I had run away, supposedly for a month's grape picking in France, I now found myself in the middle of the Great Sand Desert in Iran.

It was 24 September 1962, and the letter to my parents I started in the desert that day was my first attempt to explain the reasons for my disappearance and to try to help them understand what I was trying to do. It also tried to reassure them that everything was fine, under control, despite the fact that I was now well past my due-back date and pressing on regardless across the world - in the opposite direction to Dover. In fact I had already travelled more than 13 000 kilometres eastward!

The tone was determinedly innocent and casual - as though it was the most natural thing in the world for a sixteen-year-old Fakenham boy to be doing. In a way it felt like that too. I didn't dwell much on the bleaker side of the story in my letter, but in fact I was down to my last few pennies, sleeping under the stars, hungry and dirty for days on end. And yet I felt completely satisfied. Maybe that's what freedom represented to me then - the freedom to do what I liked, when I liked, how I liked - yet still survive and, most importantly, succeed.

The letter, penned in scratchy black ink, eventually covered eight large sheets of crested paper obviously nicked from an Iranian police station - of which I had seen many. They were always 'inviting me in' to check my passport and practise their English. My letter was written over ten days and completed shortly after I made it to the Iran-Pakistan border. It began:

'Dear M and D,
I hope you are both well and not worrying too much about my general welfare, because there is no need to worry, I am perfectly well, and am having a ball. I know you were probably rather upset when you realized I was not coming home just yet, but it was something I had to do. I left home knowing that I was going

to try something like this, but what form it would take I did not know....I will be away for a maximum of five years! But as soon as I have found what I'm looking for, learnt what I want to learn, filled my desire for knowledge, I'm coming straight home. I will now give you a rough sketch of my trip, it will only be rough because to tell it in detail would cover a full-length book, which I am in the process of writing, as well as I can.'

Of course, that's just what a penniless teenage hitch-hiker would be doing on his way to India! Well, it's taken me thirty-three years to get round to finishing that book - starting it, even!

What really gave me the idea of retracing my 1962 journey was finding a collection of my letters home in my father's safe shortly after his death in June 1991. Or maybe this was all just an excuse for me to go off wandering again. Certainly, after so many years as a foreign correspondent, what was appealing was the idea of travelling simply for the sake of travelling. Since Vietnam in the sixties, I'd covered seventeen wars and revolutions and spent a lot of time in Africa, the Middle East, Iran, Pakistan and India. Great survival training - but not very relaxing. Needless to say it didn't take long to convince myself to get out there and try it again.

With much enthusiasm, but little in the way of cash, I set off for India in the summer of 1992 to produce *On the Road Again* as a series for BBC Radio 4. The first programme was broadcast in the summer of 1993, and the series was repeated just before Christmas 1994. It was the success of the radio series that then sparked BBC TV and the Discovery Channel to commission a television version of the journey.

Retracing my steps once is fine; retracing the retrace is another thing. But somehow in the summer of 1994 the idea seemed as fresh and as exciting as it had only two years earlier. I would soon find out.

Of course it's cold and wet, and it's British - the morning, that is. It's Saturday, 27 August 1994: 5.30 a.m. is not the best time for anybody, especially when it comes to departures. Family and friends standing at the end of driveways waving handkerchiefs, that's how I'd always imagined these kinds of farewell. Shadowy figures rapidly disappearing in rear-view mirrors, hands fluttering just like my parents' all those years ago.

Except in this case it's people peering out through the steel-grey gates of a converted primary school shouting things like 'Have a good one!' An austere red-brick business centre in south-east London is hardly the most glamorous place to leave from on an epic overland journey halfway around the world.

No matter how many times I've done it, the thought of taking on this trip is always quite humbling - 29 000 kilometres from the UK, through France, Italy, Greece, Turkey, Syria, Jordan, Turkey again, Iran and Pakistan, to India and Nepal. My fellow travellers for the next six months are Ron Orders, a respected and experienced director-cameraman and a bit of an old hippie himself (he drove overland to India in the late seventies); Sean Carswell, an Australian video-age kid on board as second cameraman and sound recordist; and my nephew Dan Laurie, a film and tape editor, as the production manager. But it's the production coordinator, Canadian-born Michelle Smith, who probably has the best job of all, travelling on ahead of us - by bus, train or plane - just in case we need hand-holding somewhere down the line!

Already tired, wet and emotional: 9.30 a.m. departure for (from the left) Dan, Sean, me and Ron

Right now, though, our brains are a bit numb. We've been up all night trying to pack the vehicles - an almost new red and black Jeep Wrangler, a hard-top with its back seat taken out, and a white, eight-year-old short-wheelbase diesel Land Rover with a roof-rack. I've christened the Jeep *Wah Wah*, which is Hindi for 'the greatest'. Indian music fans shout it a lot when they get excited over their favourite track. I thought I might as well give our Jeep a bit of a confidence boost before letting her loose on the road to India.

We have also been testing our new camping gear - struggling to put up the self-standing tents in the school playground just to make sure we know what we are doing. We don't. Neither Dan nor I have ever done much camping. But, as with everything else, we are going to have to learn, probably the hard way, somewhere out there over the next horizon.

In any event we've resigned ourselves to the fact that time has already run out - and that preparing for a journey like this is, for the most part, a matter of common sense. But for all of us the trip is also going to be a demanding and no doubt changing experience. The big problem right now - with only an hour left before we must leave - is how are we going to fit everything in? We've got a 9.30 a.m. ferry to catch

Who'd take the tunnel when there's a chance for a last look at old Blighty?

from Dover and we want to take all we need with us. That's everything for four people for six months. We're trying to look efficient, but the truth is we are just winging it, bumbling around in the drizzle and half light of a London dawn showing off, not very effectively, in front of our assembled farewell team of partners, girlfriends, family and assorted production hands. There are just so many boxes: the equipment, including three Hi-8 cameras and a DAT recorder; hundreds of hours of video and audio tapes, batteries and other supplies, not to mention all the back-up gear; spare parts for the vehicles; extra fuel and water jerries; my computer and printer and all my research folders; tents; cookers, plates and cutlery; clothes and minimal personal belongings; medicines; books and cassettes; and a 'goodie' box, a surprise package packed by Ali, a long-time friend, on the strict proviso that it is not to be opened until we are in 'real need'. I can only guess it must be full of ridiculous luxuries like chocolate pop tarts and unthinkably delicious home-made jams. How long before we are really desperate? Calais perhaps?

We're going as travellers, not as film-makers, which means that all our equipment has to be broken down and packed to look as innocent as possible - a dangerous but necessary move. Countries like Syria and Iran are not known to be very welcoming when it comes to filming. It's not that we are out to spy or do anything other than follow the travellers' trail and talk with any travellers we might meet. But it quite simply wouldn't work if we had to operate under the kind of supervised filming that would be expected of us in many countries. And as far as the travellers are concerned it's important for us to be sharing the experience, not merely visiting it. How could we even begin to produce a series called *On the Road Again* if we didn't get out there and live it for ourselves?

So the journey is to be made in real time, dealing as best we can with whatever problems might arise; and with purposely limited funds of a maximum of £70 a week each to spend on food, hotels when necessary, and other travelling expenses. Still, this is doing it in style compared with my journey in 1962.

I had never been to Dover before. But I had always seen it in my mind as a town of sunlit Victorian terraces, beachfront promenades with views as far as France, and seagulls swirling over the churning wash of the ferries heading out into a blue and grey-tinged sea. The white cliffs, I imagined, would be a dramatic final curtain on my sixteen-year past.

It was, of course, completely different - but no less for that. It was the being there that mattered, even though it was wet and cold and the cliffs looked desperately in need of some bleach. I had had my first night sleeping rough - curled up in a bus shelter in Canterbury, completely confused about my new role in life, but thrilled at how dangerous and daring it all felt. So by the time I clambered up the gangplank to the ferry I was very conscious that I was already beginning to look a bit travel-worn (i.e. scruffy and dirty), but none the less congratulating myself on getting through my first day on the road. I was a real beatnik - a bum at last! My first letter home said:

> *'Well, I arrived in France on Sunday 15th of July. It was raining hard. I was lucky and got a lift to Boulogne that night with two French students in a Citroën. I was well stocked up with whiskey and cigarettes off the boat, so that kept the cold out. I slept the night on a bench in Boulogne and the next morning I set off for Paris....'*

I had £25 in my pocket, the proceeds from selling my bike and, unknown to my parents, the coronation commemorative coins. But by the time I left for Paris I was already down to £17.

Ron is like a dog in a basket - a new basket. He spends much of the trip down the M2 to Dover 'getting the Jeep comfortable', as he puts it, packing bits and pieces away under the passenger seat, beside the seat and in front of the seat, and sticking up lucky charms from his friends. He jams a wooden giraffe over the top of the

rear-view mirror and super-glues a sort of bug-eyed piece of Maori witchcraft to the dashboard. God knows what his friends are wishing on him! And then there is his large collection of music cassettes (place: beside the seat). But more about them later. My side's clear - so far!

Behind us, as they would be for most of the journey, are Sean and Dan in the Land Rover; 'the boys' are undoubtedly already having a go at 'yuppy Jeeps' compared with the 'real-man' qualities of a 'macho Land Rover'. From the way they're swaying around they must also be testing out Sean's love and joy - their 360-watt, multi-speaker, Clarion sound system. The crew car, as Ron calls it, has already become a mobile disco. We're all feeling very new.

Dover slips into view through the drizzle as we fumble around for our passports, carnets, insurance papers and everything else we haven't yet sorted out among the mountains of clutter that fill both our vehicles. Then we have to smile for the camera - PR pictures to mark the start of our trip - standing in the pouring rain in front of the P&O ferry to Calais. Photographer Peter Robain is unhealthily cheerful and outspokenly envious. How can I suggest that we might be feeling anything less than exuberant about the journey ahead? Nobody would understand. I mean, who wouldn't want to spend six months on the road - *and* be paid for it? Well, at least the crew's getting paid!

We don't bother to go up on the deck of P&O's *Pride of Kent*. The squalls of rain are so heavy and so frequent that Dover has gone before we can even find the restaurant. Despite the pitch and roll of a heaving Channel, our thoughts, of course, are on only one thing: our last English breakfast. A huge, greasy fry-up. We're so predictable! I make a half-hearted suggestion to Ron that we film ourselves eating. Idea not well received. Nobody's eyes leave their plates of bacon and eggs, their mounds of buttered toast and steaming cups of hot, sweet tea. This is like a serious religious event. A bit like arriving in France, really. We've cut the cord now. Turn left at Calais and just keep going.

They don't stamp passports in France any more. They don't even ask to see them as we drive through immigration and customs. I don't care so much, but I can see that Sean and Dan are going to make a major effort to get a bookful by the time they get to India. Perhaps they should learn to read maps first. We follow them for a while and get totally lost in the relentlessly dismal back streets of Calais - and we're only looking for a money changer. We're also looking for food. That should

have been OK, but Sean made me feel a little nervous by suddenly going a bit sur-real on us. I don't know where it came from, but the idea is immediately rejected. 'Fried thrush on toast!', he says. 'The frogs eat thrushes, don't they?'

Our first night isn't much more together, either. We drive 500 kilometres south from Calais, and end up in what appears to be a large camp site set back among the trees beside a lake near the market town of St Dizier. Ron shows immediate boy scout tendencies (he was, he tells me, banned from the real thing after being thrown out of the cubs) and starts making tent erection look easy (even in the dark) while Dan struggles, less than elegantly, trying to assemble the pressure cookers. I have a go at them too, almost as incompetently, while Sean starts being technical and cool with all the video and sound recording gear. We haven't filmed a frame yet. We haven't bought any food either. But we are all so tired, as much from the tension of the last three weeks as the lack of sleep the night before, that we turn in by ten - just before the wind picks up and a storm breaks. Well, at least it's a French storm!

The sound of the rain on the tent helps, the sleeping bag is like heaven and the stone I can feel under my back isn't yet beginning to bother me. We're abroad and, yes, I really am on the road to India again. But I know already that this is going to be a very different experience. Travelling on my own in 1962, without any precon-ceptions, without any expectations, without any planning even, is something I could never repeat. The magic of first discovery was so completely fresh. Today, try-ing in some way to relive and film that experience, and to share the discovery of others' journeys, travelling with all this equipment and three people, is going to involve a way of working that in itself will detract from that experience. For a start, we will probably have to put a lot of effort into just getting on with each other.

None of us has spent much time together. I met Ron for the first time only three weeks earlier. The only bond between us so far is our professional commitment and our shared enthusiasm for the idea. Six months is a long time to be cooped up in the same vehicle. I'm certainly not a group traveller, or a camper, at least in an organized sense. Ron, on the other hand, obviously is. Well, he knows how to deal with it, any-way. You know the type! Of course he has one of those 'go anywhere, fit anything', slimline air mattresses that keep you insulated against damp and cold, as well as stopping all those rocks from grinding into your spine and your bum; he has a miner's headlamp for easy, hands-off reading; a small, pretuned short-wave radio for bedtime listening; a special, compact pillow - and God knows what else stashed away in his tightly packed, diminutive case-cum-rucksack. Oh well, learning to share a tent with a travel genius was obviously something I would have to get used to - if I didn't kill him first!

CHAPTER 3

The Word is Out

Heading south through France and Italy

I've woken up in what seems to be some kind of Euro holiday camp. Not exactly good for my traveller's cred. Our rough-and-ready safari set-up, the vehicles bristling with spotlights and bull-bars and all the other long-distance survival gear, is surrounded by ordered lines of brightly coloured bungalow tents and caravans, red-brick outdoor barbecues and blow-up swimming pools nestling among the pine trees. It's 7.30 on Sunday morning and, thankfully, most of the happy campers are still sleeping off Saturday night. The rains have passed and a brilliant fresh sun is calling us south. Ron's up early too, demonstrating his outdoor skills again, brewing a pot of coffee to give a lift to a miserable breakfast of stale rolls and jam (with leaves in it already).

We start the inevitable 'forgotten to bring' list: a grip for the steadicam (that we'll never use); 'c'-sized batteries (of course we have every other size except that one); a set of Indian maps (for some reason we got German ones) ; a BBC short-wave band book (all Ron's presets seem to be wrong); Dan's travellers' cheques (left in a drawer); and elderflower water from the Body Shop for me (well, it saves washing sometimes!). But who-does-what seems to be falling into place: Ron puts the tent up; I take it down and pack *Wah Wah*; Dan and Ron cook; Sean and I wash up; Dan deals with the roof of the Land Rover; Sean the inside. This is all getting a bit too organized for my liking.

Ron and I are ready and off a few minutes ahead of Sean and Dan. I put my foot down, with Canned Heat and 'On the Road Again' pounding away on the Jeep stereo, and drive out on to the main road, turning left towards Paris. A mile later we stop and wait for the boys to catch up.

They don't. They just disappear. Ron and I drive up and down the road for about three hours, but they are nowhere to be seen. And ahead of us lies a maze of autoroutes, N-roads, E-roads and any number of choices as to how to reach southern France and Italy. Not a good start for us intrepid overland travellers! I wonder how the rest of the world is getting on?

After the depressive, stay-home slump of the late eighties, **Next stop: the Greek islands**

there's a new generation of young people on the road these days - doing it nineties-style, but in some ways no different from the hippie culture of the sixties. There's no trace of beads and flowers, though - this is all trainers and lycra leggings, cut-off jeans and baseball caps, Walkmans and shades, all colour-coordinated and techno-casual. Over the next few days I see them everywhere. At the height of summer the backpackers are out in their tens of thousands, heading south from Calais, crossing the borders from Belgium and Germany, on their way east from Spain and France, crowding bus stops and train stations across Europe, mostly heading to Italy and down to the cheaper, warmer climes of Greece and the Greek islands.

These are the fresh-faced first-timers in their teens and young twenty-some-things shaking up their lives before it's too late, out for a taste of away-from-home-freedom - and a bit of partying as well. They're probably next year's travellers to Turkey, the Middle East - and maybe even India. They talk excitedly of the places they've heard about, the places they're going to go and how nobody back home ever expected them to make this kind of trip. They talk big, but few have any idea what they are doing or the kind of problems they might face on the road. Those problems are mainly to do with never having enough money; losing what money they do have; or having everything stolen.

Clumps of travellers everywhere. They're slumped on the pavement outside the Gare du Nord in Paris trying to work out their next move and deal with getting by on £5 a day. They don't even know how to read a train timetable, let alone make their way round Europe on the cheap. They're going to Greece - student train tickets and hitching. They've got these books about travelling on a shoestring, but at the end of the day it's a lesson they will have to learn the hard way.

**Terry Cripps - still one
tee-shirt left**

Terry Cripps from Hackney in London is twenty-one and on his first trip to Europe - his first anywhere, in fact, apart from the occasional weekend rave outside London. He too has made it as far as the Gare du Nord, but is already beginning to look a bit frayed around the edges, with a sweaty tee-shirt, torn jeans and a plastic water bottle hanging from his belt. It's night and small groups of travellers are bedding down against their packs, in sleeping bags on the floor of the station waiting rooms, and stretched out along benches in a nearby park. There's a few hours to kill before the next train to Italy. Terry is there too - but he almost didn't make it through to the next morning.

'This place is known for being rough,' he tells me, 'but because I'm from London I thought, well, I know my way about, I can handle any problems. So I kipped in

the park where five Spanish boys approached me and said, "Don't sleep on that bench, where the street light is on. You stick with us, we'll be safer all together."

'Well, I woke up in the morning and there was thirty of them Spanish boys, knife to me throat, their hands all in me bags. They roughed me up a bit, kicked me all round the park, then run off with £120 and me best tee-shirt. And that was just me second day travellin'. It's luck, really - you can have a couple of good strokes or you can just bugger it up, you know. But hey, listen, I'm having a good time - even with an incident like that.'

Like an already seasoned traveller, Terry isn't to be deterred. Somehow, as he puts it, things will work themselves out. When I last saw him he was getting ready to board a ferry to the Greek islands, funds depleted but still smiling. 'The word's out,' he said, 'I can earn a few quid working the bars. That should do me.'

In 1962 the word was out to watch your pack as well, but it was all much more laid back. The word was also out that the hottest spot in Paris was Chez Popoff's, a café in the heart of the Latin Quarter, the centre of student and beatnik life. Chez Popoff's was supposed to be the *place - where the marijuana was the best (and the cheapest) and where you could leave your pack and it would still be there a day later.*

I had to go there. I had no idea why, but somehow that was part of being on the road. To me, going to the Latin Quarter and a place like Chez Popoff's was more important than visiting the Eiffel Tower. I was told the Latin Quarter was where love and peace, sex and drugs went hand in hand. I saw it all as part of some romantic dream: every café crowded with famous artists and writers; every huddled group in a darkened corner plotting revolution; every club le best jazz *in town; every cigarette a joint. This was life for the beat generation - and for the hippies, too, a couple of years later.*

I remember looking for Chez Popoff's, wandering down the Rue de la Huchette, a narrow, winding alley full of cafés, with the houses leaning in on each other. In the dark of a warm Paris night it all seemed very wild and wanton, recklessly subversive. I had no idea how to behave or what to do. But then I found that everybody just said 'Hi' and started talking. Forget all those frustrated dreams of afternoons on the pinball machines at the Fakenham coffee bar. This was it!

Chez Popoff's was everything I had hoped for...steep stairs into a dark and dingy basement; rooms thick with smoke and noisy with chatter and laughter from all the beats and their girls; small round tables strewn with half-empty coffee cups and wine glasses; hot, hot sounds on the turntable; and a lot of black hairy sweaters and duffel coats.

I stayed up all night; had my first (and second and third) lungful of grass; passed out briefly under a table; reckoned I really grooved at a Russian jazz club; sang in the street with a group of buskers; dozed in a doorway with a curly-haired German girl - and left the next

day, amazingly only four quid lighter but with my first dose of the runs! Then came my first piece of luck, I wrote home, leaving out the drugs and the diarrhoea:

> *'I got a lift in an E-type Jag from Paris all the way to Antibes. We touched 120 mph [190 kph], several times. He was an American student going to the Riviera to waste money.*
>
> *We reached Cannes and Antibes on Wednesday the 18th July....There I spent the days of the festival [Antibes Jazz Festival] with bums from all over Europe.... They were marvellous. We had newsreel pictures taken of us and my picture was in the paper... glued to my seat watching the jazz....*
>
> *There were riots, we slept on the beach, in the fields, and I had £15 stolen...but we used to play guitars around the cafés and on the front, sing and paint, for money of course.'*

Not enough money, considering I now had only £2 left. But somehow we all got by, occasionally supplemented with a bit of shoplifting (the odd loaf of bread and some cheese). And my sleeping bag was a green and white canvas mattress cover removed, in the dead of night, from a private beach in Juan-les-Pins. It would last for the rest of my journey.

Although eager to impress my parents with my 'Boy's Own' adventures, I was also careful to keep the letters reasonably well sanitized. I never told them, for example, about the story of another lift I got, a few weeks later, in Italy. This time it was a Ferrari, but again with a rich young American. He lavished meals on me and even insisted on putting me up in a room in the hotel where he was staying in Milan. Not just any hotel, mind you, but the best 5-star hotel in town. Can you believe I was that naive? Even though, later that night, I resisted his open flies and frantic gropes and persuaded him out of my room, he at least had the decency - and the sense of humour - to leave a few lire for me in an envelope ('for services not rendered') at reception when he checked out early the next day.

We're driving south, over sweeping green hills, through blazing yellow fields of sunflowers and picture-book Alpine towns - the palm-fringed elegance of the Côte d'Azur and the Italian Riviera in our sights. We had finally linked up with Sean and Dan again, two days after losing each other. Michelle, still back in London before flying out to join us in Istanbul, had been sworn to secrecy: we had all used our common sense in the end and phoned home, so she had been able to arrange a rendezvous. Of course Ron and I blamed Sean and Dan, and they blamed us. They had turned right because it was south - without realizing that the road swung back to the north. We turned left because we'd read the map and realized it eventually went south. We'll all read the map together next time.

The Europe we're now crossing is no longer the beat and hippie mecca it used to

be. In the mid-sixties Paris, the South of France, Rome, Athens, the Greek islands and Istanbul were as far as the trail went. Today, for example, the Rue de la Huchette looks more like a promotion for the Greek Tourist Board. Every other café is a taverna, and where once there was the sound of jazz these days it's listless, boot-stomping bazouki music. Nearly everybody seems to be called Andreas and nobody has heard of Chez Popoff's. There isn't a hairy sweater in sight - just crowds of jostling, camera-wielding Japanese and American tourists.

The journey is passing in a blur of motorways and gypsies selling terrible food by the side of the road. And on the move like us. The gypsy man's eyes are as hard as coal nuggets, darting and suspicious beneath his furrowed black brows. Stefan is about to hitch up his caravan alongside the N1 south of Paris, preparing to head towards the sun for the winter, along with all the other gypsies working the tourist routes through France. He and his brother Pedros - with crumpled white shirts, tight-belted trousers and greasy felt hats pushed back on their heads - pose awkwardly in front of their roadside stall with its baskets of hard-boiled eggs, a tray of slightly yellowing sandwiches and the inevitable cans of Coke. Centuries earlier, their ancestors had drifted west from India and settled in North Africa and eastern Europe. Time has

Assembled gypsies - not quite the kings of roadside cooking

erased all memories of that epic migration and the promise of what it must have held. Stefan says he sometimes wonders whether things might have been different, but shakes his head at the thought of any shared roots between himself and an Indian. He and Pedros really have no idea what they might be missing out on or just how much of their history - all our histories - might have worked itself out along this road east.

The South of France is a manicured and outrageously expensive glitter-dome, and snooty with it - a bleak, unpromising experience for most backpackers. Unless you're a beach-brown blonde with your top down, or your limo has Swiss plates,

don't try cruising on the Croisette in Cannes. Yes, I actually got asked to move along - or be arrested. Apparently anything less than being five-star is not encouraged. A couple of gendarmes decide that any vehicle with camping gear in the back (i.e. mine) does not belong.

There are still a few travellers around, hanging out and sleeping in the parks, but they're not having much luck. Mark Devine and Paul Dundan, both eighteen and from Ireland, are trying to busk their way to Italy.

'It's like we've got AIDS or something,' says Mark. 'The police harass us all the time and keep trying to move us along - any other town as long as it's not on the Riviera.'

Hitching is a problem too. 'Very few stop,' says Paul. 'Any sign of a rucksack and you have no chance. Still, the hassle's worth it just to be out here getting all this experience.'

Maybe - but as far as I'm concerned it's good riddance Riviera, I'm off to pitch my tent in the hills and eat one of Dan and Ron's spag bols!

And after France? The war in the former Yugoslavia only adds to travellers' problems in Europe. To reach Greece most now have to take the long way round, south through Italy. Not many are prepared these days to run the risk of following the Adriatic coastline through Slovenia and Croatia.

Seven hundred years earlier, Marco Polo, the great Italian explorer and the world's first real travel writer, was equally unprepared for what he found after he set off from Venice on his journey to the East. When he left in 1271, still only seventeen, the world was still thought to be flat - uncharted and dangerous. To most people this was a world dominated and terrorized by the advancing Mongol hordes. After Marco, his uncle and father had left they were presumed to have gone for good - and were all but given up for dead even before their departure.

More than twenty-five years later three men in coarse, tattered garments, clutching an assortment of bundles wrapped in brightly coloured cloths, stood staring up at the shuttered windows of a faded, three-storey house in the back streets of Venice. Their faces were bronzed and lined and they spoke in a slang that the servant answering the door could hardly understand. The Polos had long been forgotten. The three men had to force their way into their own house and endure several hours of questioning from relatives and neighbours before anybody would believe it was them. No doubt their argument was helped when they cut open the seams of their clothes and spilled a fortune in precious stones - rubies, diamonds, emeralds and pearls - on to the table!

The parents of the young American and Canadian backpackers arriving at Rome's Fumincino airport and of the many other nationalities, dipping their feet into the fountain at the foot of the city's famous Spanish Steps, probably feel much the same way about the world as Marco Polo's relatives did. Italy has one of the worst reputations for the mugging of travellers and in particular the harassment of girls. But all that tends to be forgotten on the beaches along the Sorrento coast south of Naples as the midday heat slows the pace of life towards another siesta. It can make all those nights sleeping out, all those days without showers, all those meals without enough food so much easier to bear. The temperature in central Italy is close to 27°C, but by the time we reach the southern port city of Brindisi, on the very heel of Italy, and take the overnight ferry to the Greek mainland, we are sweltering in the mid-thirties.

At the height of summer as many as forty thousand travellers a day bottleneck through Greece - and most can be seen on the docks at Piraeus, near Athens, the first great gathering place along the road East and the sailing point for the islands, Turkey and the Middle East. The docks here are a sea of bobbing, swaying backpacks, a mass of stooping figures on the move, searching for somewhere to settle or marking time in the shade. It's all the bare legs that strike me most - and the dirty toes sticking out through the sandals and flip-flops. I feel very overdressed and am trying hard to be eternally youthful. A few weeks around here and I might even succeed!

Nicola Cadwallader is twenty and laughs a lot. Blonde, tanned and dishevelled - and smelling of the sun - she leans against her pack in the shade of an old wooden doorway. Nicola came to Greece with £80 and now has £150. She reckons she's got travelling down to a fine art and can live and work on the road and go home with a profit to put towards next year's journey.

'Maybe I'll spend the rest of my life working in Greek bars,' she jokes, almost seriously, 'just so I can go on travelling.'

Nicola sounds as naive as I was back in the sixties, but in a way she's also typical of the new breed of nineties traveller, fired by the romance of a life that seems to offer so much more than she can find back in Oxford where she was brought up and still lives with her parents.

'I can't stand the weather back in England, the thought of a nine-to-five job and being stuck in an office,' she explains. 'I'm too young for all that. I want to go away and see mad waterfalls and huge canopies of trees - see everything.

'Travelling for me is all about freedom, about waking up the next morning and being able to go somewhere without any worries, even if I don't have a map. It's made me so much stronger, more confident, helped me grow up a lot.

Jame's left luggage locker -
home of Elvis and friends

'I just followed the gang before - now I can say to people: "I think what you're doing is wrong." Travelling should be part of everybody's education, you know. Maybe you have to go away for a year on your own, without any money, and see if you can survive.'

It's the kind of sentiment the Greeks understand. 'Left Luggage' James would like Nicola to leave her bag in his doorway. He's been there for a good many years now, with his eccentric collection of film posters and Hollywood paraphernalia hanging in the entrance to the disused customs hall he's allowed to use for his business.

'But if they no want, they don't do,' he says. 'You know these people, they are so young. So beautiful.' And he laughs. He doesn't care really.

Maybe he's got the spirit of Zorba in his soul - at least, that's what he says. He's not going to press them anyway, but produces a bottle of wine instead. They sit for an hour or so in the shade and talk.

'Somehow I never thought I would feel so free to be what I like,' says Bill, a young Canadian traveller, 'or that a sunset would look so good.'

Sarah, his friend from New York, agrees. 'I know when I get home,' she says, 'I'll be a different person. It'll be like I'm seeing everything for the first time.'

Somebody picks up a guitar and starts to strum a Greek song. Sarah, barefooted and bold in her tight tank-top and shorts, her long blonde hair swaying down her back, stands and starts dancing along the pavement. And Andreas, all black curly-chested and gold chains, slides across from the next-door ticket shop to join her. They move sensuously together, laughing in the late afternoon sun. People stop and watch. Somebody starts clapping - the slow, steady clap of a long, hot Mediterranean summer.

It's time to start filming. Our journey has begun.

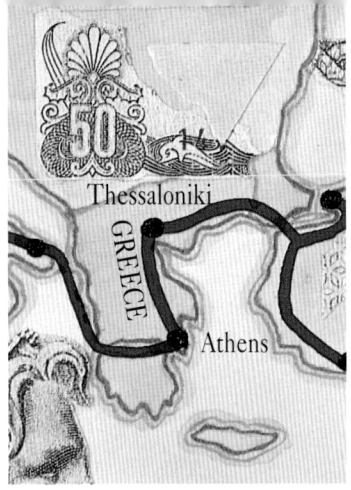

CHAPTER 4

Living Rough

Learning the hard way in Greece and the islands

It's late one evening somewhere between two Greek islands, and Captain Michalis is falling in love with Sean. You can tell from the sideways glance of his heavy brown eyes, the way they slip across Sean's face and delight in his youth, in the physical ease with which he is stretching across the table and scooping up the glistening black olives. Well, everything can be forgiven on such a sensual Mediterranean night as the ferry slides quietly into another port. In any case, it's all very unashamed and innocent. The captain's pleasure is little more than an ageing man's fantasy, an aching perhaps to reach out and touch his own youth. But of course Sean, six foot and apparently surfer fit, sees it only as an assault on his very Australian manhood. For a twenty-three-year-old taking his first steps along the road to India the world is quickly becoming a stranger, much more alien place - as threatening as it is sometimes enthralling. By my map we have now covered nearly 2500 kilometres - only 26 500 to go! I can't wait. But Sean is already pining for Kylie, hopefully still being a long-suffering and faithful lover back in Fulham.

We leave the vehicles for a few days to follow some travellers round the Greek islands. There were times when the four of us sailed into yet another sunset that we felt we must be featuring in a long-distance remake of Cliff Richard's *Summer Holiday*. In reality there's a lot of innocence being lost on our way across these trembling Greek waters.

The sun is starting to slip over the horizon. A bugler, dressed in a billowing white

Bedding down - or passing out?

smock and thigh-high black boots, steps forward. The sound of the Last Post rings out over the docks at Piraeus, and a contingent of Greek sailors lowers the flag as the evening ferries ease out to sea. Our boat moves fat, low and slow in the water, a dark shape against the pink and grey spread of a glowering sky, its engines throbbing quietly far below, its decks a sprawl of bodies - hanging out, or passing out. The air is soft and warm, stirred by the cut of the huge, gently rolling prow; the smell is of a turning, salty sea and just the faintest trace of the day's heat and oils still lingering. Scattered fragments of words, snatches of shouts and laughter, and the chords of a guitar fly with the breeze away across the waves in our wake. It's hard not to feel a bit breathless with the romance of it all - a sense of wonder perhaps, especially if you've never before been afloat in a starlit dream like this.

Settling in for the night are Will Bower, Louise Middleton, Mel McNaught and Matt Smith, four teenage friends three weeks out from the West Country, cutting their teeth on overland travel with some of the last, but best, days of the summer still ahead. And every day seems to bring a new discovery.

'When we were in Corfu, we met some Dutch people and got on really well with them,' bubbles Will. 'Then that night we were all in a restaurant eating and these two Germans came and sat down and started talking about politics, music - everything. And you know they knew how to express themselves in *our* language, which made us feel a bit small. But we have built this bond with these German and Dutch people and we've got such a good friendship now.'

'Yeah, it's amazing,' adds Louise, just eighteen, 'it's like such a unification between countries. We spoke to these Germans again yesterday before we split, and they said these have been the best days of their lives.'

So what is it that's *not* being taught at school - or at home for that matter - that even educated, middle-class kids like these should feel so isolated and should be so ignorant about some of our closest neighbours in Europe?

'I think a lot of people are quite bored in England, frustrated and cut off by the system,' says Matt. 'They don't know there are options and they don't really know what to do with themselves. They might see something like drugs and rave music as the easy way out. All some want to do is get off their heads and stuff. I think personally you can get a much better high out of life, by pushing yourself and travelling, seeing beauty and everything, rather than pumping yourself up with some godforsaken drug.'

Louise agrees. 'We've all experienced that sort of thing, but I decided before I came away that there's so much to see, so many more natural and more beautiful things to do. I don't want to sound like a hippie or anything, but I have such a feeling of freedom when I'm away from home, when nobody can touch me, you know,

when I'm in a different country and I'm around orange trees and lemon trees and all that - it's like paradise. Now I really appreciate what I have at home - I really appreciate English nature. As soon as I get back I'm going to go for a long walk and have a nice take-in of all my countryside....'

'Aah,' says Captain Stamatis, breathing deeply, sighing Greekly, leaning over the bridge of his ferry as another glorious dawn breaks. 'How good it is to pass these days feeling so free. Look at them - they are like flowers in a garden. What a wonderful morning - every morning, when everybody is so close to each other.'

Long before Marco Polo passed this way towards the East, and the Venetians and the Greeks commanded these unpredictable waters, Roman galleys forged trade and passenger routes through the Mediterranean islands between Europe and the Middle East, churning the seas with their oars, slaves dying under the flaying whips of the galley masters, while above them the privileged basked under gold embroidered awnings.

Captain Stamatis describes how in Roman days the galleys carried cargoes of oil and ingots, corn and cotton stashed in huge urns below deck. Storms often forced them to spend days at anchor near these islands, sheltering from the winds and the waves in small bays and inlets. When the storms passed, tradition had it that an offering of thanks had to be made to the gods.

Simon and Jonna, from Los Angeles, tell how earlier this summer they had slipped over the side of a rowing boat into the still, clear blue waters of the Fontana Amorosa - the Fountain of Love, a small cove on the island of Cyprus. Diving down below the surface of the water they discovered a wonderland of Roman artefacts, of urns half buried in the sand, welded into the seabed by the centuries that have passed since they were thrown overboard. The freedom for Simon and Jonna was to spend days on end sleeping out on the beach, cooking fresh fish over a campfire and not worrying or caring about the fact that they had almost no money and no idea where they would go next.

Gill and Steve - scumming out

In much the same way, two twenty-one-year-olds, Gill Handie and Steve Brand, met in Dudley, West Midlands, and took off across Europe without much thought as to where they were going and what they were doing. Not showering for days on end, not being able to afford to eat very much, just living rough is all part of the experience.

'You grab a shower when you can,' says Steve, rearranging their bed on the deck of one of the overnight ferries. 'That's part of the fun of it, being totally scummed out.'

'It's a big test for me too,' laughs Gill, her brown curly hair looking as though it's been unwashed and uncombed ever since they left England two weeks earlier. 'I've got no foundation and no hairdryer, just a bit of lipstick in the bottom of my pack. My mum would cry for me!'

'The thing is,' adds Steve, 'the harder it gets the more it makes you appreciate it when something good happens. We've had bread and cheese today and it's never tasted so nice. You just get it out of the fridge at home, but when you actually have to try and buy it or find a shop that's open it's quite an achievement.

'We know so little about all this, even about Europe. They don't teach us at school anything except things like the battle of 1066, the siege of Colchester and the Roundheads and the Cavaliers. We're very ethnocentric, you know: "The British way of life is the best way of life."'

'When we finally get to Ios,' adds Gill, 'it will be brilliant because we have worked so hard to get there. But if you don't try it you'll never know what's out there. So I think everybody should have a go.'

In 1962, I wrote to my parents about the 'liberating' experience of living rough. To them, back in Fakenham, the first month or so of my journey must have seemed like a nightmare of extremes. And I didn't always try to hide it:

> *'In Venice, I slept under a bush, and by the way, there happened to be a thunder-storm that night too. Still, that's life. And the next night it was a haystack....*
>
> *Then I got a lift to Zagreb with a French couple going to Bulgaria. By then I was down to about 5 shillings [25p], but cigarettes are only 4 pence [2p] for 20 there, and that's all I needed....*
>
> *In Belgrade I was sleeping in the local park when at 1 a.m. the Special Police woke me up, examined my papers and let me sleep in the jail, with breakfast thrown in....'*

In Greece, I told them, I lived off unripe green melons and the occasional stolen chicken, spit roasted with its feathers on because I couldn't bring myself to pluck it. I wrote to my parents about how I now knew what it was like to be 'penniless, hungry, cold, wet, dirty, smelly and really tired' and how I had had to sell 'my black sweater and several of my [twenty-two] shirts' just to get by. 'Thanks Mum, but p.s: miss your chocolate pudding. Oh, and can you make sure Viv has my address.' I obviously hadn't found any flaxen-haired girls yet. I sup-pose it didn't help, having no money.

Apart from my trade in second-hand shirts, I also sold my blood.

The bridge across the Corinth Canal

I got £3 for a pint of it in Greece - but they refused a second one. There was a two-week return limit and they sprang me when I came back to the hospital pretending to be a German student.

All this nose-down-in-the-dirt stuff made me feel much the same way as Gill and Steve. 'I'm being challenged all the time and discovering there's so much more to me than I thought,' says Steve. 'I know I'll feel more confident about myself when I get back.' With a new sense of optimism for the future too, perhaps!

Most of the travellers we meet on the beaches and islands of Greece say they're dis-illusioned with all the consumerism back home. They're revelling in the freedom of discovering it's all right to do all these things - to stay up all night and sing to the moon over Heraklion, or dance on tables until dawn at the Pink Palace on Mykonos.

Like so many travellers looking to earn money, Catherine and Dylan from Portland, Oregon, have been working tables; Jamie from Toronto bar-keeping; Spider from Sydney harvesting sweetcorn. They're saving to extend their journeys on to Turkey and the Middle East - or India even.

Today is Sarah's last day on the island of Heraklion before heading off to Turkey. She's heard that a few of her friends might be heading for Butterfly Valley, a remote beach only accessible by sea, halfway down the Turkish coast towards Syria. She climbs to the site of what is said to be Homer's tomb for a last afternoon in the Greek sun. The tomb was first discovered by Paasch van Krienen, a Dutch sailor, in 1770. It's a large grass mound on top of a high cliff with a view as far as the eye can see towards the next horizon. In the distance, we hear the steam whistle of the incoming ferry. It will be leaving for Turkey in an hour. Sarah, a country girl from Wales as she describes herself, picks up her pack and, with a last glance out to sea, heads off down to the coast again.

Like so many other writers, Marco Polo, in his book *Description of the World*, extols the virtues of the freedom that travel brings. An American woman in the early fifties, making her way to India following in his footsteps, wrote: 'Seeking out the unknown corners of the world breaks the mould of my life and liberates my soul.'

We are crossing many bridges between many worlds: Corinth, Athens, Marathon, Olympus and beyond. It's a relief in a way to be back behind the wheel of *Wah Wah* again. Only ten days on the road, but already she's beginning to feel a bit like home. She certainly looks like it. The back is more ordered, but the collected *en route* clutter is beginning to appear, especially on my side. There's a sunflower stuck up behind Ron's giraffe atop the driving mirror, as well as some Greek prayer beads of some kind or another for luck.

We're probably going to need it - sooner or later. We are struggling through the scorching heat, the eye-watering pollution and the noisy chaos of downtown Athens. From one of the city's eight hills we thrill at the sight of the Acropolis, but it's hard to recognize that, along with Rome and Jerusalem, this is one of the three great seats of culture that have most influenced the Western world. Greece today seems to have lost touch with its past - that's just preserved in a museum somewhere!

In the distance, as we head north, the great peaks of Mount Olympus, birthplace of the gods, tower over the flat and dusty lands of Macedonia, homeland of one of the most influential figures in Greek history: the legendary Alexander the Great, perhaps the most famous of the world's marauding colonizers. In 334 BC, Alexander, still only twenty-six, led a vast army east from here towards Turkey and the great lands of Persia. Over the next seven years he succeeded in driving the Arabian and Persian armies back across the Middle East to the very gateway of India. Although he was out to crush and to conquer, Alexander ended up wearing flowing robes, marrying an Afghan princess and being rejected by his men for 'going native'. He never returned home. Even Marco Polo, carrying letters of friendship from the Pope, dressed in skins during stages of his journey east. He stayed away for a quarter of a century. They might not recognize it yet, but the nineties travellers, much like the hippies in the sixties and seventies, can't fail but be affected by the experience. I stayed away four years and came back a foreign correspondent.

None of us have donned our robes yet, but we've learnt a few tricks by now - about how to survive and adjust to a new pace of life, driving up to 350 kilometres every day, camping, cooking - and filming. Ron's looking settled; Dan's looking tanned; and Sean's looking increasingly suspicious about this strange world that's unfolding about us.

We are on the road heading east along the northern Greek coast. The port city of Thessaloniki is one of the richest and most politically volatile cities of Greece. But never count on a quiet cup of coffee around here. Andreas Petronis (nearly everybody seems to be called Andreas in Greece!), felt hat firmly on head, sitting in the shade with his friends, is holding forth to anybody who'll listen. He reckons the world would be a much better place if Maggie Thatcher was still in charge. Few seem to know much about John Major and nobody has even heard of Tony Blair. Today's debate was stirred by an old farmer who had dared to speak out against Maggie. They shout abuse at him, charge all the coffees to his account and eventually throw away his tatty straw hat. Even from the political graveyard, Maggie appears to have some kind of mythical hold over the imagination of this group

of farmers and shopkeepers longing, they say, for a return to discipline and order in Greece.

A dangerous lot, these people! Don't ever try talking about the days, at the turn of the century, when this part of Greece was actually Turkey; or raise the violently unpalatable truth that moussaka, the most nationalistic of all Greek dishes, was in fact Asian in origin and was introduced into the culture by some upstart cook from the court of the Caliphs in Baghdad!

The trail east from here towards Turkey is now a heavy-duty tarmac highway, with a heat haze of exhaust fumes over what used to be a quiet backwater of white-washed fishing villages. You don't pass many kids with their thumbs stuck out any more - they mostly wait for the local buses, fighting their way on past the goats and the black-shawled grannies, squeezing three to a single loo-sized seat. Some travellers have their own wheels. Paul, Bronwyn, Nikki and Liz - one guy and three girls from New Zealand - are in a lime-green combi called *Just Missed* that has to be push-started each morning. But the spirit of it all is still alive. Just around the corner: a Frenchman and his dog, ambling along, stick in hand, pack on back.

Only 6000 kilometres to go - José Ramon and Diva

I don't suppose Diva, a six-year-old Alsatian, had much of a say when José Ramon decided to walk to the Middle East on some kind of personal pilgrimage. She's even got a backpack and has to carry her own doggie bowl, travelling snacks and a bottle of water. José, a wiry, super-fit sixty-eight-year-old retired policeman from near Lyons, thought she would miss him if he walked the 6000 kilometres to Jerusalem without her. 'Apart from that,' he laughed, 'she needs the exercise.'

All of us - dogs 'n' all - are now in head-long confrontation with increasingly strange cultures and traditions. But the small, deserted beach tucked up against the Turkish border offers little to be afraid of - its pebbled shoreline washed by a gentle morning swell of blue-green sea. The beach isn't much to sleep on and we could do with a bath, but somehow the sunrise seems all the more sweet and special for the fact that we are now already more than 3000 kilometres along the road east, and ahead of us lies Istanbul - the Gateway to Asia.

CHAPTER 5

Gateway to the East
The road to Istanbul

In many ways nothing seems to have changed, even though more than thirty years have passed since I first went to Turkey.

'Istanbul is one of the most magnificent, fascinating cities in the world, and the Turkish people are the kindest, most hospitable people in the world. I love Turkey....'

My letter home to my parents in 1962 could not have been more over the top in its praise for all things Turkish. It's not surprising, really, considering how kind and generous the Turks were to me when I first found myself, penniless and alone, on the streets of Istanbul:

'After 5 minutes there was a crowd of about 30-50 standing around. I was really lost though and could not speak a word of Turkish. Then a Turkish student, Mebrur Sengil, walked up, who spoke English, and invited me to his home. There I stayed for 10 days. They would not let me spend anything, although I had nothing. Even if I had £100 they would not have let me spend anything. I went all round Istanbul, the islands, the mosques. I swam, I sailed, and went to the cinema....'

But I didn't tell them about how my virginity was severely shaken when Mebrur and his friends decided I should visit a 'public house'. I thought it was a pub, not a legally licensed, sealed off street where every house was a brothel and naked girls sat in doorways and let you feel their breasts - for free (and none of us had even had a real kiss yet!). We ran giggling into the night, virgins still.

Thirty years later I'm walking down the narrow residential street in Topkapi, on the outskirts of the city, where Mebrur and his family used to live, hoping to find them again. The dark, wood-slatted houses, the cobblestones and the deep shade of the narrow, vine-covered courtyards have all gone, replaced by low-level concrete apartment

PALACE HOTEL
MILAN

Dear M & D,
Could you please
adress of your cousin
TO BE COLLECTED

address

SIMON DRING,
% MEBRUR SENG
MILLET CADDESI K
No. 35 Kat 3

TOPKAP
ISTANBUL

This is the only place where y
you at the moment as everyth
muddle. If you have
name will do
the ad

buildings, two-storey brick houses and a tangle of overhead power cables and television aerials competing for roof space. But the small green mosque is still there, the corner shop, and the café where the men sit on their rush-seated chairs and play backgammon all day over glasses of sweet, black tea. It's got the feel of a Turkish *Coronation Street* about it.

Word spreads fast. A crowd begins to gather. There's a foreigner looking for Mebrur Sengil. A few people shake their heads. They've never heard of him. Someone says he's moved. Then I learn that, in fact, he's dead - from cancer - but that his family is still living on the street. And he was married as well. There are two daughters.

A shortish, stocky man with greying hair, sleeves rolled up and a black flat cap pushed back on his head comes out of the corner shop, pointing at me and laughing. 'We play football here in the street many years before,' he shouts in Turkish, seizing me by my shoulders and kissing me noisily on both cheeks. The crowd loves that. More than fifty people are now getting into the spirit of what is clearly regarded as a significant moment in the life of the street. Everybody wants to help, translate, be or do something in this play.

And then Mebrur's mother arrives, old, plump and beaming, dabbing the tears from her eyes with a faded black apron. She remembers me in embarrassing detail - like when I threw up all over her hallway after my first drink of raki. The crowd loves that one even more.

The party goes on until very late. Family and friends, Mebrur's widow and their two very excited daughters all cram into a small room, drinking raki and cola, overeating on endless bowls of nuts and fruits and Turkish sweets. And I am proudly shown the pencil box I had given to Mebrur's younger sister all those years ago, the one with my name inked on the top from when I was six and planning my first great escape.

'We would like to thank you,' says a tearful uncle offering one of the many toasts of the night, 'for honouring the memory of Mebrur. When we shared our homes with you before it was not in the hope that you would repay us, but that one day you would remember us and come back.'

This is the basis of the deeply embedded sense of hospitality towards foreigners that made me feel so good about my first visit to Turkey. And Turkey today is not all that different - a bit more worldly-wise, even cynical perhaps, but no less generous in the way that even the poorest people seem willing to throw their homes open to strangers.

These days, driving into Istanbul is not exactly the romantic moment one would hope for as the door to Asia swings open. But what reality fails to deliver the

imagination can more than cover. Certainly, the promise of a spectacular dawn over this great city is all too often obscured behind a rising cloud of pollution, the legendary skyline of cascading domes and spiralling minarets having to fight its way through a murky haze to reach the sunrise sky. But the glory of this city's past is immutable. It's everywhere. No matter how overcrowded or polluted, Istanbul will always be that bridge between East and West and retain a sense of place unique in the world.

For centuries the city was the capital of civilization, a three-thousand-year-old masterpiece, its buildings, its art and its culture steeped in the history of the Byzantine and Ottoman empires. There are other churches more elegant and rich in design, but none can match the sheer architectural brilliance and scale of Haghia Sophia - for nearly a thousand years the greatest house of worship in Christendom, then a mosque for five hundred years after Turkey fell to the forces of Islam.

Everybody has loved this city - and fought for it too. In 340-339 BC, Alexander the Great's father, Philip of Macedonia, stormed its stone walls and took Byzantium, as it was called then, in a night. But in the fifteenth century Mehmet the Conqueror, the infidel Arab king, struggled for nearly two years. Marco Polo described in his book how Mehmet finally won the day. Apparently he had one of his engineers design the biggest cannon ever made, which would hurl huge iron balls from more than a mile away. It took three hours to reload between each shot - but it worked.

Ron is filling me in as I manoeuvre the Jeep through the noisy chaos of the city's streets, producing a treasure chest of information mainly, I have to say, from a boxload of Lonely Planet guidebooks. But it's mostly what you can see and feel yourself that makes a journey like this work - not what you read in books.

Today, in the old quarter of the city, just as it was in the sixties, the narrow, winding streets are full of cheap hotels and rooftop pensions where the air hangs heavy with the smell of marijuana. And the Pudding Shop, the original hippie haunt, is still there. For the price of a glass of tea or a bowl of one of its sickly-rich chocolate, vanilla and caramel 'puddings', the owner would let travellers hang out all day, shoot the breeze, strum Dylan riffs and wash in the lavatories.

Overleaf: Sun-up over Haghia Sophia, Istanbul

When I first went to Istanbul in 1962 there were no tourists - it was just the beats and then the hippies - and the Pudding Shop was the centre of the known universe for them all. It was also the end of the road. Few people went further than Istanbul in the early sixties. But one by one, the trail-breakers started drifting off across the waters of the Bosphorus and on into Asia. By 1966 the hippie highway to India was well under way. The start of the 'hash and hepatitis' trail, according to some.

It's hard to imagine all that now. The Pudding Shop is a shiny fast food showcase (all beans, meat and rice - and puddings, of course), living off its memories and a wall covered with framed newspaper cuttings. There are a few travellers around - but it's not quite what it used to be. The notices on the message board still advertise things like 'a spare seat' in a van going to India, but only the occasional classic: 'Lucky Jim,' said one, 'waited for three days, had to go. See you in Kathmandu for Christmas. Love. Thin Lizzy.' I love it. I only hope there's still a ghost army of travellers out there somewhere - pinning poems to trees, leaving messages on sticks and stones, and planting flags in the deserts or on the tops of mountains.

Russell Roberts, a thin, twenty-seven-year-old, long-haired Australian, looks like the kind of traveller who might be one of them. I find him summoning Aboriginal spirit birds through the deep, moaning sounds of his didgeridoo in a small park near the Pudding Shop. A Turkish sailor, three carpet salesmen, a taxi driver and a shoe-shine boy sit listening in amazement. Russell is typical of the new nineties' hippies, whose lifestyle and business are trading between markets around the world. He makes his own didgeridoos in Australia, sells them in Europe, then with the proceeds buys jewellery and carpets in Turkey and the Middle East to take back to Australia. He's saving to buy land for his lady and their two children.

'I see myself as me, but some people say I'm a hippie because I've got long hair and a didgeridoo. I get classed as a hippie, whereas I'm just a person. But if a hippie is about being young and free, then I'm a hippie.'

Adem, the son of one of the original owners of the Pudding Shop, remembers those days with pleasure. As a young boy, washing up and serving in the café, he grew his hair long to be like his hippie heroes. 'Things have changed,' he shouts above the noise of the lunchtime crowd and the soul music on the record player that once used to turn with Dylan. 'Everybody was so much more relaxed before. The hippies had no money, but they smiled a lot and talked with us all the time. They were a bit strange to look at, though,' he adds, laughing. 'Turkish people thought they came from Mars with all their long hair and beads. I used to see them going by the bus stop outside and the people there would watch with their mouths hanging open - and then miss their bus.'

A great deal has changed since those days - not least Turkey and the Turks. Adem now sports American trainers and jeans, his hair is short and he's quite recently shaved off his moustache. The Turks are sick of being seen as 'pot-bellied, hairy-lipped barbarians', he says.

Just down the road, in the famous Grand Bazaar, Mehmet feels much the same way. The bazaar is no longer the dark and mysterious place it used to be, with its smells of spices and leather (Turkey is famous for its leather jackets and coats) and the sound of raucous, hard-nosed bargaining. Today the act is more polished and the place much brighter. The Grand Bazaar almost looks like an upmarket shopping mall; certainly it has the prices to match. Standing in the doorway of his leather goods shop Mehmet proudly points out that 'we're nearly part of Europe now. I pay more than 2000 dollars rent a month for my store.' He's also saving for a shiny new Mercedes. 'Hey, there's a Turkish song,' he tells me, 'that says a man made good drives his Mercedes everywhere - even to the loo.' My translation, not his exact words - but accurate all the same. Mehmet is smoothly irrepressible in his search for profit, offering tea and cola to every passing foreigner, especially the girls - the thought of a potential sale, a new Mercedes, or a wife perhaps, always in mind.

In a way the changes in Turkey also reflect the changes in the travellers. Outwardly, most seem much more organized than in the sixties - quite a few accountants now, young farmers even, dipping their toes in the fast lane, looking for a taste of the exotic, travelling in organized groups. No bedrolls and joints here - this is all frame tents and cooking rotas. But there are also still a lot of people on the move by themselves - chasing the cuckoo of their dreams and living a life on the road that in many ways is no different from the one I lived. A new generation, one step further on than the first-timers in Greece, an older, restless youth, hungry to discover, in search of change, choice and opportunity. People from all over, of all ages. And there are even some who are still travelling, twenty years or so since they first set out, just like Marco Polo.

Whoever they are, Adem reckons that there are certainly more of them out on the road in the nineties than there were all through the eighties when the Iranian revolution, the war in Afghanistan and then the Iran-Iraq war effectively disrupted the route east, making overland travel almost impossible for several years.

Ibrahim at Londra Camping, Allah's little acre of grass by the side of one of the noisiest highways leading into Istanbul, agrees. He should know - quite a few have passed through Londra in the twenty-five years he's been managing it. For many this place, run down as it is, was also the start of the hippie trail. Overlanding to India makes you part of an exclusive club. Sooner or later most of its members

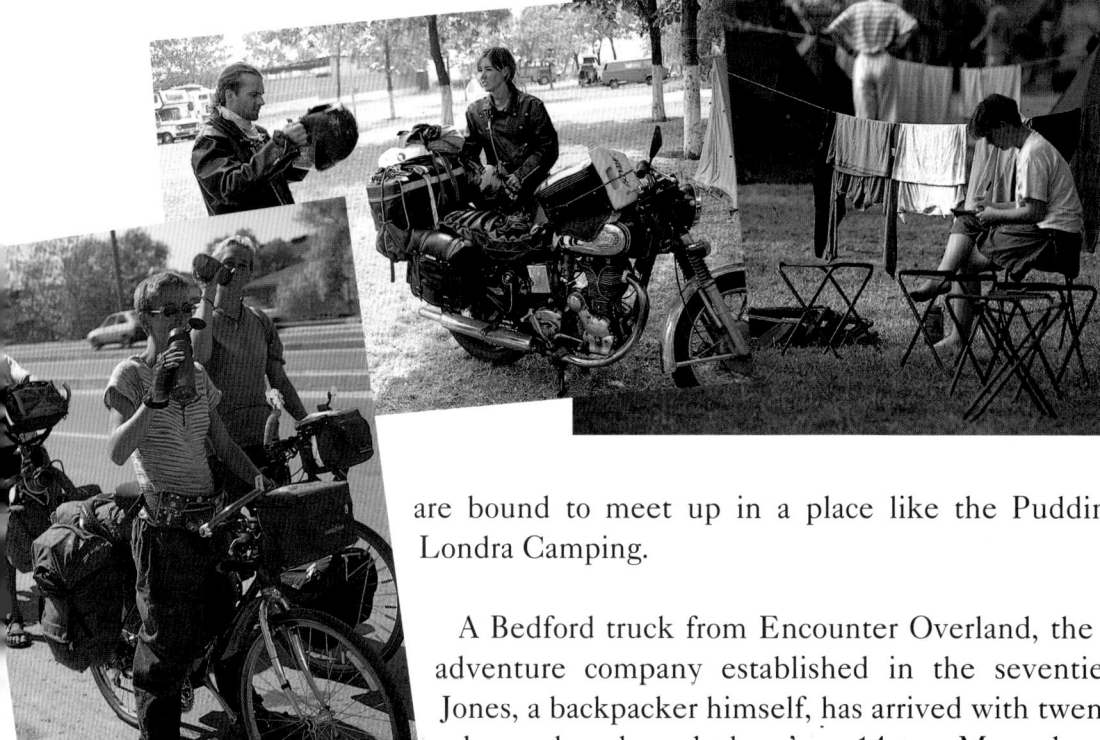

From the left: Em, Harry and Gish cycling to India; Mel and Gary biking there; wash day at Londra Camping

are bound to meet up in a place like the Pudding Shop, or Londra Camping.

A Bedford truck from Encounter Overland, the first British adventure company established in the seventies by Tony Jones, a backpacker himself, has arrived with twenty-one people on board; and there's a 14-ton Mercedes truck from Dragoman, another British overland company, here too. Melanie Burrows and Gary Swash from Islington are giving it a go on an Enfield 350; Jon Drewett from Essex is on an old Triumph, but not quite sure where he's going; Jeff Smith and Sue Rivers from Woodbridge are on their bikes; so are Em, Harry and Gish, cycling for charity; and there are two German girls living in the back of a windowless Ford transit delivery van. Nobody knows where they're going. As they only come out at night and never talk, they're known as the 'lesbian vampires from hell'. And if that isn't enough, on the road ahead, according to Ibrahim, other new members of the club include eight Danes in an old London double-decker; Pat and Graham from Basildon in an ex-army ambulance; and two German women dressed up as men on a BMW. What more could a film crew and an old wanderer like me want? Looks like heaven out on the trail to India this year!

Gillian Jones is a lawyer, and Bill Ward is in advertizing. They're taking time out too, but are typical of a new breed of overlanders. It's not the obligatory year off before or after university, since both are well into their twenties. Both seem to think they were missing out on something in life.

'I didn't really think too deeply about what I was doing,' says Gillian. 'If I had been too logical about it I probably would have chickened out.'

She gave up her job because she felt unhappy with it, and at twenty-five she thought this might be her last chance to go off and travel. 'I said to myself it would be worth the price. The fact that I might end up washing dishes when I get back was a more attractive option to staying where I was. It was a choice between dysentery and a job - and dysentery won!'

Bill, too, felt hemmed in by his work. 'There was this nagging thought in the back of my mind: is this really all there is? It's a scary thing to do, but I had to find out. I'm not sure about it being a rite of passage, but I did very consciously take this time out to think and to give myself space.'

Gillian cushioned her dive into the deep end by being far more practical about her preparations for the trip than, as she's now

A bridge too fish - Istanbul

finding out, was necessary. 'I bought loads of soaps,' she says, 'toothpaste and an electric battery-operated shaver (for my legs), a teddy bear (he's my guard dog) and moist toilet paper (it's a luxury for all those times behind a bush). And I bought two short-sleeved tee-shirts, two long-sleeved tee-shirts, a fleece, two pairs of shorts, jeans and light cotton trousers and twenty-four pairs of knickers (well, they're only very small, you know!).'

It's an old failing of mine, too - overpacking even when I know I won't need half the stuff and most of it can be bought anywhere. Surprise, surprise - they do wash and use soap in other countries! Anyway, Gillian will probably end up like me: she'll give up shaving; stop wearing knickers; use water and her left hand; and probably live with the same pair of shorts and a couple of tee-shirts for the entire journey.

Thirty-one-year-old Jon Drewett is slightly different: he doesn't even know where he's going - or how long he will go for. And he wishes he was back in the sixties. 'It's not the beads and kaftans I'm after, it's the appeal of the darker side of life - the feeling that you could change things. Or maybe it's just a rejection of the last fourteen years of government in Britain. I don't think we can change much any more. I don't know, but at least I'm freer on the road. You know, no ties - not looking back, just looking forward in my life to something. I mean, I'm finding out about me and how the world fits together.' And it's an open-ended journey too. 'What's the point in planning? Originally I wasn't going to Turkey. Then people said, "Oh, you should go to Turkey", so I've come here - because it's on the map, really. But in a way it's the journey that matters, not the destination.'

I leave Jon pondering his map, beginning to think about India but scared that he might have to endure some more jabs if he decides to go. But I wouldn't be surprised to see him in Kathmandu for Christmas!

Melanie Burrows and Gary Swash, on the other hand, are very clear what they are getting away from. 'Britain's so depressing these days,' says Mel. 'I mean, how free is it? People are so controlled. I know it's always been bred into us that what you should do is leave school, get a job, get married and have a family. In the sixties there was a revolt against that. But these days everybody seems to be going quietly - nobody tells us there are any options.'

I met them under a tree at Londra Camping, Mel trying on her new wrap-around black veil for Iran and Gary greasing up his old fifties-style Enfield motorbike - India-bound, on the cheap.

'We just want to be a bit happy for a change,' says Gary. 'The world's all there for the taking, and you know you can only try something once.'

'Yeah,' adds Mel, 'and the fun's in the trying.'

Emily (Em) Dewhurst, Harriet (Harry) Beaumont and Grant (Gish) Gichard, all in their twenties, are going there on the cheap too - by bicycle. They're trying to raise money for the Tibetan Children's School in Dharmsala, northern India, taking the hard way - 9500 kilometres via Uzbekistan and Kazakhstan. They're eight countries down already and have got the leg muscles to prove it - and a bit more besides. Harry's stopped having periods and Em's become hairier than she's ever been before. She reckons that their hormones are all over the place, stirred by heavy doses of testosterone coursing through their hard-biking bodies.

'It's certainly made us very physical,' says Em, stuffing her bits and pieces into the bicycle packs hanging across her rear wheel, 'a lot more capable. You stop thinking about limits, and our bodies have gone along with it.'

Both the girls, who were joined by Gish, a New Zealander, *en route*, have also stopped worrying about how they look. 'Not that we did much before,' says Harry, 'but it helps deter marauding men.' Gish has added another weapon to that defence. He tells everybody that the girls are lesbians - and he's their keeper.

'The problem with that,' says Harry, laughing, 'is that Em's holding out for a yak herdsman!'

'Oh, sure,' retorts Em, laughing louder, 'but really Harry's your girl for all that. Stop somewhere for a couple of days - and Harry makes a friend!'

Asia calls - only the width of a fast-flowing stretch of water away. The Bosphorus splits Istanbul in two. It's 30 kilometres long and in places less than 500 metres wide - but this glittering grey sea link between the Black Sea, the Marmara and the Aegean has always been the great divide, the most effective of frontiers where the cultures collide - where the voice of Islam is first heard. It looks as though it would take an army to hold it - but religion has been the guardian of these shores for almost as long as history has been written: Islam battling Christianity battling the Mongol hordes battling the great armies of the Greeks.

We check our route notes and say goodbye to all the travellers, knowing that we'll probably meet many of them again along the road to India. And then we swing east across the Bosphorus Bridge, the fourth longest in the world, the sun rising bright and strong into our eyes. Ahead lie the great Anatolian plains of central Turkey, the beginning of the Silk Road to the Far East - and it's still more than 2500 kilometres to go before we enter the Arab world. This is where the going gets tough.

Istanbul

TURKEY

Konya

Olu Deniz

SYRIA

CHAPTER 6

A Road Less Travelled

Turkey - and the going gets tough

The road east barrels straight ahead towards the horizon, a fine black line sweeping away into the far distance, disappearing through the yellowing, early autumn fields of Anatolia. We're nose to tail, Ron filming *Wah Wah* from the top of the Land Rover. The landscape is spectacular, mainly because it seems so vast, so endless. But Turkey *is* vast, an empire unto itself.

The going's good so far, but we know that by the time we reach the mountains of the south-east the distances will seem much longer, the heat more oppressive, the roads bumpier and more wearing. But there is also a more challenging feel to the journey now - an increasing sense of entering the unfamiliar. It's a relief to be out of Istanbul. The suffocating pollution that we've had to live with over the past few days has now given way to the fresh, clean air of these vast open spaces. Even though this is Asia, the only obvious signs so far are the pencil-thin minarets of the mosques that rise above even the smallest villages. Western influences, however, are more noticeable than before. Turkey is a modern, secular state with every intent of becoming a fully fledged member of the European Union - and it's beginning to show. The proliferation of roadside signs - for Pepsi and Coke - are just the beginning of the new, 1990s look for the road to India.

The hailstorm comes without warning, lashing down out of a clear blue evening sky, bringing traffic to a crawl and laying a glittering rainbow across the road in front of us. It lingers for almost 1.5 kilometres before we are slowly enveloped by its shimmering colours, swallowed up in a way none of us has ever experienced before. It seems entirely appropriate that we should be driving through the end of a rainbow: the pot of gold will be ours; everything we could ever imagine must be out there somewhere on the road ahead.

Travelling across Turkey is like turning the pages of a history book, following in the footsteps of some of the world's greatest adventurers, generals, philosophers, architects and scientists. It's said that this country has more ancient cities and classical ruins than Greece. Following

Heading out across the Anatolian Plains

the coast road that twists and turns along the Aegean we pass the battle-scarred beaches of Gallipoli (a mecca for Australian travellers) before reaching the walls of Troy, and further south the remarkably well-preserved ruins of Ephesus, an Ionian city that was to become one of the wealthiest Roman trading centres on the Mediterranean. Head further east towards Ankara, drop south towards the centre of Turkey and we can follow the first leg of the Silk Road to China, pushing towards what used to be the frontiers of the Persian empire.

Marco Polo says little about his thoughts when he first set foot in Turkey, but clearly he saw and felt the difference - as much in the landscape as in the people. He notes how flat, dry and dusty the land had become; the clothes more extravagant and loose. The city of Konya lay at the hub of the trading routes in those days - a brief patch of green, an oasis of relief after the dry winds and scorching heat of the plains. It was also the place where, more than two thousand years ago, the armies of Alexander began their drive towards India. Some of the settlements around here are among the oldest-known human communities in the world - dating back as far as 7500 BC. And the trade route caravanserai (a watering-hole, rest stop and market surrounded by high walls) at Sultanhani is one of the best preserved of its kind. Close your eyes and imagine what it was like seven hundred years ago: huge wooden gates opening on to a central courtyard surrounded by towering, vaulted chambers; the shuffle and snort of tethered camels; the weathered faces of the traders; the many colours of their clothes and the sound of their voices speaking in a dozen different languages; stalls selling silks and cottons, trinkets and jewels, and bowls of hot, spicy foods. Marco Polo was only seventeen when he stopped here - maybe even sat in the same spot as me. As a young man, he can only have believed himself to be on the threshold of some wondrous kingdom, or at the edge of something far more wild and dangerous.

We are heading south towards the coast. It's late in the afternoon and we are looking for a place to camp. It's a small back-road running along a lake shore on one side, silver birch woods on the other. There's never much traffic in areas like this - just the occasional tractor.

It's hard to believe, really. I do the obligatory double take just to make sure. But it is still there, a silvered, galvanized beast trundling down the road towards us, slightly tilting to one side, spotlights and bars and things sticking out all over. And there's half of another one being towed behind. A Mad Max killer drogue if ever I saw one, even though it says 'Land Rover' on the front. But the best is yet to come. When it finally stops under some trees, the wildly laughing driver leaps out followed by four dogs (two Great Danes, an Alsatian, and an Australian dingo); a cat named Oscar; and a wife called Noa!

So this is where all good rock 'n' rollers end up! Bernard Qualman, a forty-two-year-old music promoter and publisher from Germany, has been on the road for five years (six by now) in his bullet-proof, converted Land Rover - all five tons of it. Since 17 September 1989 he has covered more than 250 000 kilometres and travelled around twenty countries. There's no moss on this old rocker - and he says he intends to roll forever!

'Mad Max' is a 1980 long-wheelbase diesel Land Rover, with the back half of a 1980 short-wheelbase Land Rover towed behind. That's the dogs' kennel. The main vehicle has been adapted to sleep two and is equipped with shower, loo, cooking range, library, video - and a set of African drums. It also has a satellite navigation system and enough strange gadgets to stock an electrical shop. It carries six hundred spare parts (including three spare wheels and an axle); 300 litres of diesel; 500 litres of water; solar chargers; a generator; a small boat; a bicycle; and 80 kilos of dog food. What gives it its strange futuristic look is the fact that Bernard has covered the entire vehicle with slatted panels of aluminium, a second skin to keep down the heat.

Bernard is handsome and smiles a lot, looks incredibly fit, has a great set of teeth and seems to have absolutely no doubts about anything. Neither does his Israeli wife, Noa. They met in Tel Aviv on 14 May 1993 and were married three days later. Noa, who is twenty-one, also smiles a lot. She's perfectly slim, blonde and beautiful. God, it's enough to make you sick! Is there nothing wrong with these two?

'Well, to others maybe we seem a little crazy,' admits Bernard, 'but only because we do what is needed to make our dreams come true. I have a feeling, a very, very strong feeling, that I wasn't living before. I was not there inside, do you understand? I was working, I was chasing money, but I wasn't living. I was successful, but every day was stress. Every day I felt like a robot. Now I wake up every morning and I say to Noa, "I'm living every second." I'm writing, I'm reading, I'm discovering so many things about myself and this planet where I live. I'm always learning and growing.'

Noa feels equally positive about the prospect of life on the road for the rest of her life, though it seems more to do with being with Bernard than with what she gets from travelling. 'I saw him,' she says 'and I thought, "Right,

Bernard gets poetic in print

with him I want to spend the rest of my life.'
It's very easy because he lets me live. I'm
never alone, but I can be if I want, even when
he is next to me.'

'And it's a good life for the dogs, too,'
enthuses Bernard. 'I found them in dogs'
homes in Germany and Greece. Nancy, the
older of the two Great Danes, and Cora, the
Alsatian, have been with me for five years.'

Bernard makes some money from writing,
an art he has taught himself since going on
the road. Noa makes jewellery. They have
enough to get by - and enough saved for the
next part of their great journey, which is
already under construction in a boatyard in
southern Turkey. They are converting a wooden,
200-tonne, 30-metre traditional Turkish fishing boat
(renamed *The Noa Queen*) to take them across the
Pacific to the Americas. It's big enough to carry
the Land Rover and to accommodate many more
animals, including a donkey which Bernard has
his eye on.

'Now we'll always travel, slowly, quietly it goes, like
this. Forever. I hope for the next hundred years!' They
both laugh and look at each other. The dogs are asleep

**Noa, Bernard and family.
And next year's Ark?**
in the shade, the cat curled up on Noa's lap. There's nothing crazy
about these two.

The next day, in a small port down on the coast, we leave Bernard and Noa standing in the sun on the prow of their ark. Bernard is talking excitedly about lifeboats,
water and fuel storage and waving his arms around and explaining where the dogs
will sleep - where Noa will play her drums - how the Land Rover will be hoisted
aboard. I wish I could put to sea with them... instead we're on the road again, heading east across this huge country.

> 'So we crossed Turkey,' I wrote home in 1962, 'on the backs of lorries, sleeping
> all night on the lorries, nearly 1000 miles down to Iskenderoun - Istanbul,
> Ankara, Adana....'

I must say I had had my doubts. Stepping past Istanbul in those days was very much a leap in the dark. I remember heads shaking back in the Pudding Shop. But at least I had found somebody to travel with:

> *'I met this Englishman called Keith Altman from Swansea. Ock (Keith), who's quite old (26), was trying to get to Israel where he was going to live. Now I have always been interested, and admired the Jews and always wanted to go and see Israel. So I said do you mind if I string along. He didn't mind, so from then on we were partners. I had no money, he had two pounds, so that made a pound each.'*

Amazing how easy it is to travel without any money. No thought of India yet, but destiny was already moving me in the right direction.

> *'Oh, I forgot to tell you my hair was down to my shoulders in Turkey, but so many barbers offered to cut it for free I let the best one do it.'*

That news at least would, I hoped, have pleased my parents.

We are already beginning to meet up with some of the travellers from Istanbul. One of the Dragoman trucks thunders by, heading south towards the mountains to make camp for a few days in the pine forests around Olympos, halfway along the Turkish coast towards Syria. There are twenty-three passengers on board, many of them women, and the fourteen-ton Mercedes truck also has a female driver. Kecia Harris is twenty-six and comes from Cardiff, Lesley her co-driver is Australian. It's Kecia's first time on the road to India, although she's made several trips across Africa. She has explained to her passengers that they are now in the heartland of a Muslim country and that they have to behave differently, or at least be more aware of being in a different culture.

'It's not as strict as many Middle Eastern countries,' she says, 'but you must try to dress down, and avoid see-through tops and very short shorts.' Most of the girls are, in any case, already used to the way they are sometimes propositioned by men, even in remoter areas like this. Tonight they are making camp on the outskirts of a village in the forests high above the coast. Kecia is tired and has gone to bed in her tent. She's been

Kecia on top; Lesley underneath

wrestling with single-track mountain passes all day. The arrival of a truck full of foreigners attracts like a magnet, and soon several of the men from the nearby village have come to share raki and kebabs by the campfire - and hopefully a dance or two. The light from the oil lamps plays shadows around the clearing between the trees. It's going to be another of those long nights.

The first sign of trouble is when a furious Kecia comes charging into the clearing chasing a young man and trying to beat him over the head with a metal camp stool. It's hard to tell whether he is more alarmed by the threat of the stool or by the stirring Cardiff Arms Park expletives coming out of Kecia's mouth. 'Fuck off! Go on, fuck off!'

'I think I did the wrong thing,' she admits after things have calmed down a bit and the villagers have taken the young man away. 'I probably should have kept quiet and not caused such a scene. But I suppose I'm glad I did wallop him one - I mean, he was flashing in front of my tent! I just didn't want him around, and I suppose I was just getting back on all the men who touch you up in towns - which happens a lot. People say that some of us bring it on ourselves by dressing provocatively, but yet in some places even if you are wearing a veil down to the ground you still get hassled and abused. In the end you think, "Why am I bothering?" It beats me. What's provocative behaviour? Just being female is provocative sometimes - just being a Western woman.'

The group of young English, Australian and South African girls sitting around on the roof of the Australian and New Zealand Pension in Selchuk, a small tourist town near Ephesus, agree. They've all had problems too.

'I always get the desperadoes,' laughs Karen O'Loughlin. 'They start off offering you a cup of tea but then they've got their hands all over you before it even comes. The best thing to do is to stand up and yell: "Hey, I've got balls, baby!"'

'Because you don't have a guy with you,' adds Antoinette Beckmann, a South African traveller, 'some of the men immediately think you're vulnerable. Sometimes I'm walking down the street and they just come up and grab you and touch you and try to make you go and have tea or food with them. Others are just really friendly. In the end you don't know whether they're being hospitable or just taking advantage of you.'

Breakfast at Selchuk - with balls!

The holiday season is almost over and business is a bit slow for Ibrahim, Mehmet and Said. But a good carpet salesman never gives up. Anybody walking past their shop in Selchuk is a potential customer. And if they happen to be girls then, like most Turkish men, they don't see the harm of flirting with them a bit too.

'In Turkey,' says Mehmet, 'if Turkish woman sleep with man before marry she can never marry. But we know from newspaper and television that sex with European girl is free. Turkish man is warm and forbidden is sweet, so now you understand why he want to marry European girl.'

'Hello, excuse me, hello...' and Mehmet is off again, trying to stop two Czech girls walking down the street and to get them into his shop. This time he's promising a free lunch.

It's not just Turkish men, however. The complaints start in Europe, with the Italians rating high on the list of 'hasslers and pervs'. According to Sasha Orteng from Copenhagen, Britain's the worst. Not only did she get groped more in London than anywhere else, she says, but 'I even met English people who didn't know where Denmark was!'

But Sasha thinks it's still all part of the experience. 'You know, the other day I was sleeping out on the rocks here in Turkey, it was very cold and I was using a wet towel as a pillow, but I felt really happy. I could be back home with a good job and all the material stuff I could ever want, but I couldn't be half as content as I am here, poor, in a strange country where I sometimes get hassled but I'm learning and seeing all the time. I'm so happy just to be here eating breakfast.'

The sheltered beaches at Olu Deniz used to be a real paradise, accessible only on foot, locked away beneath towering cliffs and rolling pine forests. It was like that when Bob and Anthea Gurkan discovered it back in the late sixties and set up one of the first travellers' camps in Turkey. Bob - his English nickname - was in the Turkish Air Force until he ran into Anthea, a young London girl doing the unthinkable twenty-six years ago: hitch-hiking around Turkey by herself. Today, Bob and Anthea have found that their paradise has become one of the busiest new tourist spots on the Turkish coast. Bob's Buzz Bar certainly has one of the best locations on the now crowded beachfront and business is obviously good, with the restaurant and bar full most nights - but things aren't like they used to be.

'It's tourism that's destroying this place,' says Bob, clinking the ice in his glass of raki and being the perfect host. 'If we could have kept it just for the overland travellers then it would have been better. They care more about the natural things, about the countries they visit.'

Anthea agrees. 'So much was different when I first came to Turkey,' she says. 'As

A postcard from Pammukale in central Turkey

a hitch-hiker in those days you didn't have to put your hand out, you stood nicely by the side of the road and waited and you were always picked up.'

I couldn't help wondering. This sounded almost too good to be true. I certainly remember that in 1962, apart from the rampantly rich Ferrari owner, I often got drivers' fingers straying across my thighs - from France onwards!

'Well, there was just once,' recalls Anthea, 'when this man gave me a ride into Yugoslavia. Because I could tell he was gay I thought I was safe and broke my own rule about accepting lifts after five in the evening. But we were driving through these woods and he suddenly pulled out a gun and said, "You must kill me! I don't want to live any more." I said, "I can't possibly kill you. I've never used a gun before!"'

It was only quick thinking that saved her. Pretending to get a handkerchief from her pack, she opened the back door and ran off into the night. She spent the next six hours cowering under a bush while he rampaged around with a torch and the gun - now threatening to kill her.

Things were certainly not all sweetness and light back in the 1960s. I wrote to my parents then about how I had had my rucksack stolen when I was sleeping on the beach at Iskenderun, near the Syrian border. But I must say the police were much more concerned than they might be these days:

> *'My rucksack was soon recovered and there was a court case for the thief, who was vigorously beaten up in front of me at 1 a.m. in the morning, and stripped naked as he had my clothes on. My picture was in most of the Turkish papers and there was a big write-up. After the court case I left for....'*

In the summer of 1994 the word is out that Butterfly Valley, a remote beach in southern Turkey, is the place to go. We've left our vehicles at Bob's Buzz Bar and have taken a small boat to get there. The beach is only accessible by sea or down a very steep rock path 300 metres high. It's another one of those sunset moments as the boat edges into the long, narrow valley of cliffs that funnel the sea back towards the beach.

'I heard about this place when I was in Prague,' says Michaela Bowland, an Australian woman travelling by herself to the Middle East, 'and again when I was in Istanbul. It sounded so tranquil and beautiful. I think I'll just hang out here for a while before I head off again.'

A room with a view in Butterfly Valley

We scramble ashore through the foaming evening rollers and help to unload crates of soft drinks, supplies and fruit for the small makeshift restaurant that's been built at the back of the beach. There are about fifty or so travellers hanging out at Butterfly Valley. Some

stay for just a day or so, sleeping on the sand or in the tree houses scattered round the valley; others have been here a few weeks. It's that kind of place. A lot of lying around thinking and talking; midnight skinny dipping in the phosphorescent waters; campfires on the beach; not much food, but the grass is good and - when the boats come in - there's plenty of beer. Bit of the runs around, too, unfortunately!

Nineteen-year-old Sam Menter's almost forgotten what Bristol's like. He's been 'bumming around', as he puts it, on and off for a year now. He's as laid back as you can get and looking as though he's down to his last tee-shirt. But who cares? It's time to clamber up the rocks and watch another sunset.

'Can you believe it?' he says. 'My mum came here about two years ago and was ranting and raving about the place. I never realized it was some sort of hang-out. Oh well, I suppose that makes my mum a hippie! Because I'm here doesn't make me a hippie, though. Bumming around doesn't mean I'm out on some mission to learn the meaning of life either. I'm just having a look, enjoying myself wherever I happen to be. But I suppose it's got to end soon - I've got to go and get educated and things like that!'

The Kool-aid, acid-dream kids of the sixties and seventies who used to hang out in places like this were never so sane. Hunt around long enough and what's the betting we'll find a few still out there on the road ahead - or on another beach like Butterfly somewhere in the world.

Chiara and Stuart don't quite fit the bill - they're not Bernard and Noa either - but they do have a Land Rover and they are going to India. I run into them on the beach at Olympos, a day's drive south of Butterfly Valley. I've never met Land Rover enthusiasts before - I mean a real Rover-*crazy* couple. I'm convinced they are making the trip for their vehicle, not themselves! They are from Bristol - Stuart, a gas delivery man, is painfully thin and a bit serious compared to Chiara, who does something in customer care for an insurance company. She organizes things and laughs a lot. Well, giggles really. They've been prepping the Land Rover and themselves for this trip for a year and the conversation flows more easily when it's about mechanics or manuals, so I suppose I had better get learning. I've a feeling we're going to be seeing a lot more of Chiara and Stuart in the next few months.

Next stop Syria, Jordan and a way to be found round Iraq to reach Iran. Thirty years ago it was relentless propaganda about the threat of Communism and the fear of Reds under every bed that was fed to us in the press and on radio and television. Today the Middle East and the forces of Islam hold the front page and create the mind-set for the journey ahead.

To a young traveller in the nineties Turkey is still OK - Europe almost. But the

imagination begins to work overtime as you approach the Arab world. Suddenly everything seems very strange - impenetrable almost. The long, flowing robes; the rasp of the language; the crumbling, dusty border towns; the rusting rolls of barbed wire; and the slouch of the soldiers. All those stories start coming back to you. You move on to the defensive almost without noticing it. You've read it all before: war and revolution, terrorism, hostages, gun law in the streets, mad mullahs, fanaticism run riot - and it all seems aimed at you. It is.

Michael and Carol MacDonald (he's from Belfast, she's American) are cycling to India, taking the tough route down through the Middle East. They know all too well the risk they are taking, especially as Carol is American. At least, that's what they think.

'Our journey hasn't really started until we cross the Syrian border,' says Michael. 'From anybody's point of view, especially as Carol is a woman and an American, we think it's going to be a bit hairy. All we can do is take one day at a time and be careful. I mean, it makes you think. But you know, what you read may not be what you find. When you hear about Northern Ireland you only kind of hear about it - you know, bombs gone off or soldiers shot. It's the same for most countries - you only hear the bad things. I'm a great believer in the other 90 per cent.'

'It's not like we're flippant about it,' adds Carol, 'we are careful, we do take precautions - and we kissed the Blarney stone before we left!'

At the end of the day the only thing that's going to keep the traveller safe in this part of the world is common sense and good luck. Of course there are dangers (not normally as extreme as the British Foreign Office likes to make out), but more often than not no more than you might find on the back streets of Miami or many other Western cities. The simple fact is that if we took every warning, every sign of danger or difficulty as a cue to go home we wouldn't go anywhere. The spirit of adventure would die, the joy of discovery would fade.

Still, it doesn't hurt to be a bit nervous. Setting off from the southern Turkish port of Iskenderun, we head for the hills that mark the border with Syria. The Turkish kids who crowd around us before we leave seem to think it's very funny that we are planning to go on through the Middle East to Iran. So let's all have a laugh!

'Saddam, Saddam,' they chant, running after us. 'Saddam very bad.'

British cyclist Michael Wainwright took much the same route and ended up in an Iraqi jail. He got ten years on a trumped up charge of spying, and several travellers have been kidnapped by Kurdish rebels on their way through south-eastern Turkey. Still, what's life without a few risks!

CHAPTER 7

Never What's Expected

Syria and Jordan - a first step into the Arab world

I'm driving slowly through a valley of dry scrub. Coils of rusting barbed wire are strung across the hills that run alongside the road. Rounding a corner, I see three men running towards me. Their shirts are in tatters, their trousers torn and dirty. Their hands flap urgently and they are shouting in broken, unintelligible English as they run - dry, rasping voices calling out to me. Behind them lies, half buried in the sand, the bent and rusting wreck of an old American Chevrolet. But this is No Man's Land and I'm in no mood to slow down.

It's like a scene out of some future, desperate world - dangerous, even. In front of me I can see watchtowers along the border and a cluster of concrete buildings half hidden by the turn in the road. I can imagine the cold stare of binoculars and the barrel of a gun holding me in its sights. I just want to get away from these crazed figures and stay on the right side of the soldiers I know to be up ahead. The road-block is a flimsy red pole. Suddenly two men in uniforms, both with Kalashnikov rifles, are stepping out from behind a wooden hut. I can feel the sweat running down my back. I stop. Then they smile and ask us in for tea! Not quite what I expected. But there you are - we've arrived in Syria.

The men in No Man's Land turn out to be Nigerians, thrown out of Turkey without any money or passports six weeks ago. If the Turks didn't want them, why should the Syrians? Nowhere to go - nowhere to run. The border guards, however, are sympathetic and have been giving them food and water - as much as they can afford. Everybody seems to be very relaxed (except for the poor Nigerians) and the guns are no longer threatening; they're just there.

But no matter how much smiling goes on, borders are never the best place to hang out - especially if you're carrying as much film and recording equipment as we are. If our vehicles are going to be properly searched it's unlikely that our story about being teachers (that's me, Ron and Dan - Sean's a student) would stand much cross-questioning. We all feel a bit inadequate. For the first time, language has become a real barrier. Arabic seems so much more foreign than Turkish. I'm trying my best with the phrase book but I can't get the pronunciation right. Everybody just laughs - or, more usually, stares blankly. There's no longer anything that looks vaguely

European apart from the inevitable soft drink signs. At least the Turkish ones were in a script that suggested something almost understandable. Arabic - well, as Sean puts it: 'Even a XXXX couldn't help me read this stuff!'

Lines of trucks are waiting to cross the border, loaded with God knows what - mostly refrigerators and televisions by the looks of it. And old American taxis, yellow and battered, their roofs piled high with suitcases and boxes tied down under brightly coloured blankets and strips of canvas. There's also the occasional air-conditioned Mercedes, the back seat crammed with black-veiled women waiting for their men - or man.

I'm waving passports and papers uselessly in the air, diving in amongst the truck drivers in their long robes and head-dresses, pushing, sweating and shoving my way towards the immigration and customs counters. Beat them at their own game, I say: first come first served and elbows to the fore. The problem is that once I reach the head of the line I can't speak the bloody language. But actually I'm in my element. Don't panic and it'll work itself out; and never mind the hassle. Hey, it's fun!

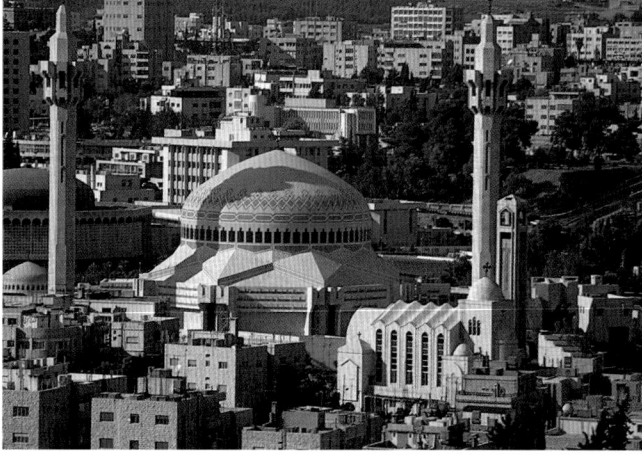

The modern face of Islam - the King Abdullah Mosque, Amman

The procedures seem endless. But this is just the way things are done here and they are, in their own way, quite organized. They can become expensive, though. Seeing the fruitless hours ahead and the threat of a lot of suitcases being emptied, I accept the help of one of the people (all apparently called 'Ali') who are hanging around and who seem to be able to get things done much more quickly and easily than I do. It costs forty dollars but we are through and on our way in only a couple of hours, leaving the struggling masses still standing and waiting to have their passports, baggage and vehicles checked and, no doubt, checked again.

Entering Syria, there's a greater difference than after any other border we've crossed so far. The faces are lighter, softer almost; the clothes more traditional, looser, longer, with very little Western influence. This has the feel of Hollywood Bible land: camels and donkeys on the roads, the villages more spread out, baking quietly in the sun. The desert stretches away towards the horizon: Iraq to the east, Jordan to the south, Lebanon and Israel to the west. There's no doubt we've made it to the Middle East.

Ahead of us is Aleppo, one of the great trading cities of the region, with its labyrinth of narrow, covered bazaars; dark, stone-vaulted souks; the smell of a hundred

different spices; the cries of the hawkers and barrow boys; the glitter of gold, silver and silk; and the hauntingly beautiful call to prayer ringing out across this bustling city of Islam five times a day. And everywhere a 'Hello, friend' or a tug on the arm and the offer of yet more tea and conversation. Syria really is different from anything most people have ever imagined.

The dusty elegance of Baron's Hotel

Coco Mazloumian is dead now, but my memory of him is still very much alive. The Armenian hotelier, with his crisp British accent, was into his eighties when I met him a couple of years back; even so, his fast-fading, rheumy eyes still managed to find me in the gloom of the bar at Baron's in Aleppo, for many decades one of the premier hotels in the Middle East.

Coco's pale, soft-cheeked face creased into a thousand lines when he spoke, a dark blue flat cap was crammed on his head, his shirt was white and well pressed, and his turn-ups flapped an inch too short over his sandals. He didn't really care about his age, he said, only that he was forgetting all the old stories. His memory was going and with it the history of his family, the hotel and the many Western travellers who had sat beneath its slow-turning fans and told of their adventures on the road to Damascus, along the banks of the Euphrates to Baghdad and further - to India and China. All through the twenties, thirties and forties Aleppo had been a fashionable stopover for some of the great voyagers of our time.

Coco couldn't remember much about Lawrence of Arabia, except that he had always seemed very much a loner; or Agatha Christie, except that she had written the first chapter of *Murder on the Orient Express* while staying at Baron's; Freya Stark, on the other hand, had been a real live wire and a marvellous dancer; Theodore Roosevelt and Lady Mountbatten were there too, as well as the aviators Charles Lindbergh, Amy Johnson and Charles Kingsford-Smith - not to mention all those minor European royals riding the Orient Express to Istanbul then travelling on overland to Aleppo and Baghdad. But the one adventurer who really stuck in Coco's mind was the eccentric, American millionaire who had driven a huge truck, complete with bedroom and sitting room, across the Middle East to India - preceded by six cars scouting the road ahead for dangerous terrain and bandits.

In the late nineteenth century Coco's family had been travellers too, humble traders and pilgrims heading south on horseback from Armenia, braving the mountains and the deserts of the Ottoman Empire, passing through Aleppo *en route* to Jerusalem and the Holy Land. On their way back Grandfather Mazloumian,

remembering the waiting list for floor space in Aleppo's overcrowded stables (for man and beast) decided to exercise his entrepreneurial energies and build the city's first hotel. With the profits from that he then built Baron's in 1909. It was an immediate success. The cool of its wood-panelled rooms; the stretch and shade of its terraces; its delicate afternoon teas and reputation for sophisticated dinners off the best English china, all gave the hotel an air of elegance well suited to this city.

Today, what's left are the shadows of that elegance. The sunlight filters through the wooden shutters to finger the fading colours of the old KLM and BOAC posters on the walls, and the yellowing photographs of the past. The beds squeak and the plumbing is ancient. Coco may be dead, but Sally, his English wife, is still there, as is his son, Ahmet - both committed to keeping alive the spirit of a hotel which will always remain on the travellers' Most Romantic list.

I had not expected to have a vision on the road to Damascus. But there I am, driving south out of the desert from Aleppo, my mind on other things (like food), when this figure appears through the heat haze, all shapeless sun visor and tattered vest, a flag flying high on a long pole. It's pushing a supermarket trolley - accompanied by two dogs on a lead!

Sadly, I have not been chosen by the Lord. This is a solidly terrestrial, eccentric Frenchman. Daniel Mariet is, he explains, a forty-eight-year-old God-fearing crusader on a mission to the heart of Islam. No doubt St Paul would have approved, but a passing infidel has driven his Dodge truck off the road in amazement - main-

Daniel Mariet, Aiza and Dokko - a vision on the road to Damascus

ly, I think, because of the dogs. All he can do is stare and say, 'It is good, it is good' and laugh nervously, no doubt wondering, 'What the hell?'

Daniel takes all this attention in his stride. After nearly 8000 kilometres and eight countries, nearly a year and two pairs of shoes later along the road east, he is obviously used to it. He fusses around, watering his dogs, Aiza and Dokko, and talking non-stop in a hurried, staccato French, eager to explain what he's doing. No, he's not going to India, but thinks he will carry on round the Mediterranean until he gets back to France again: a total distance, he reckons, of about 16 000 kilometres. And no, he's not on a pilgrimage, but God is very much part of his journey.

The first global, mid-life crisis bag-man, perhaps? The trolley is certainly laden with things wrapped up in plastic, most of which are books (including a few giveaway Bibles), together with some clothes, a spare pair of walking shoes and several

bottles of water for him and the dogs. He eats - and feeds the dogs - when and where he can, never accepts lifts and expects to be walking for another year. The dogs, he agrees, don't have much say in the matter; but they seem completely at home.

'But of course they are happy,' says Daniel, sounding just like Inspector Clouseau. 'The dogs are the tourists - me, I am the mule!'

What is it with the French - always out walking their dogs around the world? First there was José Ramon back in Turkey, also heading for the Middle East, now Daniel Mariet in Syria. Not to mention Bernard and Noa. And next?

The vision I have in the steam baths in Damascus is a bit different. This is much larger - about 32 kilos larger, I think - and much younger and taller. It also talks and laughs very loudly and has a Canadian accent. Mike Terni, a twenty-six-year-old from Quebec, has been travelling for nearly a year, wondering what to do with his degree in mechanical engineering, but having a ball spending all this time thinking about it.

He and I share the suffocating heat of one of the best hammams in the city, staggering around in the dense steam desperately looking for the cold water trough. It's like a scene out of the *Arabian Nights*. By the time we've been soaped, steamed, boiled, beaten and rinsed off in a freezing pool by some rather large, hairy Syrian masseurs and bath attendants, we are surprised to find that it wasn't that bad after all and we wouldn't mind going back for more. Maybe the real attractions are the huge fluffy towels and exotic head-dresses they're wrapping around us - and the cold drinks and water pipes we get as we sprawl around on cushions by the indoor fountain. It certainly isn't the fact that Ron is filming us. He keeps emerging from the steam to catch us in the most unflattering positions!

Mike is one of those people you meet on the road who you know can look after themselves. He's stocky and big boned in his tee-shirt and shorts with his baseball cap pushed back on his head, and he's getting into a rhythm of travel that allows him to spend as much time in a country as he likes - to go when and where the mood takes, as long as the money lasts.

'Sometimes, though, I just want to go some place which I can call my own,' he says. 'I was in Greece for four months, had my own room, worked and really had a chance to get to know the people and the culture. My initial plan was to go to India. Now I've been diverted and fancy spending some time in Syria, and then maybe 'Disneyland.' That's traveller talk for Israel when in an Arab country.

'Being here, it seems as though everything I've read about Syria is more fiction than reality. The Syrians were described as fanatical - but all I've encountered is people who really go out of their way for you, to be hospitable, to invite you to their homes and feed you. Back in Canada or the United States, nine out of ten people would tell you to go away.

Never what's expected: Khoury in his red neon nightmare

What is sad to me is that the people here look to the West with envy for all the money we are supposed to have. Yet if you look round my country, for example, the people seem far less happy than they are here. North American values are so different. We seem to have a superiority complex that makes us always ridicule things that we don't understand. Like Islam, for example.'

The last person I expected to find luxuriating in the 'peace and prayerfulness' of a Syrian mosque was an American Roman Catholic priest. But, like Mike, Father Bob Turner has been drawn to the Middle East in search of answers - and, like Mike, he finds everything so different.

'Everybody here seems very balanced and normal and overwhelmingly charitable - not crazed radicals out to get Americans. If anything, I find Australians and New Zealanders to be crazed radicals out to get Americans.... I can't say I understand it all - but I have found the Muslim people to have a real commitment to God.'

In Syria, they also have a commitment to President Hafez al Assad. His picture dominates, huge, hand-painted portraits bearing down from the sides of buildings and on the walls of every office where brownie points are important. And if there is one thing you soon learn in countries like Syria, even more so than in the UK, most of the time politics has little to do with the real aspirations and needs of the people. So if you don't demonstrate - which you can't very safely do in Syria - you tend to shut up and put up and get on with your own life as best you can.

And if it isn't President Assad it's King Hussein, supreme ruler of the Hashemite Kingdom of Jordan - next stop on the road south before we swing north again to try to find a way past Iraq into Iran. Hussein, too, smiles serenely down from the walls of most offices, hotels, cafés and shops - a bit more benignly, perhaps, but none the less dominant. A man who can get things done, according to most Jordanians.

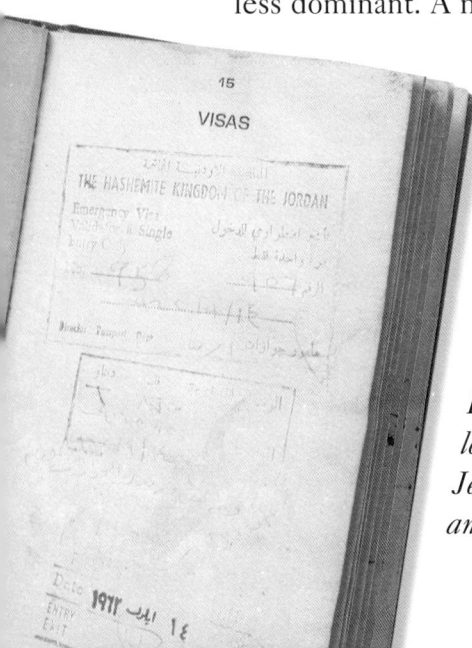

It was a long story, but I kept it as short as possible in my letter home in 1962; surprisingly so, considering that King Hussein was to be a significant influence on the course of my life. I had explained to my parents that my plan was to travel from Syria to Jordan and then cross into Israel to find work, knowing full well that once I had done that I would not be able to get back into any Arab country. But Israel had now become my destination:

'....with a pound to my name, I got a lorry to Jerusalem from Damascus, but when I got to the Jordan border they would not let me in because I had not got a certificate saying I was not a Jew, anyway I had not got enough money for a visa. I was well and truly stuck.'

I didn't even have enough to buy a visa to get me back into Syria. So after four days sleeping on the floor in a hut at the border post I tried calling the British Embassy in Amman, reversing the charges. All they told me was: 'Ring your family for money' and 'Get a certificate from your local vicar' back in England to prove that I was not a Jew. Pointing out that I was a penniless sixteen-year-old stuck in No Man's Land between Syria and Jordan didn't seem to make any difference.

> *'It was obvious now that I could not get to Israel,' my letter continued, 'so I decided either to turn back or to get repatriated. I also decided not to do either but to keep trying.... Well, then came the very thing I wanted, King Hussein of Jordan making a tour of the border posts....'*

The card up my sleeve, I figured, would be that the King had just married an English girl from near Ipswich and that I had gone to school down the road in Woodbridge. So when he started shaking hands with everybody in the immigration office I stood in line - except that when it came to my turn I didn't let go. I blurted out my story, adding, triumphantly, how I came from close to where his wife was born. I was, of course, dragged away by the security police, but not before the King had smiled and said he would do what he could. And he did just that.

That night the mayor of the local town arrived and said that the King had given orders that I was to be given a free 'emergency transit visa', put on a truck and sent to Iraq. I could hardly say that it was the wrong direction and that I really wanted to go to Israel. Thanks, King! Next destination? Well, why not India?

The problems that travellers have to deal with today are very similar to the ones I faced in 1962. Political unrest, coups and revolutions even, bureaucracy and difficulties with visas have always been part of the experience. Richard Burnett, a young English backpacker, and about twenty or so others have all met up in the Cliff Hotel, Amman, a long-time travellers' haunt where rooms cost less than £1.50 a night and the roof is even cheaper. This is where you go if you want to know what's going on. It's also a good place to find out about the stories behind all those headlines.

Abou Suleiman is a Palestinian and owner of the Cliff. More than 40 per cent of the population of Jordan is of Palestinian origin. In Amman it's almost 80 per cent. Even though most are now settled, many still feel a deep sense of anger about the unresolved issues of Palestine.

'I want my land, I want my country,' says Hassan, a long-time resident of the Cliff. 'Where is my home, where is my family? My brothers are in Jordan, in Saudi, in Egypt, in Lebanon. Do you understand? Why is all the world against the Palestinian people?'

'You don't really learn much about a country if all you do is visit monuments,' says

Richard Burnett. 'But meeting and talking with people on the streets, in the cafés and in hotel lobbies makes a huge difference.'

Night-time on the roof of the Cliff is certainly the place to fill yourself in on the nature of the journey ahead - whichever direction that might take you. Tonight there are travellers here coming down from Syria and up from Egypt, as well as others from Israel. There's also a lone Japanese girl, a hitch-hiker, just arrived from Iran.

'The fact is that if I thought I could go down to a car park in Croydon,' says Tim Jarvis from Wandsworth in south London, 'and meet all these people and learn all these things, then I'd probably do it. It would be a lot cheaper. But you can't - you have to be out of your routine situation and in the middle of it all, like this. I mean the Whitgift Centre at sunset - hewn out of the concrete as it is - isn't quite the same, is it?' Well, Tim, if my experience is anything to go by, you ain't seen nothing yet!

Lone star desert tree

The sun is setting: dark, disturbed streaks of red spread across a windy, desolate desert landscape somewhere south of Amman. I have been told to look out for a run-down building down a side road near the town of Ma'an.

It's like a film set in an old Western ghost town. An ancient artillery piece sits on a concrete pillar outside the gate of the Khoury Rest House. A single neon light winks on and off over a darkened doorway; a sign creaks in the wind; the shutters are closed. A deep voice rings out through a loudspeaker demanding to know, in broken English, what I want - and only reluctantly agrees to let me in. The door opens to the sound of bells ringing, beeping and flashing as I pass through what seem like the beams of a dozen miniature burglar alarms.

I am met in the deep red gloom of a cavernous bar by a tall man with a huge flowing grey-white beard and long hair. He's a Jordanian Jesus hippie living in a sixties time warp, in a neon world filled with hundreds of clocks and photographs of himself and the Hashemite Royal Family of Jordan. It's a truly psychedelic experience, but sadly depressing as well. Khoury is a man obsessed with being alone - bypassed by life and the main road south. He's driven his wives and all six of his children away. Nobody comes to his bar any more; even if they did, they wouldn't be welcome. He sits alone, waits alone and talks in broken, disjointed phrases about nothing, listening to Pink Floyd.

'Funny life, funny life - that's all.' And he switches off the lights.

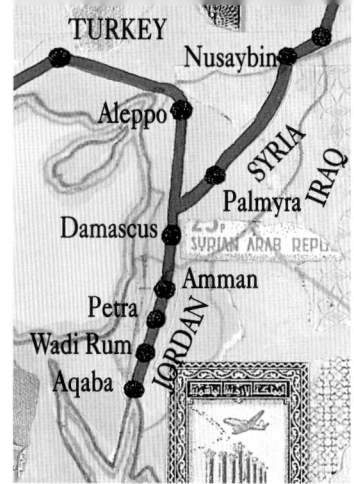

CHAPTER 8

Lost in the Desert

Crossing the Middle East trying to avoid Iraq

The first light of a brilliant dawn is breaking over the horizon. *Wah Wah* is a small speck of dust travelling through a vast expanse of desert. The sand is running deep beneath our wheels, the Jeep slewing sideways in the softer patches, showing her bum to the boys in the Land Rover who are ploughing a straight line through the dunes over to our right.

It's already getting hot and our tempers are not at their best. Ron is struggling to keep his eye to the camera, supported by a complicated set of rubber bungies and a tripod that keeps slipping. Another camera is strapped to the outside of the door. Every time we slow down, clouds of fine sand dust fill the Jeep. We are covered in the stuff and it's getting in everywhere. Then I look up.

Nothing had prepared me for the sight of Wadi Rum - an avenue of towering, rust-red cliffs rising nearly 1900 metres, running in parallel several miles across the desert. It's truly stunning - overwhelming in the way it imposes its vastness so dramatically on the landscape. We're driving the hard way through Jordan - crossing the desert from the Red Sea and the Gulf of Aqaba, north towards Saudi Arabia and Iraq. Our compass isn't working, so it's a matter of gauging our route with the help of the sun as well as having a good sense of direction and the luck to pick the right track. The desert around here is covered in the grazing trails of Bedouin camels and sheep and, these days, ancient Toyota pick-up trucks.

We come to a halt on the last rise before Wadi Rum - and switch off the last three hours of the engine straining in low gear and the crash of everything shifting around inside. The silence is wonderful - so silent it's almost painful to hear. Lawrence of Arabia rode into Wadi Rum in 1917. He wrote how 'our little cara-van grew self-conscious, and fell dead quiet, afraid and ashamed to

My first sight of Wadi Rum

flaunt its smallness in the presence of these stupendous hills'. A squadron of planes could wheel in formation between the valley walls.

Another dawn, seventy-seven years after Lawrence was here, and twenty-year-old Kate Brunner from London sits alone on the top of a sand dune, waiting for the sun as a wash of chill blue sky creeps up from behind the silent, darkened rocks.

'I didn't know I would find this here - I didn't know that places like Wadi Rum were here. When I first arrived yesterday I could literally see nobody, nothing for miles and miles - and that's the most amazing feeling. I get smothered in cities. Even the English landscape, beautiful as it is, doesn't inspire in the same way. I'll paint it when I get back.'

According to Kate, coming to places like this, walking out into the desert and being so alone is what travelling should be about: taking everything that little bit further. 'I don't think I could feel as much if I just sat at home, not pushing myself. I don't think anybody can fail to find that out when they travel. Here you are pushing yourself physically and mentally: you get exhausted, you get hungry, you get worn down - but you are always learning. And certainly places like this push you spiritually too.'

It's perhaps the emptiness that strikes me most about Wadi Rum. There are people out here - nomads and the occasional traveller - but you can't or don't see them until they are almost on top of you. The distances are enormous, the scale completely dwarfing, yet the way sound carries so perfectly and so far, allows a feeling of extraordinary intimacy.

We have made camp in the lee of one of the towering cliff faces. This is the kind of place one must stay. It's in the space and solitude of landscapes like this that one begins to sense just what it is that lies at the romantic and spiritual heart of the Arab world. In front of us, the desert stretches towards a point that could be a thousand miles away, or ten. Somehow everything seems so much sweeter. As the sunset drenches the desert in a deep orange glow Dan's pasta becomes a cordon bleu event, and bed that night beneath an all-embracing, crystal clear blanket of a sky is nothing less than a soul-stirring, peaceful experience of sensual bliss. I have rarely slept so well, or so deeply. Or woken so quickly and had the urge just to go, to walk until I might disappear. Which is what I do - stepping out across the sand, still cool to the bare foot but already beginning to warm to the rising sun.

Then - not what I expect in the middle of nowhere - I run into Jeff and Caroline. They both look very English - a bit red in the face, wearing shorts and carrying water bottles, almost with knotted hankies on their heads, but obviously at home, wandering across the desert with that kind of 'Wow, isn't this great!' look about them. A pair of old hippies, or what? Forty-three-year-old Jeff White's a sheet metal

worker from Middlesex, while Caroline Fletcher, who's thirty-seven, is a hotel receptionist. They first met in a Transit van on their way to India in the seventies. However the spirit took them then, it still seems to be there.

'Hippies are travellers really,' says Jeff, 'so I suppose if that's the case then we're hippies. But it's really about individualism, like the girl we saw the other day who - not content with just looking at the ancient Nabatean monastery in Petra - had to climb to the top of it.'

'Just like I have to walk in the desert,' adds Caroline. 'I feel real peace within myself here in all this space. I like England, but it doesn't seem to have any room for itself, let alone for me.'

'It would be a bit different if we lived here all the time,' Jeff points out, 'which of course we wouldn't. But we do find it hard not to go away - just to be able to set off somewhere. It's difficult to relate to people who don't think like that.'

Caroline laughs. 'Jeff's mates can't understand us at all. They ask why can't we go to Spain or Ibiza, like everybody else?'

Jeff and Caroline are still laughing about that and the thought of going on a package holiday when they head off again across the desert. God knows where they are going, but it can't be too far - they've only a week or so left before they have to get back to West Drayton.

The only other visitors we have this morning are a lot of goats. Unaccompanied, but with food clearly on their minds, about thirty of them invade and occupy our camp in less than a minute, viciously foraging among sleeping bags, clothes and equipment, going for anything that looks even vaguely chewable. Disaster would have been inevitable but for Ron's immediate caveman instincts - charging about waving a big stick and hurling rocks in a way the RSPCA would definitely not approve!

My turn next, when I drive *Wah Wah* too fast across a patch of sand and scrub and into enough of the soft stuff to strand us up to our axles - and wipe out the small camera attached to the outside of the door. Glad the boys weren't around to come to our rescue. What humiliation! Instead I give myself into the hands of a passing Bedouin who's driving a pick-up that's falling to pieces and has bald tyres but is still able to extricate our go-anywhere, do-anything vehicle. The cost: a stern lecture in phrase-book Arabic about how to drive in the desert. I'm going to need it. I have a feeling a camel might be easier!

Following the camel trails north, along the edge of a series of vertigo-inducing sheer sandstone canyons, we reach what many people consider to be one of the great wonders of the world. The Lonely Planet guidebook says: 'If you are only going to see one place in Jordan, or the whole Middle East for that matter, make it Petra.' The 'rose-red city, half as old as time'

Overleaf: Mrs Motor Hamdou makes us dinner

dates from 7000 BC and it truly is like reaching back and touching the beginning of time.

We park and walk into a narrow, pencil-thin space torn in the rocks, 3 kilometres long - sometimes no wider than 3 metres, sometimes as high as 180 metres. It feels damp and cool and echoes to the shouts of the Bedouin horsemen who offer to let you gallop wildly through this dark and mysterious entrance to another world.

Petra was the ancient capital of the Nabateans, nomadic Arabs who settled here and dominated this south-western area of the Middle East in pre-Roman times. At first they thrived on plundering the silk and spice caravans coming in from the East; then they got richer still by forcing them to pay protection taxes. The city they built at the end of this hidden pathway is truly remarkable. Its temples, tombs and houses are, literally, carved out of the huge sandstone rocks, secreted away within a network of interlinking valleys.

It was several hundred years before the Romans took the city in AD 106 and set about throwing up the usual run of colonnaded streets, amphitheatres and elaborate hot baths. But with the rise of other trading centres further north Petra gradually declined, and it finally disappeared into obscurity in the twelfth century.

For the next seven hundred years its existence was known only to the local Bedouin descendants of the Nabateans. Then, in 1812, a young Swiss explorer called Johann Ludwig Burckhardt, a convert to Islam, rediscovered the forgotten city, bluffing the locals into revealing the entrance to the path we are now walking down.

Just as I think there's no end to the path, we round a bend and walk into the sunlight to be confronted by the towering 'rose-red' façade of the Khazneh, or Treasury, one of the best preserved of Petra's buildings. Less than 100 metres away, in the deep recess of a bougainvillaea-covered cave, Mohammad Othman is dribbling 5-million-year-old coloured sand into a small glass bottle, creating intricate shapes and symbols. A tall, handsome woman in her late thirties, her hair covered by a scarf, sits by his side. She's talking to him in Arabic, discussing their plans to add new stock to the souvenir shop that they run inside the cave.

Margarita is a New Zealand nurse, a backpacker who met and fell in love with Mohammad sixteen years ago. They have recently moved into a small house in a village near Petra, but for most of the

Out of their cave: Margarita, Mohammad and the kids

early years of their marriage they lived together and brought up their three children in another cave just down the track.

'In fact it was a two-storey cave,' says Margarita. 'We slept upstairs, the donkey downstairs. But it was easy enough to get used to - after all, I had been living out of my backpack for a year and a half!

'Unlike most Bedouin wives I didn't have to move in with his family because he was already living alone in his own cave. All I had to do was to fetch the water every day and sweep the cave out once a week. I cooked on a small primus and had a frying pan and a little blue teapot.'

Mohammad was born in the caves, as was his family for eight hundred years before him. But, having worked with tourists most of his life, he was already much more used to Western ways than were his relatives.

'His attitude made a big difference,' Margarita stresses. 'It took a while, but I think everybody now considers me to be the same as them and Mohammad doesn't mind me wearing the trousers occasionally too.'

The only area where there has been some disagreement has been over the education of their three children, especially the two boys. Margarita would like them to get some of their schooling in New Zealand. Mohammad shouldn't worry too much - if they are anything like their mother, sooner or later they'll probably end up back in a cave in Petra!

It would take two or three days to explore Petra properly, but in a way it's enough just to walk and climb for a while, to stand at places like the Altar of High Sacrifice and look out across the city as the sun rises. But perhaps it's the Monastery that is the most emotive place in Petra. It's a long, hot climb along a tortuous, ancient rock path before I find myself 1500 metres up, looking out over an almost vertical drop, down into a valley that stretches away towards the Dead Sea and Israel. It's absolutely timeless. The air is still and slightly hazy as dusk falls. Nothing moves. It's a vast and empty landscape of towering rocks and peaks, tumbled and torn, silent and untouched for millions of years - as far as the eye can see, as far as the imagination allows. For ever.

Behind me the Monastery is now bathed in the warm orange glow of a spectacular sunset. It's an enormous solid piece of carved rock 40 metres high and 45 metres wide, a huge, echoing chamber clawed back out of the mountain. It took sixty years to create, an extraordinary testament to the whole idea of commitment. For the first time on my trip I feel really moved, perhaps as much to do with the hunger in my own life as with the thought of a lot of Nabateans spending all those years chipping away at rocks. Perhaps the moment is right.

It makes me think, too. A journey like this one, wonderful as it is in its

On top of the world -
my meeting with Dot at the
Monastery in Petra

self-empowerment, can only reinforce the need we all have to find some kind of permanence in our lives - the desire *I* have to create something, to commit to a future shared.

Several travellers have clambered to the top of the Monastery. The air is still and quiet, broken gently by the sound of a flute, by single notes drifting away towards the sunset. A bottle of arak, the fiery aniseed Arabic liqueur, is passed round, warming the spirit as well as the body. The power of this place lies as much in its desolation as in its beauty. We feel in awe of it.

A few of the people here I met before in Amman and further back down the valley. But there is one I am drawn to; she is like a touchstone for my soul and I feel as though I have journeyed far in search of her. Dot Feast is South African. She's on a journey too, a young doctor drawn from across another ocean to a point and a place in time, unplanned and unprepared, with no preconceptions. She has only the desire to listen to the songs of love, Arabic melodies entwined in the warmth of this Jordanian night. Dot's laughing, her flaxen hair pulled back from the softness and sensuality of her face, her skin a golden wash from the setting sun, her eyes alive and at peace

The hidden entrance to Petra

with the passing of these moments, with what must be the thrill of sitting on the edge of the world, of being so much higher than all she can see.

For me it's a sudden realization, a moment of true discovery and understanding. I shall never ever forget Dot's look, the glances that pass between us, the intense emotion I feel at wanting to be with her and for her - or the magic of the life we share together later that night in Petra. We will again in so many other places, but I'm not to know that when I drive off the next morning for Syria, and she prepares to return to her work in London.

The first rule is not to show anybody that you're nervous. The second is to convince yourself, privately, that you're not being really stupid. It's getting dark and I've turned off the road and started driving out across the desert towards the distant oasis of Palmyra - Tadmoor, as it's also known - about 250 kilometres away (in a reasonably straight line). We are heading north and east again, into Syria, but carefully skirting Iraq, which has refused us visas. Ultimately we are trying to find a way through the Kurdish areas of northern Iraq and Turkey. Destination: Iran.

I'm looking for Motor Hamdou, a Bedouin who appeared unannounced out of the desert one night during a previous trip and invited me to his tent. I know he lives somewhere in this area, no more than 16 kilometres from the start of the tracks to Palmyra and quite close to a slight rise in the desert. But two years have passed since I was here. Has he moved on?

Ron is being very patient, slightly disbelieving. The boys are following along diligently, doing a few wheelies here and there to exercise their four-wheel-drive spunkiness. On the horizon, a nomad is herding his sheep home (wherever that might be - there's nothing visible for miles). I drive across the sand towards him. 'Motor Hamdou?' I inquire with my best Arabic accent (which probably sounds more like Japanese), but loudly (the British always seem to think foreigners understand them better if they shout).

The shepherd looks startled. I say it again, more quietly. Three times. 'Aaaah, Motor Hamdou!' he exclaims as though he's revealing the tablets of Moses to me and I haven't just uttered those very same words four times. Then he points a finger unerringly out across the desert.

This is standard in the desert. Follow my finger (and the fact that it's pointing towards yet another piece of flat sand) and you'll never get lost! Sure enough, after a few hundred yards I

Motor Hamdou tries out Wah Wah

see the tent, and a patch of green where water is being pumped. Motor Hamdou comes flying across the desert, the very picture of a wild infidel, his long dark robes flapping about him, his red and white head-dress looking as though it's about to fall off.

'Simon, Simon!' he shouts as we come to a halt. 'Simon!' And we embrace. It's extraordinary how, after spending one night with a Bedouin farmer and his family two years back, I can return and, before he could possibly have recognized me, he knows who it is. Must be the wheels!

Now it's party-time in the desert, with friends and members of Hamdou's family appearing from all over. Blankets and mats are spread on the sand, fires lit and food prepared. The conversation is a bit limited, but there's a lot of smiling going on and hands being held. And that's enough really. Ron makes the mistake of producing his Polaroid camera: instant colour pictures can become very addictive. Hamdou poses with everybody, and everybody poses with each other. The falcons are fetched, and then even the women and children. Times are changing in the desert.

That night, as is the Bedouin tradition, the best bedding is brought out and we are tucked in by our host. Another member of the family sleeps at our feet and is responsible for ensuring that the covers remain in place and that we are properly protected from the cold desert night.

Breakfast the next morning is our treat - and the grand opening of Ali's goodies box. This is going to be the first 'Big Bedouin Breakfast' all right - global cultural harassment of the worst order! Well, they had sat by and made us taste all their weird and wonderful curds 'n' things - so bring on the pop tarts, the Marmite, the Ambrosia rice pudding, the Bird's Eye custard and the rhubarb crumble! It was hysterically successful. After much suspicious nibbling and slurping the pop tarts and Marmite are given the big thumbs up - but an Ambrosia/Bird's Eye mix gets the big finger.

We spend two wonderful days with Hamdou and his friends, smiling and learning - slowly, but always learning. On the last morning, I get up early and drive alone towards the rising sun until I feel its heat on my face and I'm on the edge of being very lost. It's the most natural thing in the world to want to run naked in the desert. I run and run until I am burning from the heat and my feet are bruised and sore from the stones. I can see for miles, I can feel everything, I can be whatever I want and shout as loud as I like.

Palmyra is another of the world's great historical sites. It was certainly one of the most important trading centres along the Silk Route between Europe and India - precisely because it is in the middle of nowhere. Legend has it that **Overleaf: Palmyra - the** Palmyra dates from 1900 BC. What we do know is that it prospered **jewel in the Syrian crown**

and grew most dramatically under the Romans, becoming a colony in AD 217. Certainly its remains show quite graphically just how wealthy a city it was during those days. Its huge temple and elegantly colonnaded central avenue are among some of the best-preserved ruins in the world. After a succession of rulers, the famous half-Greek/half-Arab Zenobia, 'the most heroic of her sex' - as Edward Gibbon described her in *The Decline and Fall of the Roman Empire* - used Palmyra as a base from which to conquer Egypt and large areas of Asia Minor. The city was destroyed by a devastating earthquake in 1089. It was not rediscovered until the late 1600s, and even then excavations did not begin until the 1920s.

'It's hot (120°F+[40°C]). It's dusty. It's old. It's in the middle of nowhere (nearest town 300 kilometres). The water's negligible and lousy. It's the desert, but I'm having a ball.'

That was a card sent to my parents in 1962 from Palmyra. I clearly didn't relate to the ruins very much, but seem determined to shock a bit and reassure a bit all in the same sentence. I suppose it was all about trying to prove something - about saying: don't worry, I can look after myself, even under the most difficult conditions. It was all about playing up the 'Boy's Own' image a bit, too.

'I travelled out to Palmyra,' I wrote, 'in a special desert bus [there were no proper roads there in 1962] belonging to the Iraq Petroleum Company, for free of course. I stayed in Palmyra (for a week) and slept with the Bedouins.'

The story I did leave out, though, would have really upset my mother - prompting, I suspect, an immediate attempt to haul me back home. On my first night in Palmyra I made camp under the date palms that lie thick around the edge of the oasis. I was almost immediately made welcome by a Bedouin family who had set up their tent about 100 metres out in the desert. It became a habit over the next four days for me to share their evening meal, consisting of a light, rather greasy soup, bobbing with lumps of very fatty meat which they scooped up with flat, unleavened bread. On the fifth night I arrived at the tent to find the usual group of four men and three boys swollen to more than a dozen people, all obviously wearing their best robes. Dinner that night was also different. Before the usual greasy soup, a flat dish covered in small strips of roasted meat was handed round to the older men in the group. Then,

after some hesitation and discussion, the plate was offered to me. As the others had done, I took only one small piece. It was slightly tough, and tasted like rather sweet chicken. Curious, I used my phrase-book Arabic to find out what I had just eaten. Again, after some hesitation and a certain amount of giggling, I was taken by the arm and led outside.

Behind the tent was a pile of rugs about 1.5 metres high. The man escorting me started to peel back one of the corners until he got to a white shroud. The dead man was very old and painfully thin, and I could see quite clearly how difficult it must have been for them to have got a clean slice of flesh off his right thigh. No, I didn't throw up. It would have been rude. But he didn't taste that bad, anyway.

It wasn't until I got to Baghdad a few weeks later that I was able to discover what might have been the reason for this bizarre ritual. An American Arabist studying at the university there told me that there was certainly no record of any kind of cannibalism amongst the Bedouin, but, symbolically, it was quite possible that an important tribal leader might be honoured in this way by other elders. There are, however, some unusual nomadic culinary traditions, like drinking the blood of living animals and eating stewed dishes such as camel hair and feet mixed with blood. And Marco Polo wrote about how the Mongol armies travelling through the Middle East kept themselves alive by drinking from the pierced veins of their horses while they rested.

Palmyra is a very different place today. There are a few good restaurants, for a start. A thriving town of forty thousand people has grown up around the ruins and there is a fast, straight road from Damascus. It's still in the middle of nowhere, especially when you take the desert trails like we have been doing. But it's a good deal harder from here on in - dangerous, even.

Our route lies due east towards Baghdad, then north close along the Iraqi border and across the River Euphrates at Deir-ez-Zur, before we head east again into Turkey and on to Iran. But the news is not good. We hear that the Turkish border has been closed, and there is heavy fighting between rival Kurdish groups in northern Iraq. And for the cream, Saddam is making threatening moves towards Kuwait again.

Khaliq Ayzaz is actually a traveller from Huddersfield. But being of Pakistani descent and a Muslim he has a distinct advantage, especially in this part of the world. He's going to Iran, too - *en route* to visit his father's village in Pakistan.

'I'm in the middle of it all,' he says, 'but I don't feel it - not even slightly vulnerable. I know it's strange, but it's all so peaceful here, isn't it? I suppose I would actually have to hear the bullets or the bombs before I felt any different.'

I'm not sure I want to put that one to the test. But we drive on anyway. There's not much choice. Nobody likes going back.

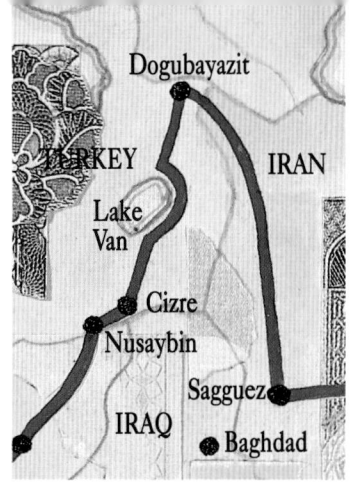

CHAPTER 9

Mama Told Me Not to Come

Running the gauntlet through Kurdistan

'**W**elcome to Turkey', says the sign. Oh yes? The Syrian-Turkish border at Nusaybin doesn't open for business until after nine in the morning. But it may as well stay closed: few people cross here. In any event it's not exactly the most welcoming place - all barbed wire, huge rolling link barriers across the road, heavily armed soldiers and enough spots for a floodlit football match. At least, that's the Turkish side of the fence.

The Syrians, as usual, are being very relaxed about it all. Tea is served while we wait for the Turks to decide whether or not it's going to be business as usual. Nobody seems very sure, which is a great excuse for the Syrian police and customs officials to come out with a lot of anti-Turkish jokes. They don't seem to have much else to do anyway.

To get to the Iranian border without going near Iraq we have to go through the far eastern, Kurdish, part of Turkey. This is a region that not many travellers see, embroiled as it is in an all-out war between anti-government guerillas and the Turkish Army. In the past few years several travellers, including British, French, Germans and Swiss, have been kidnapped by guerrillas in this area and held for a week or so in an attempt to promote the Kurdish cause. Others have been arrested and harassed by the Turkish Army and accused of being sympathetic to the guerrillas.

Common sense dictates that not too many risks should be taken in this part of the world. On the other hand we have a film to make, so Sean is trying to act casual and has been dispatched to try and get some 'hidden camera' shots of the border. He is now finding it hard to deal with the fact that one of the Syrian policemen has told him that it's OK to film. Having always imagined that you get shot if you produce cameras at places like this, Sean clearly has a major psychological barrier to overcome. Will he, won't he? He does!

But the Turks don't seem too happy, peering through the fence at us: they are obviously trying to decide whether we constitute a big enough threat to national

security to keep the border closed. But apparently not, because shortly after 9.30 the barriers creak open and, for better or for worse, we're allowed through.

The first signs of war on the road to Cizre in south-eastern Turkey

The road east from here follows the Syrian border for 96 kilometres towards the town of Cizre. It is not a very comforting sight. There are Turkish army and police checkpoints everywhere; half-deserted villages with bullet-spattered walls and shattered windows; and the burnt out wrecks of trucks and cars by the sides of the road. The Syrian border, then the Iraqi, run close by for many miles - a menacing line of barbed-wire fences, watchtowers and concrete bunkers. This is the front line, mainly there to prevent Kurdish guerrillas moving back and forth across the borders where they are supposed to have training camps. Pictures are definitely forbidden around here.

Cizre is like the end of the world. Nothing moves on the streets of this place after dark except armoured cars and tanks. We hear distant sirens and watch the sweep of searchlights targeting God knows who, what or why. More than fifty thousand people lived here once - fewer than fifteen thousand now remain in a town that is as good as dead, scarred by years of bitter fighting and oppression. Most of its businesses appear closed, its schools half empty. The war here in south-eastern Turkey is one of the most violent and unreported in the Middle East. What began in the mid-1980s as an armed Kurdish insurgency is now taking on the dimensions of a

full-blown war. More than three hundred thousand Turkish troops and police have been committed to defeat the fighters of the PKK, the militant Marxist Kurdish Workers' Party. More than sixteen thousand people have been killed so far.

It's time to move on. I feel the journalist in me coming out and must remember that I am supposed to be following travellers out to India not getting stuck into reporting another war. I've been doing all that sort of thing for too long - seventeen wars and revolutions too long already. But it's hard not to want to know, not to want to find out what is really going on.

No matter how brave a face one puts on it, or how much travelling through these kinds of areas can be justified, there's no doubt that this is out-on-a-limb time. But some travellers blunder into trouble by mistake; some are just unthinking; and others take calculated risks. Like me, Andy Ling from Goodna, Australia, has been drawn to this area because he wants to find out more. We run into him in a seedy, run-down hotel near the border. He is aware that his journey through the Middle East will inevitably entail a degree of risk, but, he believes, it is an acceptable risk:

'It's a mystery heading into the unknown,' he says. 'You don't really know what it's like unless you come here. They say there are terrorists round every corner, they warn you that it's dangerous, but you will never know unless you come here. And invariably it's completely different from what you've read or been told.

'If you listened to all the stories, you might be dead but you would never get up off your butt and find out anything in this world. This way you get to see both sides of the story. You realize the Turks in western Turkey know nothing about what's happening in the east, in their own country. Most people in Australia don't even know who the Kurds are, yet there's many thousands living there at the moment. Maybe my travelling through areas like this will also enable me to help other people understand what's going on.'

It's hard not to sympathize with or approve of that kind of attitude. Ignorance of the world we live in and the way of other people's lives is the greatest barrier to understanding and peace. Knowledge doesn't only come out of a book; more valuably, it comes from experience and consideration. That in itself entails risk. How boring and colourless, pointless even, life would be without the challenge of discovery and learning. I can remember many times during my first trip out to the East in 1962 when I used to fantasize about being a 'standard bearer for the truth', and I was always referring in my letters back home to my 'need to learn' and to get something useful out of my experiences.

The truth at the moment, though, is that the only way to deal with the situation in this part of Turkey is to get out of here

as quickly as possible. Which we do, heading north through the hills and up towards Lake Van and the town of Dogubeyazit on the Turkish-Iranian border.

I would like to drive faster, but the roads are so narrow and twisty that it's hard to make much over 50 kph. Then we follow the flow of a river through a valley of rich farmland, the fields green and sparkling with fresh-grown crops, and grasslands swarming with the slowly moving backs of grazing sheep and cattle.

Occasionally, set back in the hills, I glimpse the sandbagged bunkers and fortified positions of the Turkish Army, isolated ghettos of firepower where nobody dares step outside their perimeter without mounting a full-scale military operation. The Turkish flag flies defiantly, but the reality is much more cautious. In the towns the atmosphere can be cut with a knife: stand-offs in the street between a hostile Turkish Army and a hostile Kurdish population. Groups of silent men, flat caps pulled low, waiting for a hand on their shoulder or the crack of a bullet. Arrest, torture and death come without warning in this part of the world.

Many of the people in these areas are refugees, forced from their homes by the war, their villages burnt to the ground by the Army. Now they are taking refuge with friends and relatives before they might have to move on yet again. Nearly 2 million have fled over the last ten years. But if you are a young Turkish soldier drafted in from the west of the country to fight this nasty little war it must be impossible, looking into these faces, to decide who is your enemy and who is your friend. Probably the only time you will ever know is when it's too late.

Earlier this year I travelled through this area with a Turkish militiaman by the name of Black Eyebrow (that's the literal English translation). We followed an army patrol to the scene of an ambush where we found the body of a young soldier, returning from home leave, lying by the side of the road. His hands had been tied, his shirt stripped from his body. The PKK had dragged him from a taxi in the middle of the night and ripped his twenty-year-old body apart, spraying him with at least sixty bullets from a sub-machine gun. Black Eyebrow, tears coursing down his face, bent and gently gathered up the boy's brains from the verge, placing them carefully beneath a mound of fresh earth and grass. It's hard to push those images out of my mind as we drive through this wild and beautiful land.

It's getting late, and we know we must find a place to stay. If you sleep out, the chances are that an army patrol might find you and shoot you before you have a chance to explain. Or the PKK might get to you first. Sometimes you just can't win.

Driving round a bend in the road near the town of Batman, I spot a figure standing under the tree-line about 30 metres off the road. My instinct is to put my foot down and drive like hell. But my curiosity gets the better of me when the figure waves, and then another appears,

Overleaf: Safety still some way ahead - in the shadow of Mount Ararat

with a guitar. There are six of them in the group. Young guerrillas fresh from the villages, their job is just to watch the road and make note of every military vehicle that passes. They don't even have guns. But they sing very enthusiastically and couldn't be more friendly. I sit with them with my feet in a stream, take cover under the trees when an army helicopter flies high overhead, and wish them luck when I leave. What else can I say? They look very unsure of their future.

We are spending the night in a town on the edge of Lake Van. Within a few minutes of us checking into a small guest house, three cars and an armoured personnel carrier full of Turkish security police arrive and demand our passports. We are told not to leave the guest house, although after much debate we are finally allowed to go to a local restaurant - but only under guard and only for an hour. Even while we are there, and being watched, more leather-coated police demand our passports. It is a relief to drive on the next morning - short-lived though the pleasure is to be.

Sean has drawn the short straw again. He is doing some 'hidden camera' work from the inside of the Land Rover, using the smallest of our three cameras and trying to film an army convoy coming down the road towards us. I can see him and Dan in my rear-view mirror, but I only recognize he is filming because that's what I know he is doing. Then I lose sight of the Land Rover as I drive up over the top of a hill and past an army checkpoint on my left.

About a mile or so down the road Ron and I realize the boys are no longer with us. We stop and wait for nearly fifteen minutes before I decide we should go back and look. We turn back towards the hilltop and, edging very cautiously over the brow, I see them - stopped in the middle of the road, surrounded by soldiers, two armoured cars blocking their escape. I start to reverse, but it's too late. We've been spotted. Several soldiers start running down the road towards us, waving their rifles. One of the armoured cars swivels round and lowers its gun. We know the game is up. A soldier in the convoy using infra-red binoculars had spotted Sean filming, and radioed to the army camp on the road ahead to stop his vehicle.

We spend the next six hours trying to look innocent and waiting for orders to come down from on high to tell our guards what to do. Sean plays at being one of the boys and tells stories about being a Manchester United fan (a favourite in Turkey after Galataseray, the Istanbul club, beat them in the European Cup); I play the slightly stern group leader demanding to know, all bruised innocence, what is going on and how much longer we will be inconvenienced; Ron and Dan stay in the background looking bored. Spies? Dangerous? Us? You can't be serious!

But the soldiers are only doing their job. It never hurts to stand back sometimes and remember that. The inconvenience of a group of foreigners is really irrelevant

when you are trying to fight a war. It can only make matters worse if you start jumping up and down and shouting in a language they can't even understand. That's how people get shot.

Eventually we are taken under armed escort 48 kilometres to the military police headquarters in the town we left earlier that morning. Here, in front of a fire in the officers' mess, a major views the tape taken from Sean's camera. It soon becomes apparent that we must be tourists after all - there are more sheep on the tape than soldiers! There is relief all round. And then we are free to go - with much back-slapping and more laughter about Manchester United. By now we've decided that we will tell everybody we're from Manchester. It worked a charm!

It is shortly after one in the morning and the wind is getting up. Within an hour the tent is being lashed by a ferocious storm, the rain flying almost horizontally off the turbulent waters of Lake Van. Every rope is straining at its pegs, the whole tent flapping violently and threatening to tear itself apart at the seams.

I'm very sick. Headache, nausea, the runs, the spectre of that bug, *the* bug: giardia (or giardia lamblia, as Dot would say, being a doctor and wanting to be a proper doctor about these things!). I don't want to go home, but I wouldn't mind going back to Motor Hamdou's tent in Syria. It's hard to think that only two days ago we were in the middle of the desert and the temperature was up in the thirties. Now it's almost zero. I feel terrible - and very cold.

Everything is wet. I'm wearing two pairs of trousers, three tee-shirts, a sweater and two jackets and I'm in my sleeping bag, but I'm still freezing. I dread the thought of tomorrow. There's a snow line up ahead and we will be driving some 2700 metres up into the mountains. Please let this be our last night in south-eastern Turkey.

We have to make the border town of Dogubayazit before nightfall. Once again we are running late, slowed down by army checkpoints and the long climb through the mountains. The road we are following is closed after dark and even the army stays away: this is PKK territory. Our window of daylight fades fast, but the last roadblock before the pass waves us on. We must go, they say, quickly. Before we know what's happening time has run out, it's dark already and there's another 100 kilometres to go.

We drive very fast, with our lights out. Even though it's a brilliant moonlit night, there's no way we can be distinguished from an army vehicle - and many have been ambushed along this stretch of road. The stereo is off, the windows are open. We are alert for the first sound of gunfire. It's the longest (and the hairiest) 100 kilometres we've driven since leaving London. At least I've forgotten about being cold.

Overleaf: Short-haired, tight-thighed and super-fit - India the hard way

The voice of the law makes itself clearly heard in Dogubayazit. Police tannoys ring out across the rutted, rainswept roads, a constant reminder of the war. This sprawling, dingy border town is the last stop before Iran, and the place has the feel of Vietnam about it. Helicopters clatter overhead, bombs get thrown and people get shot - unexpected, unexplained and judiciously ignored. There's an underlying, unsettling fear here that makes it feel like nobody can be trusted, that a door is being opened on an oppressive world where the only law is the law of the gun.

Travellers call this place 'Dog-in-a-basket' or just plain 'Dog'. It's the pits, even if it does lie within sight of the sparkling snows of Mount Ararat and the jagged rock slopes where Noah's Ark is supposed to have foundered. Alexander the Great passed through here in 333 BC. He would have known nothing about Noah's Ark, but he would certainly have known about the Great Flood. That had been a story floating around the ancient world for hundreds of years before the Bible was ever written. But in the summer of 1270, Marco Polo actually went hunting for the Ark. He had been told that the 'ship of the world' might be visible as a black patch of snow on the slopes of the 5000-metre mountain. He didn't find it, but he did discover what must be the first-ever use of petroleum. Not far from here, just north of what was then the border with Persia, now Iran, 'there is a fountain of oil which discharges so great a quantity as to load a thousand camels,' he wrote. 'It is not used for food,' he adds, sounding rather surprised, 'but as fuel for lamps'.

Travellers these days are not likely to discover very much around this region except roadblocks. But, like it or not, Dogubayazit is another one of those inevitable travellers' bottlenecks. Today it's the only overland route through to Iran. Eventually anybody India-bound will meet up here - slightly apprehensive, no doubt, as they gird up their loins before taking on the Islamic revolution.

Chiara and Stuart, the English couple whom we last saw on the Turkish coast, have arrived in their Land Rover. They have a couple of new passengers on board: John Lowe, an Englishman hitching and bussing his way to India, and Sumela, a small roadside Turkish dog bought in exchange for a cigarette. John's getting a lift into Iran, but the dog is going all the way, her life changed forever on the whim of a passing traveller. Chiara and Stuart don't seem to have changed much, though: they're still up to their ears in Land Rover problems. But space must be a bit tight - and a dog can't do much for Chiara and Stuart's sex life either. 'Ha!' explodes Chiara, with that laugh again, 'It might just improve it!' Stuart, who has definitely put on weight and is beginning to look a bit wild now, blushes deeply and pats the dog. What else can he do when Ron's filming the whole scene?

There are a few cyclists here, too. Well, Paul Dixon and Brian Kinsella from Dublin are supposed to be cycling to India but nobody's yet seen them on their

bikes. Now they're loading them on to the roof of a Land Rover owned by a Spanish couple from Barcelona on their way, they think, to Mongolia. There are some German and Swiss cyclists on their way through, too. Short-haired, tight-thighed and super-fit, they are working on their mountain bikes and racers before the long haul through Iran. Rob and Karen are eleven weeks out from London, greasing up what look like a couple of shopping bikes.

And there's another Dragoman truck with twenty-one people on board, including the two drivers, Anne Ford and Lindsey Grimshaw, and thirteen other women, getting their black Muslim veils and chadors ready to cover up what one of the women laughingly describes as their 'heathen bodies'. In a semi-darkened room on the top floor of a seedy backstreet hotel Anne is giving the group a run-down on the do's and don'ts of Iran. Lit by a single, naked bulb, the room dances to the shadows of the women as they try on the swathes of black cloth they are supposed to wear. The rules are harsh and simple: no hair can be shown, and the shape of the body from the shoulders to the ankles must be properly covered. It can be a daunting thought - hot and sweaty too.

Several of the travellers, including the Dragoman group, have decided to cross into Iran in convoy: safety in numbers, not out of any fear for their lives but simply because they are apprehensive about their first confrontation with the Ayatollahs. I have been there and done it all before, but for us too these next few kilometres could make quite a bit of difference. The Iranian border is known mainly for the thoroughness of its searches: cars, trucks and vans are taken to pieces and searched down to the last pocket of the last coat. It's not bombs or guns they're after, it's things like pictures of women, Western pop cassettes - and, of course, video cameras! We are now 12 250 kilometres out from London. I say a little prayer to Allah that our trip to India isn't going to end with us looking out from behind the bars of an Iranian prison.

CHAPTER 10

Into the Land of the Infidel

Taking on the Iranian Revolution

Another day, another border, another tightening of the stomach and a dose of the cold sweats. The road that runs towards the frontier is beautiful, rugged and wild, stretching eastwards towards a horizon of snow-capped hills. We stop for breakfast beneath the soaring slopes of Mount Ararat, but even that can do little to calm our nerves.

As we approach the frontier there are clearly no guns - none of the drama of the Syrian-Turkish border. But it still feels rather ominous. The Turkish customs and immigration police let us out of the country far more easily than they let us in, and even have the brass to demand some pay-off ('Hey, you have cigarettes?') for doing just what they are supposed to be doing - stamping our passports. Then it's the usual mêlée of people, pushing and shoving their way round the customs and immigration offices on the other side under the eagle eye of the late Ayatollah Khomeini, staring down from officially sanctioned, strategically placed posters.

I have no answers for what happens next. Because, in effect, nothing happens. Rather bizarrely, my conversation with one of the senior customs officers starts off with questions about English country gardens, but quickly switches to whether or not the British people really support John Major. I sense he wants to hear the worst. Being an *ex*-country boy I fail miserably with the *Gardeners' Question Time* bit, but being a *now*-journalist I succeed brilliantly at the second, painting a picture of

Time to wrap up

terrible national disillusionment with our Prime Minister, especially with his policies towards Iran. I then rubbish Douglas Hurd for good measure. I think I hit the nail with that one. All I know is that we are through customs in a record one hour (as opposed to the usual six or seven) and, even though all three of our video cameras are burning holes in the vehicles, we congratulate ourselves on having pulled off the impossible. (Last time I went through, in 1992, they even took my condoms!)

The 'Drago girls' are not being so lucky. There's a great crowd of them milling around their truck like a whirling flock of crows, their

The Drago girls sizing up their chadors

chadors flapping in the breeze. Only the occasional cigarette disappearing in through the folds of a veil gives them away. No chaste maidens among this lot. One of the women, a young writer called Hannah Vincent, is stirring things, getting dangerously close to Bosey, her boyfriend. Her chador is threatening to fly up at the front in purposeful defiance at any moment.

The problem is in a small, dingy office at the back of the customs building. An Iranian health officer has got it into his head that the Drago group should have AIDS certificates. 'But we don't have AIDS,' protests Anne, one of the two drivers.

'No, no - certificates to say you have been tested against it,' the officer persists, looking a bit puzzled himself.

Lindsey, the co-driver, has a go too, suggesting that perhaps the yellow vaccination certificates they all carry may be of some help. But she fares no better. 'Polio' and 'tetanus' don't even begin to look like the word 'AIDS'. It takes the mass entry of a few of the women, all fussing and shaking their chadors at once, that finally decides him: perhaps this is a problem best resolved as quickly as possible. A face-saving call is made to 'a senior man' and the Drago girls are let loose on Iran.

There's a lot of laughter on the Dragoman truck about wearing the chador, but there's also anger. Many of the women feel they are being forced to compromise what they consider to be some very basic principles.

'The bottom line,' Anne keeps reminding them, 'is that you've got to forget about being a woman. At least to look at.'

'You mean no shoulders, tits, bums or knees,' laughs Hannah. 'In fact nothing must be seen of my terrible, unholy body at all!'

'I think most of us feel that this is an infringement of our rights to have to cover ourselves in this way,' adds Alice Troughton. 'Nobody should be allowed to dictate what parts we should or should not cover.'

'But the fact is that we have chosen to travel through this country,' Alice continued, 'and therefore we must respect their culture and try to take on board their systems and values as much as we can. When in Rome, right?'

It's not a viewpoint accepted by many. 'They say this is to protect us from men,' adds Hannah, clearly annoyed. 'Well, I don't need my chastity being looked after by a bunch of priests or revolutionary guards, thank you very much. I'd rather look after it myself. If I show my legs to you it doesn't mean I want sex with you, it means I'm quite happy with my legs. Apart from that, I don't want to have to pull this thing on every time I go to the loo in the night.'

The argument is still going on next morning as the Dragoman truck goes through the first of what are going to be many police checkpoints and then off down the road towards Teheran. The look is compliant - the women models of hairless, shapeless chastity. But their flashing eyes and smiles do tend to give the game away.

We've all probably heard or read more stories about Iran - most of them bad - than about any other country along the route to India. It's some fifteen years since I was in Iran to see the Ayatollah Khomeini raise the sword of Islam and the Shah was overthrown. Confrontation between the Islamic fundamentalists and the great Satan America led to years of increasingly bitter conflict and mounting hysteria in both Iran and the West. For nearly ten of those years, too, Iran was at war with Iraq. Hundreds of thousands died.

Despite the death of Khomeini, the end of the war and the softening of attitudes on both sides of the political fence, this huge country still remains a threatening mystery to most outsiders. It's hard not to imagine the worst. The road swings south under the

darkening clouds of a winter sky, across great plains that stretch as far as the eye can see, away towards distant hills as high as mountains, horizons hundreds of kilometres wide. What an extraordinary place.

It all seemed very different in 1962. In fact I didn't seem to register much at all as I made my way across it, accompanied by two other English hitch-hikers I had met on the road in Jordan:

> *'We got a lift to the border (from Baghdad) by bus. We then travelled all the way to Teheran in another bus, for free of course (900 kilometres).*
>
> *On the way we went through an earthquake disaster. It was too dreadful for words, people sitting everywhere doing nothing and all the houses flattened. I will tell you more of that in my next letter.'*

I can't imagine how my parents must have reacted on reading that I was passing not only through an earthquake zone, but through a real earthquake. I hadn't, however, made as much of it as I could have done. Maybe I was beginning to understand how they might be feeling.

We are travelling down the western part of the country, following a road that runs almost parallel to the Turkish and Iraqi borders. There can't have been foreigners here for many years. There's no doubt that some of the younger people have never seen one in their lives. The revolution of 1979 and then ten years of the Iran-Iraq war have isolated much of this country from any kind of Western influence or presence. Very few people speak English or any other Western language in this area, and in most banks it's impossible even to change money. Dollars or any kind of foreign currency have not been seen since the revolution.

When we drive into the towns sometimes a thousand or more people will gather round, blocking the streets and pressing to get as close to our vehicles as possible. There is nothing threatening, but smiles don't come easy. We must smile first before the ice can be broken. Everybody

Wot! No driver?

wants to listen to our music and practise their English, most of it spoken with a strange, lilting Russian accent. Many of their teachers, I am told, have been taught by Russians. I go shopping with Dan in one town, only to find that three hundred people are blocking the entrance to the small produce store where we are buying cheese and bread. When the revolutionary guards or the police arrive

A roadside 'caff' - Iranian style

they move, but with a slowness and surliness that demonstrate defiance. There's never any trouble, just occasional tension.

As in south-eastern Turkey, our passports are examined at least three or four times a day. We find it impossible to stop in any of the towns without eventually being approached by the guards or the police. But the reason is usually the chance of a conversation and not anything sinister. It's only when we are in the more remote villages that we feel as though we have the chance to get out there a little bit on our own.

We decide to stop for the night near the town of Sagguez, where a farmer's son invites us to sleep in his parents' house. Kamman fought in the Iran-Iraq war and several of his friends were killed. But he is a staunch supporter of the revolution. He believes Khomeini was good for the people and explains how the poor in his village have been given land by the government.

Thirty of his friends are crammed into the house, a simple white brick building, the worn dirt floors covered in rugs and carpets. They are hungry to talk, to listen to our short-wave radio, to get a taste of our world and tell us more about theirs. Then they ask us to sing. The best we can do is groan our way through 'Yesterday'. Why is it that other people invariably manage to sound so much better? Kamman and his friends sing a Persian love poem - beautifully, almost faultlessly. In the end it doesn't really matter that none of us can speak each other's languages - sitting in the half-light of two flickering oil lamps, we make off-key music and laugh for the rest of the night.

Bordering as it does on two highly volatile Kurdish areas in Iraq and Turkey, this area of western Iran understandably has a high-profile military presence. It is one of the most sensitive regions in the country, and also one of the most fundamental in its beliefs. Women are rarely seen except in the evenings, when swarms of veiled figures gather like blackbirds at sunset in the gardens and parks. It's all totally alien to us, well to Sean and Dan.

We drive up a dirt track leading into some hills to set up camp beneath the trees by a small stream. We have just started cooking when we are surprised by a man in a smart black suit who appears unannounced out of the dark. Jalal, another farmer's son, was educated in Europe and speaks almost perfect English. He tells us how much of

his father's land, on which we are now camped, has been divided up and redistributed since the revolution. 'We've only 2500 hectares left,' he says, 'but we get by.'

But life is not quite as difficult as one might imagine, he adds. They can still do business and he is able to travel abroad quite freely. He also believes that the West makes too much fuss about issues like the veiling of women. 'I think these guys [the mullahs] have a point,' he says. 'Every time I go to Europe, I just have to have goddam sex. The girls show so much. Back here it's very different. You should know too,' he adds, 'that women in this country have almost the same rights as men in all the jobs and professions. But you never hear anybody in the West complaining about women's rights in a place like Saudi Arabia, where conditions are really bad for women.'

It's Saturday night in Esfahan, a large, sprawling city with a population of nearly a million and more turquoise-domed mosques and beautiful examples of ornate Islamic architecture than any other city in Iran. Most Iranians reckon it's the most laid back and cosmopolitan place, too.

By 7 p.m. the fruit juice stands, snack bars, and take-away kebab houses are packed. Most shops are staying open late, and lines are already forming for the 8 p.m. shows in the cinemas. The tree-lined avenues, the spacious parks and squares, the walks alongside the Zayande Rud River and the delicate arched bridges are crowded. Couples stroll, not hand in hand, but as close as is possible without attracting attention. The women here make a point of showing at least a bit of hair from under the front of their veils and many seem to delight in flashing a pair of jeans or a particularly colourful skirt beneath their chador. I don't think many of them would agree with Jalal, the farmer's son.

In the Sahel Snack Bar I run into John and Andy. John, who had hitched a ride from Turkey with Chiara and Stuart in their Land Rover, has now left them for a night on the town with Andy Stevens, a British cyclist going through to India. They have spent the afternoon at the Martyrs' Cemetery, where long,

The Masjed-é Emān Mosque, Esfahan

silent lines of photographs mark the gravestones of hundreds of people from this city - most of them still in their late teens and early twenties - killed in the Iran-Iraq war.

'This is a world of such different values,' says John, stirring his banana juice with

Faces of the revolution

a travel-worn finger. 'The young people I've met have such a totally non-Western attitude to life.'

'They also have totally the wrong idea about so many things in our lives,' adds Andy. He's drinking pomegranate juice. Everybody in the snack bar is watching with fascination as we talk, and Ron ducks and weaves around the table with his camera. A young woman adjusts her veil and lets slip a bit of hair. Her father looks disapproving and she pushes it back up again.

'I mean I met somebody,' Andy continues, 'who thought that AIDS was something that you caught from kissing or from holding hands and that it was a Western evil come to destroy the world. I was absolutely flabbergasted.'

'Yeah,' said John. 'This young guy asked me what it was like to drink beer and why we had to have alcohol and fall about all over the place to be happy when all you need is good friends. It really made me think.'

John is so hungry to learn. It's very inspiring to meet somebody with so much enthusiasm for discovery, and so open to ideas and change. He has left home driven by the desire to travel and by the overwhelming need to escape the personal tragedy of his parents committing suicide together. I wasn't prying. This is something he tells me about in a careful, controlled way, his words catching slightly in the back of his throat.

'Leaving England, I felt a huge sigh of relief. It's not the hardest decision I've had to take. But it's still pretty hard. I have a huge amount of emptiness in me and I don't want to face those things now. I want to be a lot more ready to listen and to relax.'

I last saw John that Saturday night in Esfahan laughing with Andy in a brightly lit cake shop, telling jokes and trying to explain them to a young Iranian student whom he had met earlier in the evening.

Bam comes up just like that. Bam - and there it is ahead of me in the desert, a sprawling oasis town famous for its dates, dominated by the walls of a mud city dating from the twelfth century. I am driving south across the Great Sand Desert, travelling fast towards Pakistan, some 400 kilometres away now. Esfahan is two days behind me already. The final leg of my trip through Iran is passing in a blur of sand and scrub, a 1500-kilometre heat haze running parallel to the border with Afghanistan,

before swinging east again. We only have a seven-day visa to get across the country.

I've already come across two French cyclists, a married couple heading home after two years on the road out to and around India; two Norwegian brothers heading to Bhutan to join their parents on holiday; and a Canadian who has been cycling for nearly five years and can't quite make up his mind whether or not it's time to stop. What is it with all these cyclists? None of this straight-out-and-back stuff. It's all epic, back-breaking, long-term commitments. Bam cannot have seen anything like it before.

They certainly had not seen many foreigners when I went through there in 1962. It was when I was in the desert outside Bam, on my way through to the frontier town of Zahedan, that I wrote my first letter home on crested Iranian police paper. I was travelling with Peter and Arthur, two other English hitch-hikers, both in their twenties. We had got separated but had agreed that if this happened we would meet up again in Zahedan. Now I was alone in the desert outside Bam, sheltering from the heat in the shade of a rock, and writing home.

My parents must *have been concerned. Even though I tried to make the tone of the letter as upbeat as possible I couldn't resist mentioning the shock-horror aspects of my journey that somehow proved to me (and I hope to them) that I was really challenging myself and learning, making use of my time. But I missed them too. It was always the thought of home life, the sense of security and love - and the food, of course.*

I vividly remember one Sunday lying on the floor of a small military guard post in southern Iran where I had spent the night. One of the soldiers had brought me a bowl of fresh, clear spring water and some dry bread and dates for lunch. I sat there looking at the food for a long time and then I just started laughing. I couldn't stop thinking about Sunday lunch. The dining-room table shining with new polish and glittering with silverware and glass, our places marked by freshly pressed napkins and big china plates waiting to be filled; the roast beef, still pink in the middle; the vegetable dishes piled high with glistening green peas and steaming white-flowered cauli; tight new potatoes straight from the garden, dripping with butter and covered with sprigs of mint; the rich stock gravy; and, of course, a golden brown-sugared apple or rhubarb crumble and thick yellow custard to follow.

I could see them sitting round the table. I could see my empty place. I could see my mother's face, my father pursing his lips as he carved the joint, probably muttering about how I used only to pretend to run away; my sister, Susan, up from London and getting fed up with hearing about me. And I imagined that even my banished blonde girlfriend Viv would have been there, suddenly welcomed into the fold as somebody who might be another arm out across the world to bring me back. I could see it, taste it, smell it all. I longed for it. But yet I had no regrets. It just made me all the more determined to fly. Memories of home would always serve me better than having to be there.

The mud city in Bam - not to be missed

Akbar loves the old mud city of Bam. To him its narrow, deserted streets and court-yards hold the spirit of all his life and his family for generations past, and no doubt for generations yet to come. Akbar is a poet and a romantic, a good Muslim and an English teacher. He smiles a lot when I tell him an imaginary story about an English traveller (me dreaming about Dot) going to India and leaving messages everywhere for his lover, just in case she might be following on behind: notes on sticks planted by the side of roads in the desert; flags on hilltops; her name spelt out in stones across a mountain face.

Akbar, his dark grey suit freshly pressed, white shirt open at the neck, and an Islamically correct two-day growth of stubble, comes to the old city nearly every day. He's Bam's only English-speaking guide. But he likes to be here anyway. Today he is showing Anne and Lindsey and all the Dragoman passengers around. Akbar is too polite to express his discomfort at the way in which some of the women are cavorting in their chadors; or the fact that a couple of the men are giving the girls piggy-backs along the ramparts. He would definitely be appalled by Hannah's stories.

'Having sex in my chador was really the ultimate kind of get-back, I suppose.' She laughs loudly and flicks a mock-flirtatious look from beneath her veil at Bosey, her boyfriend. 'And he loved it, of course!' she adds.

Bosey grins enthusiastically, ignoring Akbar's attempt to interest everybody in another part of Bam's history.

'I can't stop feeling angry about it,' insists Hannah. 'I mean it is so demeaning. I just felt I had to find a way to break the rules a bit.'

Dragoman had not been having an easy time. In the southern city of Shiraz, close to the ancient ruins of Persepolis, the truck was broken into and several things stolen. The police and revolutionary guards came, but instead of investigating the robbery, one of the senior officers got furious at the way, according to him, the women were showing too much hair.

Debbie Reith, a Canadian woman in the party, explains: 'This man came after us, clambering onto the truck and ranting and raving. He was so angry. There was this kind of rage and hatred in his eyes as though we were evil, that we were invading his country. It was really frightening, but if that hadn't happened we would have come out of Iran thinking everything was just great and that, apart from the dressing up, it had all been really fun.'

'Sometimes, though, it can just be small things,' points out Heather. 'A group of us were invited by this man to visit his house and meet his wife and children. They told us we could take our chadors off and relax. They had a cassette of Western music and we were all laughing and dancing when there was a knock on the door. Even though it was only his brother we had to dress up again quickly and switch off the music. So even within the same family people have opposite views.'

'What really upsets me,' says Pene Childs, an Australian dentist, 'is the hypocrisy of it all. Do you know that male teachers are not allowed in girls' schools any more? That means the only contact most females have with males in their entire lives will be with their fathers, uncles, brothers and finally a chosen husband. And with the chador, that means the whole system is just the total domination of women. I hate it. I hate it.'

Akbar later tells me about his concerns - he feels that the arrival of so many travellers and tourists will perhaps cause problems among the young people of Bam.

'You see, we are Muslims living in a Muslim community, and in my opinion the behaviour of some of these travellers can only influence our young people in a bad way. Everybody is welcome here, but they must try to understand our ways. In my school we teach our children to be kind and nice to foreigners, to respect their culture, but to protect their own first.'

The sun is rising over our last day in Iran - and I'm sweating already, dressed up in a full-length black chador. We've stopped for breakfast near the Pakistan border, and the Drago girls have decided that I should find out just what it is they've had to put up with over the past week. I'm trying to eat and avoid the flapping bits getting into my mouth; I'm trying to clamber up into the truck; I'm just trying to walk normally - the chador gets in the way of everything.

'You see what I mean!' shouts Hannah triumphantly. 'Try squatting - then you find you've peed on your chador or fallen in the toilet.'

It doesn't take long for me to get the message - the hard way. I give up after an hour. It's time to leave Iran. The Iranians look the other way; the Pakistanis laugh - they've seen it all before. As the gates to Pakistan swing open and the Dragoman truck lumbers through, the women run on ahead, throwing their veils and chadors into the air, shouting and whooping, shaking their hair loose in the wind. From the wall of the Iranian border post the face of the Ayatollah Khomeini glares after them.

All veiled up - now I know how it feels

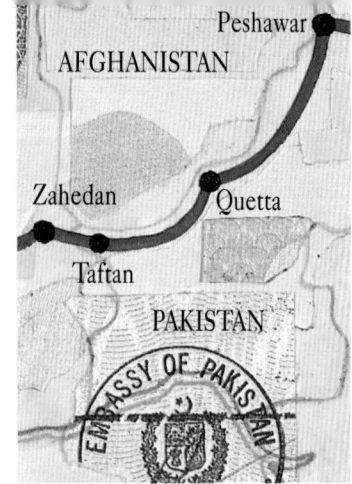

CHAPTER 11

Kalashnikov Country

Pakistan and the Afghan border - where the gun is law

Taftan is another run-down, fly-blown border town, except that this must be the true arse-end of the world. But there's nothing silent or even remotely sinister here. After Iran it's wild and exotic, strangely thrilling, with so many people carrying weapons. Squalling babies and a scrum of men, women and children, dragging their possessions with them, are being shuttled on and off a succession of brightly panelled and painted Pakistani buses. The faces are darker, the beards more dramatic, the clothes all blacks, greys, browns and whites. Heads are wrapped in scarves and turbans, bodies lost in loose-fitting smocks with baggy, draw-string trousers, shoulders draped with shawls. Some of the women are hardly veiled at all, others are covered even more than in Iran.

A dry and dust-laden wind whips around this sprawl of single-storey concrete and brick buildings, swirling the litter across the pot-holed dirt roads that stitch Taftan together. The heat settles over everything, slowing it, dirtying it even more than it is already. Traders squat in the doorways of their shops, bargaining and bartering mostly smuggled goods - cloths and prayer mats, cheap shoes and bags, belts and sunglasses. Anything, really. When I shelter from the heat in a ramshackle tea-house, money-lenders wave bundles of well-worn, tatty rupee notes in my face. Between sips of warm cola, I keep my hand over the glass to keep away the flies. I try not to smell the meat before eating it, but I'm hungry.

There's not much relief in the landscape, either. In the distance, to the north, a low range of blue, heat-hazed hills stretches away towards Afghanistan; to the east, the stone - and scrub-strewn desert seems to go on forever, crossed only by a thin trail drifting off through a darkening sky, the dull black sheen of a single railway line running alongside. Taftan is the end of the train line to Quetta, 650 kilometres away. It's the end of the line in many other ways, too.

It was almost the end of September 1962. I had been hitching in fits and starts across southern Iran before finally reaching the Pakistan border. It was here that I met up again with Arthur and Peter, the two other British hitch-hikers with whom I had been travelling on and off since Iraq.

'We are stuck now for a while,' I wrote to my parents, 'because we have to wait for the water train that will take us to Quetta for nothing. We are staying in an Indian church here, which is rather weird.'

In fact the whole thing was rather weird. This area was more unnerving than any other place along my route east. Not hostile, just suspicious and not very friendly. Strangers were not welcome, except at the 'Indian church'. This was actually a Sikh temple or gurdwara, and my first taste of the free food and accommodation traditionally provided to travellers by members of the Sikh religion. That was great. The outside loos, however, were terrible. I used to dread the trip to the squatter in the middle of the night. We soon learnt that the only safe way was to set fire to a wad of paper before lowering oneself anywhere near this deep, dark hole in the ground. That was how we drove off the monster cockroaches. Unless you did, they came out of the bowels of the earth like a bad, black moment in a Hitchcock movie, leaping up into the air and clinging on to anything they could find!

Taftan looked a bit like the cockroaches made you feel - not much different from today, more than thirty years on. You can imagine how glad we were to leave - once I had sold a few more shirts. I was now down to fewer than ten!

Packing them in in Pakistan

The water train ran once a week. We joined the scramble to cling on to the sides of the coaches and crawl up on to their flat roofs as it rumbled slowly out into the desert. I described to my parents how we had eventually been allowed to sit in the old wooden guard coach once used by troops of the British Raj. There were bench seats and grooves on the floors into which the soldiers slotted the butts of their rifles. I could imagine them sitting side by side, upright and unsmiling, buttoned to the neck in their glittering Frontier uniforms, their weapons held between their knees. Ambushes were a regular occurrence in these parts, especially in the hills.

It was to be a long slow ride to Quetta, crawling across the desert like a wooden snake on the end of a string.

Ron and Sean are filming everything that moves - revelling in the fact that we don't seem to need permission for anything. The border couldn't be more relaxed. We wander in and out of the immigration and customs offices at will. Even the police want to be interviewed.

Taftan is where we all start piling up on top of each other again. Rob and Karen are here, pushing their bikes across the border. Karen's chador is a novel combination of what looks suspiciously like a Hermès headscarf and an ankle-length light brown mac! Now why did nobody tell the Drago girls about that as an option? And coming up over the horizon, are Chiara and Stuart again, hot Land Rovering from Esfahan where I had last seen them. Chiara's definitely going native, with ethnic baubles hanging from her scarf. Stuart's still driving and looking dustier and more 'traveller' by the mile. Paul and Brian from Dublin have arrived too, and they're *still* not cycling - in fact they're in real trouble. They don't have a visa for Pakistan or a return one for Iran, and they are being bounced backwards and forwards in the 12 metres of dusty No Man's Land that separates the two countries. Their bikes and their luggage have been off-loaded from the Spanish couple's Land Rover. They look rather sorry for themselves, peering out through the railings that separate the two countries. I can't help laughing: will these guys ever get on their bikes?

But we can't afford to wait to see. The last bus is leaving, the driver hanging a Russian Kalashnikov (the ultimate status weapon in these parts) over the back of his seat. We are going to drive in convoy across the desert with some of the other travellers to try and make it to a safe place to sleep before nightfall. There is a Pakistani army and customs post at Nokkundi, a small village about 100 kilometres east.

This is definitely the badlands. It's barren and inhospitable, peopled only by nomads - some of the toughest and bravest anywhere, and fiercely independent too. The Afghan border is only a few miles away and the area is plagued by bandits robbing smugglers; smugglers killing bandits; and the police and army trying to knock them all off. Not long ago six foreign workers were kidnapped along this road; a

driver for Encounter Overland got a bullet in his leg trying to outrun a bunch of rifle-waving bandits in a Toyota pick-up; and a German woman was machine-gunned to death in her tent during a bungled robbery. Everybody seems to play by different rules. There's the customs officer who says he's single-handedly shot eight notorious smugglers to death; and the drug lord who openly boasts that he's got most customs officers eating out his right hand. Being a good Muslim, he probably keeps his left for his enemies!

Whatever the stories, there is a certain thrill in it all as we head off towards Nokkundi, the big orange and white Dragoman truck kicking up the dust in front of us; Chiara and Stuart tucked in behind - in our dust! Ron's doing one of his balancing acts out of the sunroof of *Wah Wah*, a red bandana tied tightly around his dangerously thinning hair, his eyes narrowed against the wind, the camera shuddering on its tripod. The boys are off to the side again, cutting their own track across the desert. In the evening air the Land Rover leaves a rising trail and the echoing sounds of a Cowboy Junkies tape. We're running free!

Nokkundi is just a cluster of buildings in the middle of nowhere. A small village, a customs post and the neat, whitewashed barracks of a Pakistani Army contingent. It's strange to find turbaned soldiers standing guard out here in front of tidy fences and polished brass signs on gateposts saying 'Officers' Mess' and 'Residence - Commanding Officer'. Just down the road, we are offered a corner of the customs compound for the night and an invitation to spend the evening sharing a liberal supply of imported whisky and cigarettes pulled out from under a few of the officers' beds. Dragoman cook up a meal for us all to share, then darkness falls behind a huge red sun dropping down over the desert.

It's cold. The night seems quieter than it's ever been. Our little camp, the rows of figures bedding down on the ground, is lit by the flickering of single lamps and candles. It's hard to sleep. In the far distance is the occasional sound of a passing truck. A shot echoes briefly. Somebody shouts. Then silence. No self-respecting policeman or soldier - or traveller - moves from their compound this night.

Of course we make it to Quetta - a city now better known for its swollen population of Afghan refugees and its blanket of pollution than for its glorious past as the desert fort of the British frontier forces. It's a bit of a struggle, it's hot and dirty, and yes, we have to be careful. And yes, we run low on fuel a couple of times and run into some dangerous-looking guys who wave their Kalashnikovs around. But in a way it's all par for the course. More than 15 000 kilometres out from London we're beginning to look and feel like well-seasoned overlanders. We don't change our clothes very much any more; we can eat anything that's going; even the most basic roadside diet (like the Afghani burgers with flies!) gives us some kind of pleasure; we sleep like babies in the most uncomfortable situations; we hardly flinch at the sound of gunfire; we're cool dudes, as Sean puts it, stripped to the waist and looking serious about the Land Rover in a way that makes me think he and Stuart should start travelling together.

Lourdes Hotel

Tel : 829656-60 (five lines)
61488, 822352
Fax : 0092-81-61463

College Road, P.O. Box-68, Quetta Cantt.

Lourdes Hotel is a rest stop for 'seasoned travellers', a green oasis after the long haul through Iran and across Baluchistan. It's one of those comfortable colonial bungalow complexes set among manicured lawns and flower beds, and for some reason the hotel has always allowed travellers to camp in the gardens. It's become another of those clubs whose membership is obligatory for anybody India-bound. And it's just across the road from the Café China, too - the first and only Chinese restaurant in Quetta. Travellers fall on its food like vultures on a carcass. Believe me, after eating kebabs for as many weeks as we have this place could serve Kit-e-Kat and noodles and there'd still be a queue right round the oasis!

They're all here, many old friends from back down the road: a dusty van, two trucks, a bus; three motorbikes and six bicycles; many brightly coloured tents; and washing everywhere. We're still running neck and neck with Dragoman. Anne and Lindsey have got their Mercedes truck on blocks and are doing a major oil change. This is the glam team, as everybody calls them, except that the glam's gone a bit greasy and mechanical today.

'I'm not looking for a job driving a truck,' explains Lindsey, a tall, striking brunette from Edinburgh, and the glammer of the glam two, 'but this is a great way of going to India. There are a lot of advantages for us as women. We get through all the red tape much quicker for a start.'

'They look at us,' says Anne, the lead driver, 'then they look again and wave us on. In countries like Iran and Pakistan they can't deal with the fact that we are women and are, in their terms, doing a man's job.'

Lindsey and Anne, the glam team, getting greasy

With a huge, warm smile like Anne's it's not surprising.

I should imagine there must be a lot of double-takes going on as this lot pass by. A couple of days back, I remember a Pakistani café owner pointing with amazement at Rob and Karen as they cycled down the road. 'Why they not fly by plane?' he asked. When I told him people did this sort of thing because they enjoyed it, he could only shake his head and laugh: 'Incomplete man, incomplete man.' So what brings an English double-decker full of Danes to the middle of Pakistan? That's what I want to know! Parked up under the trees is a 1960 red London bus, lumbering its way to India with eight Danish men and women on board.

'Adventure, friendship and fun - and a lot of maintenance,' says Erika, who is blonde and breastily Scandinavian. She and her friends got together and paid equal shares to buy the bus and equip it for the long overland trip. The top deck has been turned into sleeping quarters with double bunk beds, the downstairs a kitchen and sitting area. It's all very basic.

'We are going to be travelling for a year and we thought this would be the cheapest and most fun way of getting to India. It is. The only problem is that it's like a magnet. We count seconds from when we stop in a little village to when we can't see out of the windows for crowds.'

Well... they could have travelled more discreetly.

François Xavier tends to attract a bit of attention too - mainly for his equipment and its obvious antiqueness. François is all French khaki shorts and plaid shirts, with a dusty Chevy van and an attentive lover called Brigitte. It's hard not to imagine the pith helmets. But it's the explorer clutter that comes out of the back of the van that's arousing everybody's interest. Much of it must be at least fifty years old: a number of large, battered tin trunks; an ancient iron cooking range; and a rusting contraption on three tepee-type legs for cooling water. Not to mention, of course, plenty of gifts for the natives.

'Sometimes we have to thank someone for a particular service and then to express our gratitude we give them a small gift,' explains François. 'Even needles. In some places there is a real demand for needles. And small samples of French perfumes. People are very pleased for things like this.'

François, a senior administrator with the European Parliament, is taking six months out for what he calls 'a

A quarter-pounder with flies, please - but no chips

voyage of discovery' around the Muslim world. Full of theories, very French, he and Brigitte are now on their way back from China. François has obviously done this kind of thing before, and he is meticulous in his organization. Breakfast with him

and Brigitte is a 'civilized way to begin our day', as they explain it, sipping fresh coffee in a choice corner of the hotel garden. Of course, they are the kind of travellers who always manage to get the best spot by the pool - by default almost.

Another eccentric Frenchman? Perhaps. But thirty-nine-year-old Dave Woodburn's a bit like that too. He's a long-time traveller and fireside philosopher driving out to India on a much-tinkered-with BMW motorcycle and sidecar, accompanied by Emy, his Filipino wife, who's thirty-four, and Mattea, their six-year-old daughter. In fact Dave and Emy have already done the trip twice before, once when Mattea was eighteen months old. She's now on to her third passport, with thirty-one countries under her little belt. Snoopy playing at being the Red Baron springs to mind. Here they are, the happy Woodburn family, all leather flying helmets and goggles, trundling along on top of their own style of dog kennel.

Dave, short and bearded, works carefully on the art of maintaining their motorbike-home; Emy cooks and washes and gives their daughter her lessons (a properly prepared, school-approved curriculum) every morning and evening; Mattea does her homework diligently and plays quietly beside their small tent. Sometimes, they

The Woodburns: Dave, Emy and Mattea on the road in Kalashnikov country

all read the Bible together. It's impossible not to like Dave and Emy, and not to fall in love with Mattea. There's nothing pushy or precocious about this skinny little dark-haired girl. Mattea's bright and alert, well behaved and happy. She relates as much to adults as to other children she might meet. And she has an extraordinary sense of the world around her, of people and places.

'You know,' says Dave, 'a lot of parents use their children as an excuse for what they can't do in life, and then they end up asking what went wrong in their lives.

Do you think it's fair that a husband and wife go to work and the TV is used as a babysitter till somebody comes home? Mattea has always been given our love and been properly cared for. We spend all our time together, and because of this I believe we're more than the average happy family. Mattea's already a year ahead in her lessons and has a deeper understanding of many things, far more than I did at her age. This can only be good for her education and for her character.'

One of the most misleading things about Pakistan is the maps. I'm travelling north along what is supposed to be the main road to the North-West Frontier and the Khyber Pass that leads into Afghanistan. But it's little more than a rock path in some places - if we're lucky. The desert is past us now. This is a relentless landscape of rugged, arid hills funnelling down through narrow, fertile valleys of corn and fruit. This is the homeland of the Pathan. It's as dangerous here as it was on the road to Quetta, and few people travel alone or at night unless they have an armed escort. Most only stop in the main towns or in govern-ment police posts. These are self-governing tribal lands where the only law comes from the local chiefs and the threat of the gun. The inhabitants are the descendants of the lost tribes of Judea - warriors who have guarded these desolate frontier regions for centuries.

So here I am, eyes peeled for bandits, when I run into thirty or so wild-looking men with beards, turbans and guns, kicking up the dust and shimmying down to a small fiddle and a bit of hip-shaking like they're out for somebody's blood - mine, maybe. But this is the thing about travel. You can set out expecting to find a war and end up at a wedding - even if they are firing in the air. This is, however, no shotgun marriage. The boy's parents have had to come up with 90 000 rupees for the bride - that's about £2000 and enough to buy 1.5 hectares of land in this part of Pakistan (or five Kalashnikovs, for that matter).

My arrival is obviously seen as a good omen and I am hustled into one of the village huts. Surrounded in the dark by a hot, sweating press of warriors, I am then fed and watered with choice selections from the wedding feast. If I can forget the guns and the sinister machinations of my preconditioned Western imagination, I should have a good time.

Amir Mohammed, a friend of the family, says that finding the money to pay for a wedding can sometimes mean having to rob the rich to pay the poor. But maybe there's not that much choice. A Muslim boy must marry and have children, and his family has six sons. Women are rarely seen around

**Overleaf: A tribal stag party
in Baluchistan**

here - and even if they are, there can be no contact, visual or verbal, through the suffocating, all-embracing walls of the full-length purdah (veil) that is favoured in these parts. This is a land where the husband can still exercise his right to shoot his wife if she dares to step out of line - or leave the house even - without his permission.

'There can be no change in this system. One hundred years more still no change,' explains Mohammed. 'One hundred years.' And he sighs. Very little has changed in the social fabric of these remote villages except perhaps the level of frustration among young people, especially the boys, as they become increasingly exposed to images of an outside world dominated by money and sex and the apparent freedom to have both at will.

Guns, on the other hand, are as normal a part of their culture and growing up as, say, cars are in ours. Guns have also become big business in this border area with Afghanistan, where war and conflict have ruled for more than fifteen years. In the villages around the town of Dara in the North-West Frontier province there are nearly forty thousand people in the arms business, producing as many as seven hundred weapons a day. Walk down the main street of wooden and adobe buildings and you will find the shops filled with assault rifles, machine guns, pistols and grenades, while out the back are artillery pieces, recoil-less rifles and anti-tank weapons. They are all made locally, some of them almost perfect copies of standard military hardware from Russia, Europe and America.

For most travellers it's mind-blowing stuff - even more when they notice that some shops also sell marijuana, hash and opium in the same way that back home a stall-holder might display fruit and veg on market day. And nobody's going to stop you buying or trying anything. Smoke a joint, eat some opium, or blow away a mountain top with a recoil-less rifle. Nobody will say no. It can be a strangely liberating experience, a bit like the sensation you get when you play those 'smash all the china you can with three balls' stands at English country fairs. Breaking the rules is in everyone's blood.

'It's amazing,' says Mark Anderson, 'just to be able to walk around and see so many things which you hear about and read about and here they are - right in front of you. In our society drugs and guns are so hidden they are all underworld stuff.' Mark's an accountant from Glasgow. He's been on the road for a few months now and is already sensing a change in his lifestyle. 'I suppose you have to appreciate that this is just business really. Profits and loss like anywhere else. It's just that the product's different.'

Everything is very different around here. For me the best way to travel is with the freedom to head off down that unmarked track. It's all to do with things you don't plan and people you never expect to meet.

Night is falling and yet again we're looking for a safe place to sleep. Ahead of me is a small village encircled by high mud-brick walls, silhouetted threateningly against a rapidly darkening sky. Dogs bark and there is the sound of a simple flute playing. I've fallen into the hands of a local Pathan chief, who, to my great relief, seems delighted to welcome me into his home.

Saddar Abdul Quadir, as broad as he is tall, his head swathed in a swirling white turban that befits his rank, is chief of the Hamzazi, a tribe of some thirty thousand people.

With his Kalashnikov to hand, the chief sits cross-legged on the richly woven carpets of his receiving room. He talks fondly of the days when the British brought a sense of honour, justice and discipline to the hills. Right! All his sons, family and friends crowded into the room with us nod vigorously in agreement.

Getting into the spirit of things

'And the BBC very good too,' the chief suddenly adds, firmly. 'But it is no more proper BBC without Mark Tully.' He sounds almost threatening.

Now this is what I like about travel: roll up to a Pathan village in the middle of nowhere and find a tribal chief bemoaning the loss of the BBC's Delhi correspondent and muttering darkly about the declining standards of the venerable British Broadcasting Corporation. The chief does indeed still tune his little battery-operated portable radio into the stately, if crackly, airwaves of the BBC World Service every night. But now there's a new voice finding its way into the consciousness of these people. In the nineties no village is too remote for the global programming of satellite television - it's a huge new cultural footprint (principal shoesmith: Rupert Murdoch) planted firmly across Asia. And the chief's already got his dish balanced on a cattle pen behind the house.

The authoritative, middle-aged Mark Tully used to be as close to God as any mere mortal could ever hope to be. Today, super-slick teenage DJs, repackaged pop promos and a string of commercial television stations command the airwaves, dishing out diets of sex, soap, sport and other current affairs to an audience that includes some of the world's most impoverished and illiterate people. But the chief is adamant that this change can only be for the better - that the coming of the TV age is of real educational value. This village of farmers only got regular electricity in 1994 - and already three of the richer families have hooked themselves up to the

multi-channelled Star TV being beamed out of Hong Kong seven days a week, twenty-four hours a day.

'Our traditions and our ways will survive, but we must move forward. This is progress. I still listen to the BBC without Mark Tully, so why should I not still read the Koran even if I watch *Dallas*.'

In the market town of Dera Ismail Khan, Allah Nawaz is less sure. Drinking tea on the banks of the mighty, slow-moving Indus River, this educated fifty-year-old businessman believes that the influence of the new media age has been mainly for the worse, encouraging only a preoccupation with material things and, yes, he sighs, with sex.

Many of the women travellers I meet along this stretch of the road are experiencing what people like Allah Nawaz believe is a direct result of too much exposure to satellite television and Western books and magazines. As in Turkey and some Middle Eastern countries, the belief among Pakistani men and boys is that somehow Western women are different from their own and that they expect and want to have sex. The harassment here is more a matter of attitude than physical assault, but it does tend to colour, if not spoil, the experience for some female travellers.

A view up the Khyber - the gateway to India and the backstreet bazaars of Peshawar in Pakistan

But the impact of all this is more far-reaching than just changing attitudes towards sex. It's to do with a not-so-gradual and fundamental shift in every aspect of life in this region of the world. This is part of what we, as travellers, are passing on as we journey east. Round every dusty corner the changes can be seen - and more and more dishes are appearing. The increasing reach of the satellite has brought with it an onslaught of Western imagery and consumer advertizing on a scale never before seen in Asia.

Policing the Pass with Pepsi   It's not the view of the Khyber Pass, but the *idea* of the place - that's how one guidebook describes the classic invaders' gateway to India. But today the stone-walled forts that stand proud on these hilltops, lost and won many times over the centuries, look down on a new world order. The wars being fought these days are between the drug barons who use the Khyber Pass to move heroin and hash along the road to the West; the arms smugglers feeding weapons through to the factions struggling for power in Afghanistan; and the soft drinks giants of America.

Driving along the twisting road that leads through the pass to Afghanistan, I can't help getting the feeling that the fiercest and costliest battle must be between the Coca-Cola and Pepsi Corporations. At stake: a multi-billion-dollar business that stretches from here to the far shores of India - potentially the biggest soft drinks market in the world after China. Imagine: more than a billion thirsty people. Buildings, walls and rock faces are plastered with the big red, white and blue cola logos. Even some of the police checkpoints have slogans on their barriers.

Somehow the legends of the great invaders - of Alexander the Great and the Persian and Mogul emperors - seem far removed from the Khyber Pass of today. Far removed even from the hippie days of the mid-sixties and seventies, when the trail came down through here from northern Iran. Dave has driven to the top of the Pass with us, leaving Emy and Mattea back in the provincial capital of Peshawar. In the distance we can see the border post with Afghanistan. The soldiers travelling with us have refused to let us go any further.

'It's not the wild place it was when I first went though here in 1978,' Dave says, 'but I still get a feeling of excitement, of being in some kind of storybook. I can't help thinking about when the British were fighting the tribes to get a foothold here. All the different regiments that struggled up through these hills. All those soldiers in their red and white uniforms, with no sense of history or any understanding of why they were there, grumbling about the heat and just wishing they were back home with a plate of pie and mash. And the sergeant giving them a bollocking because they were marching too slow, even though he probably knew that they were going to their deaths.'

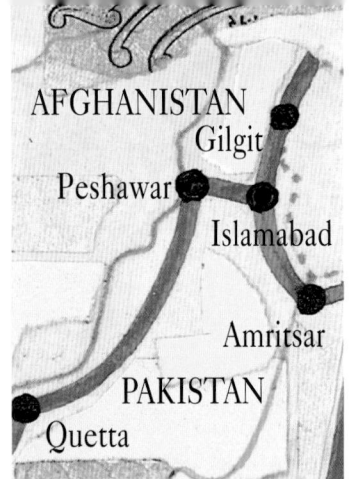

AFGHANISTAN
Gilgit
Peshawar
Islamabad
Amritsar
PAKISTAN
Quetta

CHAPTER 12

A Time To Pause

Stories round the campfire in Islamabad

The noise is deafening - and very Australian. 'Waltzing Matilda' goes punk - or just plain out of her head every Thursday night at the Colabah Club in Islamabad. This is the big promise at the end of the trail through Pakistan: Victoria Bitters, Fosters, XXXX and anything else you want to drink for six sweet hours of music, shouting, snooker and greasy beefburgers. It can only be the Aussie Embassy. The Brits would never do anything like this - God forbid, we might be hippies on drugs! And no screams of 'That's unfair!' It's true. British Embassies and High Commissions worldwide have a reputation for being generally aloof, unhelpful and unsympathetic, especially to anybody who might be 'on the road'.

The Colabah Club is one of those places where bored diplomats and expats get their knees up - a couple of rooms and some duty-free booze at the back of an embassy. Like minds always stick together, especially when they're a long way from home in a dry, Muslim state. For the traveller arriving in Pakistan after weeks of prohibition during the overland haul through the Middle East and Iran, this *is* heaven. A chance to let one's hair down before taking to the road again.

Oh for a baked potato

John has been tending bar at the Colabah for a couple of years - but the Club's been up and running since the mid-seventies. 'We've been at it for nearly twenty years, a sort of open house for non-colonialists - and hippies. You see,' he says, pouring my third rum and cola, 'the coolabah is an Aussie tree that grows in the desert with lots of shade - a place where people can rest, get drunk and not have to eat any more bloody dal!'

The formula's certainly caught on. By ten the Club's like the Tower of Babel - a kind of twentieth-century licensed McDonald's caravanserai. They're piling in here from all over, mixing in with a crowd of local expat contractors and diplomats. Most of the travellers, like us, are heading east to India and have journeyed through from Iran. But others are going north across the Himalayas to China, and some are on their way back.

The Drago girls are here in force, and thirty-three-year-old

Making sure the bugs don't bite

Faith Hawley is confessing all about sex on the road with fellow New Zealander Jonathan Sowerbutts. There's a couple of over-forties on motorbikes from Basildon, in Essex, talking about life as wandering wrinklies. Gary, a hairdresser from Devon, has fallen in love with Huy Lin from Beijing and persuaded her to cycle back to Britain with him. Lisette is pregnant after she and her husband Fritz got stuck without their condoms in the snows of Kazakhstan on their way through from Holland to Pakistan in a twenty-four-year-old 2CV. Emile and Lillian from Switzerland have been on the move in their Toyota Land Cruiser for more than ten years, and are now trying for the *Guinness Book of Records*. Pasi Sivunen from Finland is on foot, flat broke in a corner and hoping somebody will buy him a drink. Everybody does.

Islamabad Camping always stirs late on Friday mornings. It's a jigsaw of tents and vehicles and figures sleeping curled up on the ground, spread out across the grass beneath clusters of trees and bushes. There's a run-down concrete block of loos and two cold showers. The first thin light of the sun makes the heavy, early November dew glitter, but the air's damp and chills to the bone.

Dave and Emy and daughter Mattea arrived a few days ago and, as usual, are the first to wake. By eight Dave's cut wood and got a good fire going and there's some coffee on the brew; Emy's making pancakes in an iron frying pan; Mattea's sitting on a log keeping warm and doing her homework.

'I'm nearly forty, just a bloke staying alive in the recession, really,' says Dave. 'Apart from that I like knowing who I am and living life a bit closer to simplicity. I work for a while, then we go off and travel. Travel can be escapism, but so can being in a bank. I believe our journeys help us find out who we are and how we should live our lives. In our society people grow old, but they don't seem to mature the way I think people should mature. Travelling is a good way to mature.

'We are a very close family and close to God, and I guard all that jealously because I think it's very important. It makes both Emy and me sad to see how society is tearing down the structure of the family. We'll know when it's time to stop travelling - when Mattea tells us she's tired of it, when we sense that it's better for her and for all of us to go back to Australia or to England. Until then we meet many people in many places and make many friends.'

Mattea's home is the sidecar during the day and the tent at night. She plays with her dolls and toys like any other girl her age would, but she asks far more questions and has many more answers.

'I think children should travel to learn languages,' says Mattea very seriously, probably because she already speaks two and has a smattering of three others. 'I'm learning how they do things in all these countries. But India is my most favourite because the people are so kind. They talk with us and ask us to their homes.'

'We always try to stop in places for a while,' explains Emy. 'It gives us time to do her lessons properly and to write to all her friends and relations in Australia, the Philippines and England. She's a very happy child, and she has no problems making friends with other children everywhere. She plays with them, even if she doesn't understand their language. But, of course, in many ways she does.'

Friendship is one of the most common themes that travellers talk about: freedom, fun and friendship - more or less in that order. Friendship can also be romance - or wonderful, abandoned love. Or just straightforward sex. Somehow all these emotions and involvements can be made and established so much more easily, and often more honestly, away from the luggage of our lives back home.

Faith and Jonathan are trying to sort out their tent. It's a small one at the best of times, but at the moment it's strewn with crumpled sleeping bags, pillows, blankets and dirty clothes tumbling out of half-open packs. Faith is short and blonde, a self-assured, attractive nurse. She's travelled around India before - alone and

probably very competently. But this is her first time making the overland journey from Europe, and the first time travelling with an organized group. She and Jonathan met when they boarded the Dragoman truck back in the UK. But it wasn't until the Middle East that they started their affair.

'We became good friends quite quickly after we left,' explains Faith, to my surprise a little sheepishly. 'Obviously there was that initial chemistry, but we didn't let anything happen spontaneously. In fact we talked about it for about a week and a half before we decided to share a tent. I had some reluctance because I felt concerned about what other people on the truck would feel, and I didn't want the whole thing to turn into "who was pairing off with who" sort of gossip. Then I thought, well, if we can feel comfortable about it and handle it between ourselves, then it shouldn't affect anybody else.'

'What's been interesting,' adds Jonathan, 'is that we come from such completely different backgrounds. I'm an engineer, Faith a nurse and masseuse who's into New Age things. We would never have met normally, even though we are living only about ten minutes away from each other in Melbourne. Now here we are together.'

'When I came on this trip,' Faith admits, 'I said to myself I was not going to have an affair. I suppose knowing that Jonathan and I will be going our separate ways in a few weeks made it much easier to handle. The end result is that we've been able to share some very good moments - as friends and as lovers. But after you've been bouncing around in a truck all day and you've pitched your tent sleep sometimes comes before sex - and then it's been great for the cuddles.'

At which point Jonathan leaps on Faith and shoves his tongue in her ear.

Sarah Hodgson didn't get it together in quite the same way. She's much younger than Faith, still only twenty-one, but she thought she could handle it. She and Charlie, the co-driver of an Exodus truck going out to Kathmandu, began an affair back in the Middle East somewhere. Now Sarah's leaving. She had only booked her place on the truck as far as Islamabad. Suddenly it's all over. The truck's going on and Sarah is standing by the side of the gate with her bags at her feet.

'God, I don't want to say goodbye - to any of them. I really don't. I'm such a bloody fool for not booking all the way to Kathmandu,' she sobs as the truck pulls out. Charlie's waving from the window. He probably feels the same way. But there again, life on the road's full of surprises. They say that the rule for overland truck drivers - men and women - is: 'No fucks before Folkestone!'

Sex is probably the last thing on the mind of young Pasi Sivunen this morning. Or maybe it's right up there? Who knows? But if nothing else he must be bloody cold.

He's a huddled shape under a damp blanket, curled up beneath a tree at the back of the camp. He's set fire to a few twigs and some leaves and is trying to keep himself warm. By his head are a piece of dry bread wrapped up in a newspaper and a plastic bottle of water. His eyes are closed. He looks pale and close to some deathly sleep, his long brown hair ruffled and greasy over his angular, poetically thin face.

I sit looking at him for a few minutes and can't help remembering what it was like for me back in 1962. I was scraping the bottom at times as well. Nothing but a few pennies to my name, no food, nothing except the pathetic bidi (the cheapest, hand-rolled Indian leaf cigarettes) dog ends I lit up first thing every morning to try and kill the hunger. I was often so cold when I was in Pakistan and India that I used to dig up bushes and pile them on top of the green-and-white striped mattress cover I slept in.

But it never seemed that bad. Mind you, I was only sixteen and eternally, youthfully, naively optimistic about everything. In any case, there's a really strong feeling when you're out on the road that somehow, soon, everything will always work itself out.

Not everybody felt that. In the late sixties, when the hippie trail was well under way, I was amazed during a visit to India to see travellers begging on the streets. And I heard stories about girls sleeping with local men in return for money and drugs. Incidents like this were rare, but the extraordinary level of hospitality shown to foreigners by people along the road East has been and still is often badly, outrageously abused.

Pasi has been travelling for two years. 'Now I feel like going back home. I'm a little bit sick, I'm missing my mother, my sisters - and I'm missing my girlfriend.'

Girlfriend? After two years?

'Well, I'm hoping.' He looks sad suddenly, and even more frozen than he must be with nothing but a thin shirt and tee-shirt and ridiculously inadequate cotton trousers. Pasi has spent the last two years travelling around India and doing the odd job to survive. He claims he has nothing to regret. Living rough and almost down-and-out, he explains, has enabled him to go further, stay longer and see more.

'Now I've had to sell most things I'm beginning to regret it,' he explains. 'But I'm not begging, I'm not depending on other people. I have eight dollars left and I've bought a bottle of whisky on the black market which I can sell for a profit. Then I can move on. '

Finland must seem a long, long way away this cold November morning.

Switzerland must seem even further away for Emile and Lillian Schmid. I'm morbidly curious about this obviously middle-aged couple and their well-worn, Toyota four-wheel

Sarah and Charlie - time to say goodbye

drive. Every corner of every corner is packed with battered boxes and possessions - and the roof's creaking with it all too, held down with ropes and orange canvas covers. They never seem to go anywhere, but there's a lot of eating going on. Long, leisurely breakfasts around a picnic table next to the vehicle; and what smell suspiciously like steak dinners in the evening. I should have guessed they were well into a long-established routine - but *ten years*?

'It's a long time,' admits Emile in a classic understatement. 'But we didn't mean it to be this long. Initially it was only for one year - then it became more and more and we still enjoyed it, so we drove on and on.'

'If somebody had told me I would sleep ten years in that car, I would have said, "You're mad!" Lillian laughs. 'It was just a never-ending story. It still is. But I have to say it's not always easy.'

I'm exhausted just by the thought of it. How can anybody live in a car for ten years - especially one that has no space left in it except for two people in the front seat. To go to bed they have to take a whole layer of things from the back and move it to the front seats, and then return it all when they get up in the morning. I should imagine it must get a bit close in there at times! All the time?

'Human beings are so adaptable,' explains Emile. 'They can live in the snow, in the desert, in the jungle - so why not in a car? You just get used to it.'

Emile and Lillian - ten years after

But the end is in sight. They are now in their early fifties and their savings are running out. So is the Toyota, with 351 000 kilometres on the clock. And everything else is getting very old and falling to pieces; layers of boxes contain things that they've probably already forgotten - hidden treasures perhaps, or just plain junk in the trunk.

'I'm beginning to imagine a different life now because I want to have more space around me,' says Lillian. 'Emile doesn't understand that - I think he's frightened about going back and would probably like to continue this way forever. But I am missing a bathroom sometimes, and when I look in a mirror I think it would be nice to dress up.'

The problem for both of them is that they have lost contact with their previous life and their expertise as computer programmers. What will they do? After they've made the *Guinness Book of Records* for the greatest distance travelled in the same vehicle with the same engine over the longest period of time (or something like that!) they plan to go home. That, they believe, will take them until well into their eleventh year. In the meantime, Lillian's diary and collection of stones expands rapidly, filling the entire roof-rack, while Emile's list of statistics convinces most of us that these two must be Switzerland's first genuine travel loonies: 69 countries; 351 408 kilometres in 9105 driving hours (251 544 on the right side of the road and 99 864 on the left); 3650 driving days; 1600 different night stops; 84 818 litres of petrol; 41 tyres; 103 punctures; 16 batteries; 72 spark plugs; 50 air filters; 26 oil filters; 36 shock absorbers; and 52 oil changes.

'Oh, and we've taken 13 450 slides since we left Switzerland.' No doubt just in case they might forget anything!

Rob and Karen, our friends we first met in Turkey, have only been travelling for about sixteen weeks, and they're already arguing. Being together twenty-four hours a day, seven days a week is obviously not quite as laid back as Emile and Lillian like to make out.

'You see, in London we both had jobs,' says Karen, 'and sometimes we would only meet briefly in the morning and then again at ten o'clock at night. Now we're on top of each other the whole time.'

'What winds me up more than anything,' adds Rob, 'is that because I ride in front I carry the handlebar bag with the map on top of it. Karen has this habit of wanting to look at it every ten minutes and I find this so annoying. I keep ending up throwing the map across the road at her.'

'But I'm interested in knowing where we are and where we're going,' Karen interrupts, 'and whether or not there are some hills up ahead or maybe a river nearby.'

'Yeah, but having it happen every ten minutes is a bit of a pain,' Rob laughs, not without a bit of an edge.

'Well, you know what really gets on my nerves about him?' Karen leaps in. 'It's his smelly bum!' What? That must come from riding behind your partner for sixteen weeks. Give up the lead, Rob, and hand over the map!

I like Rob and Karen but I have my doubts as to whether I would want to travel with them. Take this for a touch of cultural oppression.

'We got into a situation when we were in this tent with two Turkish nomads,' recounts Rob, 'and we all got very drunk and started singing.'

'And they gave us names,' Karen adds. 'I was Asha and Rob was

Overleaf: Rob and Karen - still on their bikes

Mehmet, and all their songs had our names in them and told of our adventures in the world.'

Then it was Rob and Karen's turn. 'Well, all we could think about was "On the ball, City" which is the Norwich football team song. So we taught them to sing it. And then we got this rhythmic Turkish dance going with everybody singing "On the ball, City, never mind the danger, steady on, now's your chance - waaho, you've scored a goal!"'

I couldn't help having terrible visions about the cultural impact of this event on the future of Turkish nomads and tribal folklore everywhere. God knows, it might even spread into Baluchistan!

No such cultural ambitions among this lot, my second bunch of over-forties. Pat and Graham Seeley, ex-Basildon in an old army ambulance, and Philip and Dorothy Spain, up from Ramsgate on a motorbike, are self-proclaimed wrinklies on the run, their teenage kids left at home to fend for themselves.

'We wanted to do this when we first got married, when we were eighteen or nineteen,' says Graham, 'and then we fell into the trap of mortgages and children and it just didn't happen. Now I've got caught in the economic decline - the company I worked for collapsed and I was made redundant. So we thought there's no point sitting around hoping another job will come along - let's clear off for twelve months. China, India... it all seemed such a great idea - except they said China was impossible.'

'At first,' adds Pat, 'everybody told us we couldn't do this and we couldn't do that and being the middle-class English people we are we accepted all that without question. I think now we could get to the border and try and cajole our way in, bribe our way in or just plain ram our way in. This is what the whole journey has been about. It's opened our eyes - and it's all possible.'

'Out here,' says Dorothy, 'you have to take much more responsibility for your own safety. In England, the authorities make sure you can't even fall off the edge of a cliff or into a hole in the street. Here, you've got to watch out for yourself - and it's so much more satisfying.'

Philip admits to being quite conservative. 'But it's not until you get to a country like this that you realize how conditioned we all are to accepting and following the rules. It's really good to break the law sometimes. I'm beginning to think our lives are lived for us to a very great extent back home. The longer I've been here the more I've understood that there is, in fact, some kind of real order in the chaos out here. You can go round the roundabout the wrong way and nobody will bother you. They'll accommodate you. But in England people would probably collide with you deliberately just to make a point.'

'Oh my God, look who's here - again! Where did we last meet you?' Chiara and Stuart have arrived with their dog Sumela (who is now looking incredibly fat and nothing like the roadside hound they first adopted back in Turkey) and their faithful Land Rover. They've just driven down from the Khyber Pass and should be in good spirits with India now only a day away. But Stuart's looking worried. There's one of those noises in the engine that nobody but him can hear. It sounds, says Stuart, like something serious. Chiara's beginning to look worried too.

I can't believe it, but there they are: Paul and Brian, the Irish bikers who have yet to be seen biking anywhere. Now they're unloading their cycles off the top of a bus! I last saw them at the Iran-Pakistan border, clinging on to the railings in No Man's Land without a visa for anywhere! It seems a Pakistani immigration officer took pity on them and gave them a temporary entry permit to enable them to get to Islamabad and apply for a full visa. The trouble is that they ended up getting stuck for far longer than they expected on a bus with a lot of smugglers.

Paul describes how the bus had a false bottom and all of the seats were mounted on a floor that was about 2 feet above the real one. 'But it wasn't until four in the morning and the third customs check that they discovered this. Then the soldiers started to pull out prayer mats, rubber shoes and wellington boots in vast quantities - thousands of them.'

Clearly Brian still can't quite believe all this actually happened. 'It was just so funny. No sooner was all this stuff thrown out of the bus and loaded on to an army truck than somebody else would start off-loading it and sneaking it back again.'

'Now we have to race off and try and get our life in order - by rickshaw, probably. So there we are - we Irish cyclists

Brian and Paul - still not on their bikes

are still using alternative means of transport - but eventually we'll get on our bikes. Oh well, *c'est la vie*!'

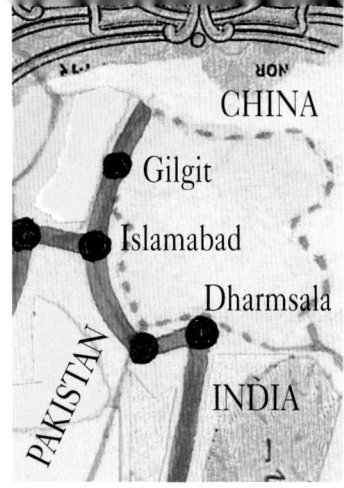

CHINA

Gilgit

Islamabad

Dharmsala

PAKISTAN

INDIA

CHAPTER 13

The Bridge to Beyond

A journey to China - and the roof of the world

It will be a race against time to reach the Chinese border and get back again before the snows set in. It's the second week in November, and we've heard that some of the passes in the Hindu Kush and the High Pamirs are already closed. More disturbingly, there are reports of armed uprisings against the government, with militant Islamic groups throwing up barricades across one of the two major roads leading into the area.

We decide to take the plunge and go anyway. Who can resist? I have always wanted to follow the Karakoram Highway to the roof of the world - to stand 4730 metres up where Marco Polo must have stood all those years ago when he looked out towards a warmer sun, where eastward the road led to the glittering court of Kublai Khan, and southward it led to India and another fabled land of vast, untapped resources and riches.

The old story went that hidden away in these mountains was the kingdom of Shangri-La, a land of peace and prosperity, where happiness and good health supposedly flowered all year round. I want to believe it. For centuries the passes through these mountains and valleys were the overland key to China from the West - the last leg of the Silk Road. No doubt the travellers in those days wanted to believe such things too. From China, seven hundred years ago, intrepid traders led pack trains laden with silk, tea and porcelain along these terrifyingly high trails. Returning from India, they brought spices, jewels, gold and ivory. Today, as China slowly opens its doors to the west again, this has become the new frontier for travellers. The 1300-kilometre Karakoram Highway, the highest public road in the world and one of history's biggest engineering projects, is now another way of getting to India via China, east along the Himalayas and south via Tibet and Nepal.

The journey north to the Chinese border from Islamabad is magical and mysterious, difficult and dangerous - as full of promise as the lost kingdom of Shangri-La itself. From the air-conditioned capital of the new Pakistan to the old British hill station of Murree; across a 2700-metre mountain pass to Abbottabad; north between the Swat and Kagan valleys, where Buddhism came of age two thousand years ago, to Besham, Dassu and the mountain trading town of Gilgit, the entrance to the

Hunza valley - Shangri-La, they say; and finally to Sust, the last stop before the Khunjerab Pass and the doorway to China itself.

Do not pass go - guns on the road to Gilgit

As dawn breaks over the hills around the low-slung wooden colonial bungalows and houses of Murree a slow mist obscures our view, drifting through the pines, lifting occasionally to reveal sheer valley walls dropping precipitously away below us. In the early morning damp the road winds like a wet, black-mirrored knife through the forests, glinting in the sun, climbing slowly but steadily along the edge of the Kagan valley and the banks of fast flowing, ice-cold glacial rivers. We are trying to take a short cut through the valley and over the mountains through the 3750-metre Babussar Pass to the small town of Chilas, in the shadow of the 8126-metre Nanga Parbat. Incredibly, there are more than thirty peaks over 7000 metres in this area. The road becomes narrower and rougher, steeper, higher, colder and, after four hours, impassable as the snows pile up. We are forced to turn back, and six hours later rejoin the Karakoram Highway.

The drive to Gilgit is awe-inspiring. I've been to many countries and made many

journeys, but I have never travelled along such a road, for the Karakoram Highway crosses the highest peaks in the world. It's hard to understand how some of it was ever built. We are following, back towards its Himalayan source, the mighty Indus, a great rushing torrent that after the winter is 60-90 metres deep in places. The road has been carved out of the towering rock faces of the valley that can rise 1000 metres or more from the side of the river.

In places the road is so narrow that there's hardly room for two vehicles. The drop is an unimaginable horror. I find it hard to look - and yet I have to. I have to stop and stand on the edge and look down. And I have to be behind the wheel too - staring straight ahead, concentrating on the driving. I need to be in control and in that way also fight off being scared of these unnerving heights. It might sound over-dramatic, but if you don't like heights you'll know exactly what I mean. There is the constant danger of rock-falls and landslides and much of the road is littered with debris washed down from above. The Pakistani trucks making the trade run between China and Pakistan know the way to go: slow and straight down the middle. I always stop and pull over. I don't care if Sean and Dan think I'm a wimp - I know better. Ron just has to trust me.

But for all the obvious dangers of driving a road like this it's impossible not to marvel at what is undoubtedly an extraordinary piece of engineering. It took a work-force of fifteen thousand Pakistanis and as many as twenty thousand Chinese twenty years to finish this road, to replace the even narrower, more dangerous dirt tracks that once linked Pakistan and China; and it cost more than five hundred lives. Most of all, though, it is impossible not to wonder at the vastness of the landscape, at its overwhelming physical presence and its primeval beauty and savagery. The sun shines for very little of the day; the shadows are long and cold; the rock faces broken and worn, uncompromisingly sheer; the sky so small and far above. And in the river below, enormous boulders and the debris of 50 million years of landslides and the infinitely slow, grinding movements of the two continents that touch and crush against each other in these mountains.

There are few people around here. Across the valley I can just make out a group of four - a man and his family, by the looks of it - moving slowly down one of the rock faces. How can anybody live up there? There's a small hut, their home presumably, perched at the back of a huge, flat rock perhaps 900 metres above the river. The struggle to live, to graze and grow even the most basic food means that the few inhabitants of this area often have to migrate between the high plateaus in the summer and to the river in the winter. They are tiny figures walking down an impossibly steep goat track. Where are they going? What are they doing? What kind of life do they lead? There is nothing here: no town or village for miles in any direction, no land to farm, no choices even. Just nothing - except solitude and space and whatever life they are able to create for themselves.

In the distance the narrow, winding line of the road fades into a shimmering haze of diffused light that blurs and finally engulfs the valley, leaving only a distant horizon of snow-capped peaks. It's not difficult to feel very alone in this part of the world.

We are close to the town of Besham when we run into the first sign of trouble. Rounding a sharp corner in the half light of an early evening we come upon a hundred or so men, mostly bearded, with woollen rolled hats on their heads and wrapped in shawls against the chill air. All are carrying guns - ancient muskets, old British .303s, shotguns, Kalashnikovs and sub-machine guns - and walking down the road towards the town.

Silent, unsmiling faces again. They turn to look. I've seen them like this before: not hostile, just suspicious. It's always best to smile and wave, or even drive straight on. The feeling is very tense. I note the rocks piled up ready for roadblocks at the corner we have just turned. I decide it's about time we try to find out what's happening on the road ahead.

A victory for Allah

Besham does not look like a good place to stop: nearly everybody in the town is armed.

It's dark by the time we reach Dassu, the next town and the seat of the District Commissioner, the government's senior representative in the area. His house is surrounded by police and armed guards and there are a dozen cars and four-wheel-drive vehicles parked outside. We are told to wait as he is meeting with village leaders and local imams - Islamic religious leaders. The police are surprised to see foreigners out here alone at night.

'Not a good time, not good,' a sergeant explains, shaking his head. 'DC sahib talking to find peace and stop shooting.'

We wait for an hour before some twenty people come filing out: bearded imams in sombre dark grey tunics; village elders in browns and blacks; intense young men with glasses and white pyjama shirts; and heavily built bodyguards with

Kalashnikovs. They don't seem happy. It's impossible not to feel caught up by events. Something is going badly wrong.

Muzaffar Ali Afridi, the DC, seems relieved to have somebody else to talk to. He welcomes us into his house and insists we stay for dinner. Of course we can sleep at his guest house - but first we must eat. He explains that Islamic fundamentalists have cut the main roads in the neighbouring Swat valley; several people have been killed, including a government official; more than a hundred hostages have been taken; and now the army is moving in to try to clear the roadblocks.

The people are protesting because the government is not acting fast enough to implement new Shariat (Muslim) laws. With the trouble spreading to this area it looks as though the road here, the Karakoram Highway itself, might soon be cut too. He advises us either to go back or to get to Gilgit as quickly as possible. He can offer us no escort or protection of any kind.

'I am supposed to be the law here,' he explains, 'but I have no real power. The only law is the people's own law and the law of the gun. This is not a tribal area, but when I can't phone any of these villages, and not even reach some of them except on foot, how can I expect anybody to take any notice of me?'

Not very comforting. No doubt the DC's next message back to Islamabad will be signed 'Desperate in Dassu'. We decide to press on at first light. Going back isn't a realistic option - we are much closer to Gilgit.

It's a bright, crisp winter morning. We are climbing steadily through range after range of mountain peaks, the snow glittering against a crystal-blue sky, the Indus flowing fast down the valley to our left. We pass several small villages. It's the same story in all of them: the local police have shed their dark blue uniforms and locked away their guns; the streets are full of armed civilians; again there are tree trunks and stones beside the roads ready for the order to put up the barricades. It's only a matter of time. Cut the Karakoram Highway and Pakistan's links with China and the whole of this north-west province of Kohistan will be severed - and we will be stranded.

We know we have only a few hours, if that, to make the last 250 or so kilometres to Gilgit. The roads are empty now. We haven't seen a truck for at least an hour. But we do run into our first traveller. Of course, it's a bloke on a bike - only mad dogs and Englishmen.... It isn't exactly a Stanley-and-Livingstone encounter, but given the remoteness of the area it could have been a bit more dramatic:

Me: 'Hi! My name's Simon - we're making a series of TV films for the BBC and Discovery.'

Biker, looking totally unfazed by running into a film crew: 'Oh, right.'

The high road to China

CHRIS RHODES
CYCLIST

___ ____, Knapton
York Y02 6QG, England
Phone: (0___ ____69

Me: 'Are you OK? You look exhausted.'

Biker: 'Yeah - bastard kids.'

Me: 'Er, what?'

Biker: 'Back there, about 50 metres, a lot of kids amusing themselves by throwing rocks at me. Still, I'm used to it.'

And then he hands me his card: 'Chris Rhodes - Cyclist' and an address in Knapton, Yorkshire. Not that he's been there much. He's been cycling for three and a half years since he left England and is now on his way through Pakistan to India and Bangladesh. This last leg has been five long, hard months across China from Hong Kong.

'I originally cycled from England to Poland, to the Soviet Union, Mongolia, China, Korea, and then China again with a stop-off in Hong Kong. That's about 41 000 kilometres. Now I've got enough money left to cycle for about another two years.'

Oh no, not another marathon man, a forever traveller! 'No, I'll go back home one day. I'm only twenty-eight, so I'm not sure when. But really this is nothing. I met a German guy in Siberia who's been cycling continuously for thirty-two years!'

He's also met an English couple on a tandem - going towards China.

'They're going to have real problems,' Chris says. 'The Chinese thought my bike was a bloody spaceship or something. They couldn't get over all the gears. God knows what they'll make of a tandem.

'It's strange, really. Here they throw stones at you and don't give a damn about the bike. In China they're not interested in you - just the bike.'

As Chris charged off down the Karakoram again, all muscled up with his bum in the air, hugging the outside edge of yet another hairpin bend and several hundred feet of precipitous canyon, I couldn't help feeling that this man could get himself through anything.

Gilgit is the hub of the Karakoram Highway and the oldest trading post on the Silk Road between China and Pakistan. Its markets date from the first century AD and the place still bears the cultural scars of many lands, its shops full of goods from China, Kashmir, Uzbekistan, Tajikistan, Afghanistan, Iran, the Soviet Union and the many regions of Pakistan.

Stand on the outskirts of Gilgit as the sun sets and watch the magic of a golden light slip down behind the panorama of towering snow-covered peaks that surround this town. Stand in the same place as the sun rises and watch how the shadows of night pull back to reveal a network of valleys spreading out between the peaks.

Buddhism laid its roots here two thousand years ago. Today Islam rules - and divides. Ismailis, Shias and Sunnis all overlap in Gilgit and sectarian tension is never far below the surface. More than a hundred were killed in clashes between the Sunnis and the Shias a few years ago. In the last twenty-four hours the spectre of that violence has risen again as the fundamentalists move to cut the Karakoram Highway.

The small, spartan rooms that surround the gardens of the Madina Hotel, the traveller's favourite rest-stop in Gilgit, are full of stranded foreigners. There are a South African and a couple of Japanese, the new travellers of the nineties, on their way through from China; a group of middle-aged Frenchwomen in a truck on their way to China; a Czech couple, both students; Dave, an artist from Glasgow; and Faith, the New Zealand nurse from the Dragoman truck, is here with an Australian lawyer, Fiona McPherson. No sight of Jonathan - *l'affaire de la voyage*!

The steel shutters are down at the Pakistan Airlines office in the centre of town and an angry, restless crowd - Pakistanis and foreigners - has gathered, demanding to know when the next flight is due. Troops and police are patrolling the streets, with heavy machine guns mounted on the backs of Land Rovers and Toyota pick-ups.

The normally cool and decisive District Commissioner Haji Sanaullah is beginning to look a little bit frazzled. A dozen foreigners are sitting round the DC's huge desk, all claiming priority on the first plane out of the town. The captain of one of the local polo teams is hobbling up and down the room clutching a bloody head and demanding the reversal of the result of the match he's just lost. And an old man from one of the nearby villages, accompanied by a family of sniffling wives and daughters, is going on and on about getting compensation for being knocked down by his neighbour's tractor.

'You see, I love my girlfriend,' explains Michael Neklapil, a German law student, 'and I know she is missing me. I must get on the plane.'

The DC, trying hard to ignore all the waving hands, wagging heads and weeping women, looks incredulous. 'You mean I should put you on the plane before anybody else because you are in love? Maybe we should fly her in rather than you out, because this is a wonderful place to be in love,' he adds drily.

Michael seems bemused by the response, then annoyed when some exceedingly minor American official and his obnoxious, buxom, blonde-rinse wife butts in and starts shouting about showing respect for his diplomatic status. The bloody headed polo player is behaving in a positively deranged and possibly dangerous manner; and the old man going on about the tractor is becoming increasingly incoherent and, we hope, is close to death.

'Panic Grips Gilgit!' I can see the headline now. The Karakoram Highway was cut by the Islamic fundamentalists only a few hours after we arrived here. Fuel, fresh food and other essential supplies have dried up. All buses have stopped and only one plane a day is getting in. More than six hundred people, including a hundred foreigners, are now trapped here and the word is that the 'rebels' are planning to blockade the town as well. But although Haji Sanaullah might be a bit strung out by the three-ring circus going on in his office, he is quietly confident that time and patience will solve the problem. He's too polite to say it, but he's clearly offended by the high-handed, demanding attitude of many of the foreigners. At his calmest and most soothing, Haji Sanaullah has taken to telling the increasingly impatient crowds gathering outside his office every day: 'Why not make good use of your time in Gilgit? Travel north and explore heaven. Have a nice holiday.'

Oh, right!

Shangri-La come to life

The Hunza valley is the final drama along the Karakoram Highway - the myth of Shangri-La come to life. The legend began with James Hilton's 1933 novel *Lost Horizon*. Hollywood films and media hype added further mystique, claiming that the people of the Hunza had extra-ordinary good health and led exceptionally long lives. I drove into the promised land wanting to believe nothing less. I couldn't imagine going to the top of the world and not being romantic about it. That has to be what much of travel is about. Life, after all, is how you choose to see it and live it - nothing less than a series of selected fictions.

The people of the Hunza have certainly selected theirs well: this is a valley of neatly packaged fertile fields tucked in beneath a great mountain range, a mass of white and pink blossom in the spring and yellows

and golden browns in the autumn. In the summer, its orchards are full of apricots, peaches, plums, apples, grapes, cherries and walnuts; the fields are rich with wheat and maize; the villages sheltered by clusters of rustling poplars. Even now, as winter threatens, the sun warms the fresh November air and makes the heart soar with the way it lights the sweep of the valley as it dramatically widens and narrows between the peaks. And through the middle of it all flow the rushing waters of the Hunza River, spanned by precarious rope and wood bridges between the villages.

The people here are different too. We see no guns and the smiles come much more quickly. The Ismailis who live in this valley do indeed seem ageless and happy. The troubles on the road behind us are quickly forgotten.

Sust is the last stop before China. The small town 3100 metres up is the Pakistan frontier even though it's another 190 kilometres until we reach the actual border. It's not much of a place: a few scattered houses, some travellers' lodges and buildings for customs and immigration. There are several Chinese trucks loaded with construction equipment parked along the road, and three buses carrying Chinese Muslims - men and women - on a pilgrimage to Pakistan. Everybody is waiting to hear when the highway south of Gilgit will open again.

The temperature's down below freezing tonight, but there's no electricity, no running water, no heat. A group of eight travellers, cold and hungry, sharing soup and bread around some candles, have all ended up in the Mountain Refuge. Five of them are leaving for China in the morning. Louis de Kok from Holland, with a Chinese hat bought in Amsterdam, is on his way to Tibet and Nepal with Hélène, his German girlfriend; Dave from Glasgow is here, just to travel as far as the border, paint it and say he's been there; Faith and Fiona too. But Roy and Stacey from New Zealand are going all the way. One might say they have been for several years already. Stacey Walters froths unashamedly and enthusiastically about being here on the roof of the world - about everything. She's twenty-three and has been travelling since she was eighteen.

'I had always wanted to travel and my parents, who are separated, always encouraged me. One night I dreamt I was going, so I just went, travelling first with a Russian circus in Australia. I was just seating people at the shows but I saved some money and then went to Africa.

'Now I don't want to stop. But in any case I don't really feel I've got a home any more, so maybe I won't. I love New Zealand, but I have this thing about just putting my backpack on and going somewhere. I might not be happy later on in life and not have a proper career - I don't know, I'm just bumming around. It's wonder, magical wonder, you know!'

She met Roy Hamilton, long-haired and forever smoking soggy roll-your-owns, in a brothel in Mombasa, Kenya about three years ago. He's just a lucky old hippie really, considering he's thirty-three and was minding his own business in a cheap room at the time.

'We hitched together for a bit and then sort of kept going,' adds Stacey. 'We have a lot in common and it's easier when there's two of you, especially for me as a girl.' Roy doesn't say much. But there again, he probably doesn't have to.

From here to the border the road climbs steadily another 1200 metres, in places running close alongside the river between very narrow red-brown canyon walls covered in huge icicles. It's getting colder and colder, more and more isolated as we climb. Some of the peaks are beginning to drop below us now, the vast snow-covered ranges rolling away towards a slowly widening horizon. The air is thinner and the breathing harder. We stop to film, but have to move more slowly. We pass a couple of checkpoints, but see no other life except for the occasional goats. Not a fox, a snow leopard nor a Marco Polo big-horned sheep in sight.

In the late nineteenth century this area swarmed with bandits. The Wakhi and the Hunza used to prey on the caravans travelling between the Chinese city of Kashgar and Srinagar in Kashmir. It was only fit for horses and donkeys until the first Jeep track was built in the fifties; and in the sixties work began on the Karakoram Highway. The pass was formally opened to road traffic in 1986, although even when I went through Pakistan in 1962 I heard stories about some travellers making it on foot across into China.

The final turn into the Khunjerab Pass lifts one up on to the roof of the world - and a crowd of Chinese soldiers and Pakistani border guards all shaking hands and posing for pictures. It's hard trying to be Marco Polo when some guy in uniform is beaming into your face saying, 'You me picture.' Needless to say, Captain 'You me picture' wins the day. This is the 1990s, after all. It was none the less special for all that.

But an hour is too long to spend at 4730 metres, in the cold and running around filming. All of us begin to get headaches and feel slightly nauseous. We've driven the last 1200 metres from Sust too quickly, and we are going to descend it again too quickly. By the time we set off I've begun to throw up and nearly pass out. 'It's the bends,' says Dan cheerfully, at which point I do pass out. The return trip to Gilgit is a fourteen-hour nightmare of roadside vomit stops accompanied by a continuous blinding headache.

In Gilgit, it takes another day to recover. But since there is nowhere else to go, it doesn't matter. The road south is still cut and the Pakistani police are preventing anybody from even trying to get out. This is the first time we've actually stopped travelling. *Force majeure*. We pass the days thinking and talking about 'what if' the

road remains closed for much longer; and about India and how exciting it's going to be to get there. But all I could really think about was 'Come to Kathmandu for Christmas, Dot.' She is working in England now, but somehow we have travelled together all these weeks since we met in Jordan; keepers of each other's secrets, chasers of a time to be shared and questions to be answered, searchers for an innocence and a dream not lost - just waiting. How much I wish she had left with me that morning in Jordan. I fax her and wait - but I know she will come.

We are going to be lucky to make it anywhere at the moment. But DC Haji Sanaullah finally agrees that we can give it a go. He has given us permission to make the run back to Islamabad 'at our own risk'. A deal has been negotiated between the government and the Islamic fundamentalists, but it has not yet been finalized. This means we might have to negotiate a minimum of nine major roadblocks.

We don't talk too much, we just drive down the empty, silent road - watching for the first sign of trouble. It's like a scene out of a movie. There are at least three hundred armed men at the first roadblock, and they are not happy. The only way to deal with situations like this is to be polite, friendly and firm. But I do feel a bit naked walking across the sun-parched ground to the group of four village elders sitting by a large rock. They are all armed and are surrounded by another twenty or so armed men. More gunmen are silhouetted along the skyline above us.

Faith in Allah and a double dose of Kalms is in order. They smile (well, some of them do) and invite me to sit. We converse in a mixture of sign language and my few words of Urdu. I listen to their grievances, which I understand only by knowing or recognizing perhaps one word in a hundred. But I am genuinely interested and concerned, and that always shows. Surprisingly, a suggestion that we should film them also helped.

Situations like this can turn on a single word or a sudden change in somebody's mood. It took nearly an hour, but, for whatever reason, the word was finally given and the stones were pulled away from the middle of the road to enable us to pass through. Our journey continued like that for many hours until finally the word came through from somewhere or other. The sixth roadblock turned from being more hostile than most to thunderous shouts of 'Allaho Akbar' ('God is great') and spontaneous volleys of rifle fire. It scared the hell out of us - but it was obviously all over and victory had been claimed.

As always, in hindsight, it's never as bad as it seems - but at the time.... India, here we come!

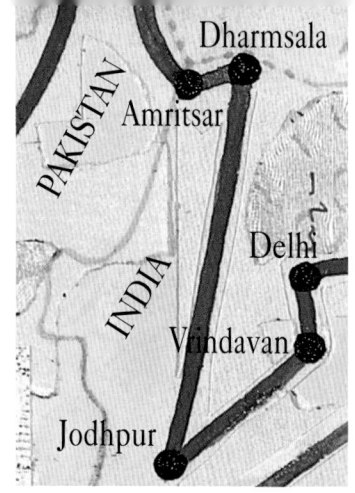

CHAPTER 14

A Magical Mystery Tour

India at last - but still a continent to go

I feel a rush of blood to the heart and the realization that in many ways my journey has only just begun. Ahead lies a patchwork of chaos and confusion. Be as intellectual as you like about it, but India is brilliantly mad. And if you want to love it, you have to hate it first.

We arrive in Amritsar in the middle of the night - and in the middle of a full-scale war. But the constant clatter of what sounds like gunfire, the thundering explosions and the bright flashes of light, turn out to be fireworks. It's Diwali, the Hindu New Year, and it feels as though the whole country is here celebrating out on the streets. But this is not the normal, carefully orchestrated five-minute firework display one might expect back home. This is a no-holds-barred, ad hoc, non-stop, twenty-four-hour affair that seems to be blowing up every corner of this teeming border city of eight hundred thousand people.

I decide to take the plunge and leap aboard a cycle rickshaw, clinging on to the seat as it hurtles through the Diwali traffic. I feel as though I'm having a fairground ride on acid. The city is a riot of sound and colour, of cattle and cars swerving round each other in the smoke-wreathed dark. The air is heavy with the smell of incense and the putrid stench of open drains; the shop-fronts piled with layers of techni-coloured sweets and cakes; and everywhere smiling faces and pointing fingers lit by the tumbling sparkle of the fireworks. Madness it might be, but in many ways it's no different from normal, everyday India. Amritsar, the principal city of the Punjab, the centre of the Sikh religion and the site of its holiest shrine, the Golden Temple, seethes with it all.

For most travellers, it's the experience of arriving in a place like this that will be their first confrontation with the thrilling, often appalling extremes, contrasts and contradictions of this land: its opulence and its poverty and dirt; its richness of languages and cultures; its blurring of politics and religions. If nothing else the shock of it all will probably change their lives forever. Many have little idea why they are here in the first place. Some are following the trail to the Krishna ashrams and the communes of the various gurus preaching their mystic **The Golden Temple, Amritsar -** message around the country; others are heading north to **the centre of the Sikh world**

the Himalayan retreat of the exiled Dalai Lama. What never changes is that, despite its conflicting cultures, India still seems, for most Westerners, to be the place to look for answers.

My journey so far has covered 19 935 kilometres and there's still a whole continent to go - that's 900 million people, 250 million cows, 225 languages and too many gods to count. Oh, and about 9500 more kilometres. I know I keep saying it, but I really do love it! It's around now that I throw away the book and tear up the map: 'Roll up, roll up for the Magical Mystery Tour - step right this way....'

Roll call at Mrs B's

The thing is that it always *feels* really good to be back in India - especially sitting out on the terrace of Mrs B's Guest House. It certainly doesn't hurt to take things a bit gently at first. And there's no better way of doing that than spending a few days here, putting on weight perhaps with some good home cooking at one of the oldest travellers' stops along the road East.

It's time for tiffin, and white-haired, eighty-seven-year-old Mrs Bandhari - the 'B' in the Guest House - is pouring tea for me in the strictly formal gardens of this red-brick 1930s colonial mansion. The routine is perfect. A tall, turbaned man, his back stooped from age, slowly sweeps the jacaranda leaves from the paths; a young servant girl polishes gleaming silver pans on the kitchen steps; a water buffalo moos softly in the background; barefoot servants pad backwards and forwards across the lawns to receive their instructions for the day. It all seems very orderly. But scruffy overlanders sleeping out on the manicured lawns!?

'Well, you see,' says Mrs B, leaning slowly forward in her wicker chair and adjusting the folds of her elderly white cotton sari, 'after my husband died in 1955 I started the guest house in order to maintain the house and to keep on the servants. It was the only house in Amritsar at the time that had the space and the style to cater for foreigners. In those days we had thirty-seven servants. Now,' she adds, with a note of regret, 'we have only twelve.'

But Mrs B's is still very much 'a proper British paradise, a decent sort of a place,' she says, 'maintained to the highest standards possible' on the income of a few travellers and tourists paying to rent the colonial-style bungalow rooms or to pitch their tents and park their *Wah Wahs*.

In 1962 I had no tent, no *Wah Wah* and no money. Mrs B's was just one of those things I had to miss out on. But Amritsar did have the Golden Temple and, as I first learnt with the Indian Sikh community back on the Iran-Pakistan border, an open door for travellers to eat and stay free of charge in their temples. I didn't write about it in my letters back home, but I remember it vividly. And it hasn't changed. The Golden Temple, gold leaf covering its elaborate carved stone walls, balconies and turrets, sits in the middle of a lake, shimmering brilliantly in the water, catching the sun at all its different angles, divine almost in the extraordinary visual impact of its goldness. The food wasn't much, though, consisting mostly of hand-rolled, sweet concoctions of flour, water and flavouring - but no doubt they were good for my soul. I wore the Sikh bracelet I was given for many years.

Mrs B's is altogether a different culinary experience. Breakfast is a feast of porridge and eggs, toast and marmalade, served on willow pattern china. Lunch and dinner are discussed solemnly at the beginning of each day and served in the colonial splendour of the wood-panelled dining room with its gently burning log fire.

But most of the action in this house takes place on 'the commander's bridge'. Mrs B's kitchen is a large, two-room affair with very tall ceilings, the walls hung with iron and brass pots and wooden-handled ladles, the shelves full of glass storage jars and stoneware bowls and stacked with chinaware. Slowed now by age, Mrs B is none the less an outspoken and single-minded woman who sits at the head of her table, allowing little argument and almost no change of routine. But the business these days is much more of a family affair, with Mrs B's daughter, Rattan, who is a former tour guide and teacher, doing most of the work necessary to keep things going - under instruction from Mum, of course!

A good deal of Rattan's time is spent problem-solving and question-answering for shell-shocked travellers trying to come to grips with the drama of being in India for the first time. How do you deal with all the dirt and poverty? How do you cope with all the chaos and the confusion? Just as importantly, how do the Indians view our intrusion into their lives? I often try to imagine what must be going on in the mind of the slum-dweller or villager suddenly confronted by a foreigner wielding a camera, waving his hands around and asking questions. One minute you are

Phone : 43737-41237
Grams : "RAMMA"

Cantonment,
AMRITSAR

PLEASE
NO TIPS ALLOWED

Mrs. T. Bhandari/Miss R. Bhandari

quietly minding your own business, sitting in the door of your hut maybe, when out of nowhere all these people arrive, probably red-faced and sweaty, and start shouting, smiling and pointing, demanding to look in your home, say hello to your wife, pat your children and shake your hand. A few minutes later they're gone again!

'I have people who go to villages,' says Rattan, 'and when they take photographs the villagers have turned round and said, "Why do these people keep taking photographs? Do they just want to show in their country that we are very poor?" I tell them it's not that. I explain that many of the foreigners I've spoken to are questioning themselves, saying, "We keep running after materialistic comforts, but are we any richer inside? We want to show the world," these foreigners tell me, "we want to show our friends that there are people, millions of people, who are living very very simply and get by with it."

'Even as an Indian,' says Rattan, 'I find it hard to understand. What really amazes me is that when there's somebody begging at your car window, you shake your head and try to say no and you sort of smile, and this person smiles back at you - laughs sometimes! I have never been able to explain this laughter and this smiling attitude and patience amongst people living in such terrible poverty and often illness as well.

'Does this mean they don't care? Of course they care, of course they would like to live in a home like mine. I won't say either that these people are richer within themselves, but there is a certain strength to be able to live on like this, a sense of community and of belonging where everybody helps everybody else. We seem to have lost that in our society. We grow apart and become less generous in every way. Even the poorest family in India will invite a passing stranger in for a cup of tea. I don't know how many people I would invite for tea without thinking, "Hmm, that's ten bucks down the drain!" So when I ask them, "why? what do you expect in return?" they say, "If we give and we share with others, maybe others will share with us."

'Simon, perhaps there are no simple answers. But as far as the chaos is concerned, the Hindu philosophy says quite clearly that the world is composed of chaos and that we must try and find some order in it. If there was no chaos, we would find no order.'

The school is only a short walk from Mrs B's, so it's not difficult to find out where the screams of the children are coming from. I've met a lot of interesting travellers over the last three months - nice people, fun people, strange people and crazy ones too. I had very few preconceptions when I set out and really looked forward to being surprised. I have been - and I am again today, wonderfully.

There must be four hundred boys and girls between the ages of six and twelve sitting out on the hard ground, in the heat and the dust of the school sports pitch. Nobody seems to care. They are screaming and laughing, their eyes wide with excitement. Even the teachers, sitting stiffly on a row of chairs behind the kids,

Curtain up in Amritsar for
The Starbug Review

seem caught up in the occasion. Dancing around in front of them all is a 4-metre black-and-blue striped insect - a baby daddy-long-legs - with huge tentacles sprouting out of his head, being chased by a magician, juggling clubs and singing badly off-key.

I have stumbled on *The Starbug Review* - not that Steve and André called it that, but *Starbug* is what they've christened their ageing Land Rover and *Starson* its titchy, two-wheeled blue trailer. Steve's an actor doing it on stilts; André a social worker who loves kids. There are fairy lights, a striped awning, banners and flags, startling costumes and lots of music, with speakers everywhere pumping up the volume of this roving kids' theatre. Not exactly *Shakespeare Wallah*, the family of Shakespearian actors who travelled around India in the forties and fifties, but in many ways more ambitious. These two have got everything packed into *Starbug* and son, including an oven because Steve loves to bake cakes and André will always eat them. The double bed that drops out of the artificially raised ceiling looks a bit dodgy, but I'm assured by them both that it's quite secure. The only problem is there's not much headroom.

The minute I meet them I know we are going to follow them for a while. What more could we want than to film two actors with a kids' roadshow heading for the villages of Rajasthan? That's what I mean about India - it's throw-away-the book

time. Steve Keen and André Bresten are a gay couple from Amsterdam. Steve's British, André's Dutch. Steve's long experience producing and acting in youth theatre projects and André's job as a social worker with children made the idea of driving to India - and putting on shows along the way - even more of a turn-on. The show in Amritsar is their first major performance since Turkey - a story about the birth of a daddy-long-legs who thinks he's human - and how, with the help of the magician, he learns to live with being a daddy-long-legs, and then how to walk. There's really no need to know more than that. Needless to say, it all ends happily with the daddy-long-legs celebrating his dream to walk by releasing dozens of balloons into the air and wishing that everybody else's dreams come true too.

The kids love it, we love it, the teachers love it. 'This was something special,' the headmaster of the school gushes afterwards, 'something new for all of us. I think we will remember this for a very long time.' But it is the kids' appreciation, the way they cheer and applaud and mob them afterwards, that really moves Steve and André.

'I feel as though something has been exchanged in all this,' says Steve, 'that we've been able to touch people, communicate with people in a way we could never do if we were just travelling. Creating theatre like this, there's always something that has to be learnt or built or borrowed, and that in itself opens so many doors. Just finding a tailor to make a new costume takes you on a path through a town or a city you wouldn't normally follow. Language is one of the greatest barriers to understanding, and I feel a responsibility about how we communicate and what we show and say to people. That's what they will remember and how they might judge other foreigners in the future.'

Both Steve and André agree that the reaction they got to their show in Turkey summed it all up: 'Several hundred children came round, and they were so enthralled and in love with what they saw and they radiated that out so strongly that we'll never forget the look in their eyes, the joy with which they received and gave so much back. It was like magic.'

There are several things very special about driving in India. Everything seems to happen along the roads or by the side of the roads. If all you ever do is drive up and down India you will see all that there is to see. The roads are truly a stage for every aspect of life in this country. There's always something to shock and amaze, but more often to make you smile, to delight you.

Early morning in the Punjab can certainly be magic: when the dawn mist is rising off the fields and life is stirring in the rich green farmlands and villages around Amritsar, there's a freshness and serenity about India that is unmatched. The smell of the wood fires; the slow, creaking movement of the ox carts down the sides of the

roads; the milk sellers on their old-fashioned shopping bikes pedalling side by side into town, their pitchers balanced over the back wheels; the splashes of colours from the saris of the women already at work in the corn; the naked children playing amongst the goats and the cows in the neatly brushed courtyards of their mud and wattle houses. For me, too, it's the trees that line so many stretches of these roads, the huge overhang of the banyans and the twisted clasp of the silk cotton trees creating long avenues of shade and dappled sunlight stretching away into the distance.

But there are many other things about the roads in India, the highways in particular, that also make them impossible to forget. They are mostly bad. They roll us around a lot and have strange cambers, for a start. Many are full of holes, too. I suppose they are not as awful as the Pakistani roads, but they're probably a good deal more dangerous. Which is another reason they can never be forgotten. I call it the 'truck in trouble' syndrome. India depends on trucks to move itself around, economically speaking. And there must be many, many thousands on the roads at any one time. Huge, lumbering home-made things always overloaded and overtired - and that probably goes for the driver as well. Quite a few end up somewhere other than on the road. Follow any major highway in India and I guarantee you will see at least a dozen accidents a day: truck on truck; truck in truck; truck up tree; truck in ditch; truck on tail; truck on nose; truck on side; truck in shop; trucks in trouble everywhere. We've started filming them. A trucking shot, Ron calls it. Thankfully there are not too many fatalities. It's only when truck hits bus or truck tops taxi that the casualties begin to mount. But it's altogether a sobering experience and a clear warning to give way rather than challenge, and certainly never to drive at night.

Next there are the two-wheel crazies: the motorbikers and the cyclists - none of whom seem to have the faintest idea about anything even remotely resembling the highway code. They either trundle along in the middle of the road until the following vehicle is on the verge of giving it to them from behind, or they appear under your wheels from the wrong side of the road, going in the opposite direction.

Then there are the millions. I have never been on a road in India, unless it is in the middle of the desert or in the highest and remotest mountains, where I have not seen people. Where they come from I have no idea, but stop for a pee (or anything else for that matter) and you'll attract a crowd. The problem is that they all amble down the sides of the road and, like the two-wheelers, don't move until the last minute. They don't even look round!

The end result of all this is that I have perfected the art of noise, as Dan puts it. It's quite simple. Fit the loudest airhorns you can find - and then use them, *all the time*. I get hell from everybody for this - but by the end of the trip Ron, Sean and Dan will all have fallen into line. In India, they say, better horny than dead!

Following Steve and André across Rajasthan promises to be another kind of travelling experience. We haven't gone more than 30 kilometres before we come round a corner and find them stopped in the middle of the road, dancing madly with the guests in a wedding procession. Much discoing ensues. The bridegroom, done up in a glittering silver turban and a high-necked red marriage suit, seems to have forgotten entirely that he is supposed to be at the temple on time and has abandoned the head of the procession to get down to a bit of hip-swaying with André.

Everybody is laughing and clapping and joining in. We film, of course. Can you imagine? The pre-wedding march is the beginning of what will probably be the most important day in this young man's life, on the edge of an eternal commitment to a girl he's never met. Then along come Steve and André dressed up like Boy George and Vivienne Westwood on a rag trade summer outing - and a film crew too! Out come the juggling clubs, and there's a change of pace to the dancing when the trumpets and drums of the Hindi wedding band get usurped by Boy George doing his Hare Krishna thing on *Starbug*'s sound system, singing 'Bow Down Mister'. Meanwhile the traffic backs up in both directions. But it doesn't really matter.

Dancing in the desert with Steve and André

Of course, all good things have to come to an end, even at a wedding. Relatives of the bride finally persuade the bridegroom to remember his duties. After much hand-shaking and address-exchanging we head off south towards Rajasthan.

Rajasthan creeps up on us. Slowly, mile after mile the lowland forests of the Punjab give way to dry desert scrub. There are fewer villages now, fewer people on the roads - and they look very different: the Rajput men wrap bright pastel-coloured turbans around their heads and sport soup-strainer moustaches, while their women wear dazzling mirrored skirts and heavy silver jewellery.

This is India at its most colourful and exotic. Further to the south and the west lies the Thar desert with its rolling sand dunes and camel trains, heading towards Jaisalmer, a famous frontier fort and perhaps the most romantic city in India. To the south are the grey-stone towering fortress of Jodhpur and to the east the pink city of Jaipur and its fairy-tale palaces. This is the land of the kings, of the great maharajahs and their lives of total excess; of unimaginable wealth, of terrible cruelty, of self-sacrificing bravery and obscene decadence. I can see that Steve and André are going to have a ball.

We are spoilt for choice when it comes to bedding down for the night. We can take our pick of desert on all sides: a low, miserable, dry gorse scrub and a few shrivelled trees. We drive off the narrow road and down a sand track, *Wah Wah* in the lead, *Starbug* second and the boys bringing up the rear. A mile or so in, close to a low line of trees and bushes, we form a circle and start setting up camp. We think we are well away from any habitation; we should have known better.

As the sun sets and the shadows lengthen, several young men and children appear and squat down to watch; then a handful of women and one or two elders, obviously from a group of huts that must be hidden away behind the trees. There are a few smiles, but mostly they just watch with both amazement and acceptance as we go through our getting-ready-to-eat-and-sleep routine and Steve and André rig up *Starbug*'s fairy lights for a special desert dinner. Steve is going to make apple crumble and custard. Yo!

It is in the watching that they can see how ill prepared we are. First they start to help clear the ground for us, then they bring firewood, then milk, then pitchers of water. For people of such obvious poverty, their spirit and generosity are very moving. Surprisingly, it is the women who are the most forward. While one of the elder men is the first to accept our offer of tea, a group of four young women soon start to laugh and joke about what they obviously consider to be our very strange ways. Not to be left out, the young men and the children then join in.

The women are slender, dusky girls and walk with elegance and sensuality: their jewellery glinting; their stomachs exposed, flat and smooth; their hips and buttocks swaying purposefully beneath the flow of their thin, brightly coloured cotton saris and veils. It's extraordinary when there's no common language how the learning of each other's names can become such a major breakthrough. Googly certainly thinks so - she can't stop giggling and showing her amazingly white teeth, flirting outrageously with

Blue horizons in Jodhpur

163

The gorgeous Googly

all of us, occasionally hiding her smile provocatively behind a lifted corner of her veil. We are completely captivated, each individually convinced that he has been chosen. She is like a *Vogue* model, the tallest of the four, the youngest of the four and, we suppose, unmarried. The village boys do not look impressed; but for us, after all those weeks of travelling through the Muslim world, the open sexuality of these women, Googly in particular, is something for which we are totally unprepared.

A returning herdsman arrives with his goats, a farmer with his camel and some more young men pulling a water tank. It feels as though the whole village is now here to watch these strange foreigners settling down for the night, in particular how Steve and André are preparing the apple crumble, and how I'm setting up my tent with its portable light and computer (I have to write this book on something!).

In a perfectly natural way we all start sharing and showing things to each other. Somebody takes over the chopping of the wood from Sean. A young man insists on putting in the guy pegs for my tent. Another starts clearing the brush from where we will sit to eat. A boy stokes the fire for us. Steve and André give cookery lessons to the girls. The camel man decides that we should learn how to ride. Steve and André are not exactly a couple one would expect to see on a camel. The camel isn't so sure, either. The result is hilarious, with the camel grunting and screaming, Steve and André grunting and screaming, and everybody else falling about in tears of laughter as the two of them hold on for dear life and clutch each other in fear on the back of this truly pissed off camel. Suddenly we are all friends.

Everybody leaves not long after the sun sets and we gather round the fire to attack our crumble. It's as though it's only polite to let people in peace to eat their food, and our new friends absolutely refuse to share it with us. They just melt into the dark, leaving us to the flickering flames and silence in the night - no doubt Googly's smile still lingering in all our minds.

'For me, tonight has been one of the most special nights,' says André, 'because it's closer to how I imagined this journey would be, just stopping in the middle of nowhere and sharing with people.'

'In a way this is what our theatre is about,' adds Steve. 'It gives people like this a chance to see how we cook and what we eat, and they teach us how to chop wood and how to ride a camel. Important things in both our worlds. I don't think they necessarily know why all this is happening, but it's also a kind of entertainment.'

'Really, what they probably want to know,' says André, laughing, 'is why we aren't eating chapattis and curry.'

'It's good, too,' says Steve, 'that there's no asking about André and me being gay. They might wonder, but I don't believe they'd question it.'

If they ever did, they would discover in fact that Steve and André are no longer lovers. The trip brought an end to their relationship after about three months.

'Before we left,' says Steve, 'we were so very much in love and so excited that all we could imagine was dancing and singing and spreading that love across the world. That's what we imagined and that's what it should have been really. We both feel very sad, but it just didn't work being so close to each other like this in the back of a Land Rover when in Holland we didn't even live together. But we will continue with our journey and try to learn how to channel the love that was, and is, there into a new direction.

'We started together, we drove ourselves into this together and we're going to get out of it together. How, we don't yet know - but we must carry on and still find the joy within ourselves to spread the happiness that I know we can.'

It's just after dawn when daddy-long-legs rises up from behind *Starbug*, all trembling 4 metres of him, silhouetted like a creature from another planet against the brightening morning sky. Slowly he lurches off down the path towards the village, followed by the juggler, dancing and laughing and tossing his clubs high into the air.

It's two little kids who see them first. Skinny legs in tattered shorts, skinny arms in tattered shirts, they stand frozen to the spot by the side of the path, clasping each other's hands, their mouths hanging open, staring. I have never ever seen such wonder, or heard such laughter. One child is screaming, screaming so much with excitement that it makes the hairs stand up on the back of my neck and tears come to my eyes. Everybody's running out of their huts, some shouting, some holding their hands over their mouths, some just pointing, speechless, as the apparition moves towards them.

I am sure this village has never seen anything even remotely like this. I very much doubt if anybody - Indian or foreigner - has ever actually bothered about this village before. Googly is really giggling now, and so are all the other women. Some are laughing so much that they are crying, while others have started dancing round Steve as he looms over them, swaying dangerously and knocking on the roofs of huts, demanding to know, 'Is anybody in?'

André's dancing too, with the fattest woman in the village. Some of the men have joined in. The children are still screaming. The camels and the oxen are threatening to stampede. Every dog is barking. Mothers start thrusting their naked babies up into

the air like some medieval offering, demanding that Steve hold them just for a few seconds. Some of the men bring their baby lambs and goats and do the same thing. It could be the arrival of a Messiah - but no, it's just Steve and André spreading a little bit of joy where before I suspect there was precious little.

It's a long day that follows that morning - our last day with Steve and André. We leave them on a hill at sunset, near another village on the edge of the Rajasthani desert. *Starbug* and son are silhouetted against a brilliant red, orange and yellow sky. Coming over the rise towards them, with the soaring sound of an Indian love song echoing out over the hills, Steve is making daddy-long-legs' dreams come true again and André's waving a huge, fluttering Balinese prayer banner on the end of a long pole. Together they dance across the face of the setting sun.

Don Quixote tilting at windmills in a far and distant land. I can hear that little boy screaming with excitement. I can see the look of wonder on his face, and the women as they lift their children up into the sky. It *is* magic.

A special kind of magic

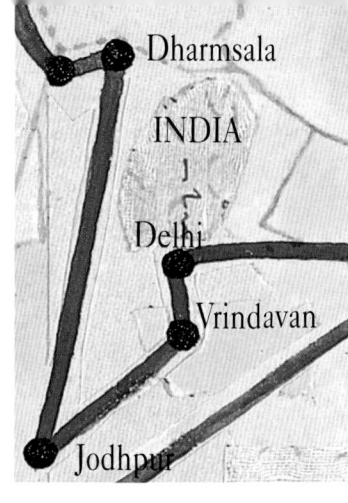

Dharmsala

INDIA

Delhi

Vrindavan

Jodhpur

CHAPTER 15

Some Kind of Pilgrimage

In search of answers - from the High Himalayas to the Ganges

I don't think I was looking to find any specific answers when I arrived in India in October of 1962, but clearly I was expecting it to be a special experience, 'very mystic and full of Eastern promise, and the highlight of my journey so far,' as I wrote to my parents in an aerogramme from the Indian capital.

'Delhi is a fantastic place, fascinating and filthy in the extreme. Old Delhi is full of snake charmers, bear wrestlers, opium dens and dead bodies lying in the gutter. But New Delhi is beautiful, modern, airy, green and lush. Amazing.'

Come to think of it, calm as that letter sounds, I must have been blown away. I was only sixteen. Sure, over the last four months I had had a chance to get used to some fairly dramatic changes compared with life back in Fakenham, but India was certainly a land of ultimate extremes. Mum and Dad must have shuddered at the thought of bodies in the gutter and opium dens (not that they probably knew anything about opium), but, once again, I had at least left out more of the gory detail. It was hard not to be shocked: there was the beggar in Old Delhi, a 'mother' who seemed to have a different dead baby laid out on the pavement in front of her every day; the legless, armless, ash-covered torso propped up in a toy trolley surrounded by incense and candles; the children with their legs broken and strapped back over their heads; the corpses that just lay there because nobody bothered to move them. I remember walking down the street in awful fascination, returning again and again just to make sure I wasn't seeing things.

But then I was also thrilled and excited by the energy and strangeness of it all: by the seething, narrow streets; the wooden shacks and tin-roofed houses falling in on each other but somehow still standing; the darkened, noisy tea shops and restaurants smelling of a thousand and one spices and serving food on banana leaves; the crush of brightly coloured rickshaws, bell-ringing bicycles, lumbering bullock carts and, of course, slow, calm cows everywhere; the shouts of the traders and the excited crowds gathered round the street performers; the

BY AIR MAIL

हवाई पत्र
AEROGRAMME
NO ENCLOSURES
ALLOWED

MR AND MRS JOHN D
THE LITTLE
FAKE
NO
ENGL

people just casually peeing and pooing, apparently wherever they liked; the total lack of any form or order that I could understand. And it was so suffocatingly hot, smelly and dirty. 'P.S. Average temp. 92°F [32°C]. No rain since Italy.'

I had been sick as well, and, while trying to get by on nothing much more than a few pennies, I was also having to ward off what I thought was a move by my father to have the British High Commission take my passport away and repatriate me. But on the other hand he sent me a fiver!

> *'Thank you for your letter, but let me say that just because I am in India and not France [doesn't mean] that you must immediately send money, it was very good of you though. Now it happened that at the time I was broke and needed money for medical expenses as I have a throat infection and an infection of my right hand so I couldn't earn my own money. But you will be duly repaid...'*

My parents were probably also concerned about the threat of war between India and China. It must have been reported in the papers back home. In Delhi there were headlines every day, and the fear was that Chinese troops might be preparing to 'parachute into Delhi'. As war fever mounted, gifts and donations were being requested to help the soldiers fighting the advancing 'red hordes' up along the country's Himalayan frontier. My early journalistic instincts were clearly showing:

> *'By the way, don't believe all you read about all this so-called war going on with the Chinese. That's all I'm going to say about it except that if you were here you would see what degree of fanatic patriotism the Indian nation has been driven to. I saw some of the worst riots in Delhi....and met Nehru outside the radio station after he had been broadcasting to the nation.'*

Doorstepping in India - that must have been my first freelance assignment!

More than thirty years on, India is still on the verge of war - once again with Pakistan. The age-long conflict between the two countries over Kashmir seems no closer to being resolved. There are daily reports of shelling along the border and fighting between the Indian Army and Pakistani-sponsored separatist groups within Kashmir itself. Travellers coming out of the area say it's now almost impossible to travel round what was once India's premier region for tourism.

Delhi is the place to pick up all this kind of hot gossip. The capital is one of the last great gathering-points for travellers along the road East. Like Istanbul and Dogubayazit in Turkey, and Quetta in Pakistan, sooner or later every traveller ends

up in Delhi. They crowd the seedy, mozzy-ridden hotels in the back streets of the old city or in the rabbit warrens behind Connaught Circus where, in a place like the Ringo Guest House, you pay £1 a night for a place in a fourteen-bed dorm. Let's hope you're not sharing with somebody who's got the runs (which you probably will be). Or else you can go pitch a tent or rent a room at the Tourist Camp, more commonly known as Delhi Camping. Surrounded on three sides by roads and with the outside wall used as a tethering spot and open loo for what seems like every horse-drawn cart in Delhi, it's a bit like sleeping in a stable on a traffic island - only much stinkier and noisier. But it's fun at least, the showers are hot and there's a reasonable café. Listen, after nearly four months' travelling, this can easily be mistaken for luxury! And it's been a long haul driving up from Rajasthan in one day, too.

Once again there are many familiar faces here and a whole lot of new ones as well. Stay a few days and there will be even more. There's a yellow bus from Germany with six passengers, including a little boy of seven, happy at last to be in Delhi and get the chance to recuperate from several weeks of dysentery on the road through Pakistan. There's an Italian couple in their late fifties driving a very fancy sort of seaside camper. She's got high heels and a pleated skirt while he's dressed in something nautical; they make us all seem a bit like drama queens, haggard and knackered as seasoned travellers like to imagine themselves to be. These two haven't even run out of espresso or fresh pasta. There's a Hare Krishna van here too with four shaven-headed Irish disciples being very earnest, very persuasive and very nice - and quite happy to talk about why this is a more fulfilling life than being back at university in Dublin.

Major Singh runs Delhi Camping with military precision. He doesn't much care where you come from or what you worship as long as you pay your bill and follow the rules. He takes great exception to anybody camping on the grass - which is just where my tent is pitched. I'm not feeling confrontational - but I am. I want to sleep on the grass and not some hard-packed red dirt path. Everybody else has fallen in line and nobody has complained. But I have no intention of moving - and I don't. And that's what Delhi's about: not moving, but sleeping, eating, collecting mail and getting your strength together to take on the rest of India - and your visa for Nepal if you want to make Kathmandu in time for Christmas. Which I do. Very much.

The first step in meditation is clearly an impossible walk up a very steep and rocky Himalayan path, albeit through a fresh, sweet-smelling pine forest. If nothing else, it certainly takes discipline.

I've just arrived in Dharmsala, the village home of the exiled Dalai Lama 800 kilometres north of Delhi, and I'm following a group of Tibetan monks and their

**Dharmsala - the exiled Dalai
Lama's Himalayan retreat**

Western disciples up to a Buddhist retreat - 2000 metres up to be precise - in the mountains. The rocks are loose beneath my feet. I keep my head down and my eyes fixed on the deep burgundy of the robes of the monk in front of me moving slowly up the mountain. The only sound is the steady breathing of the monks - and the panting of the rest of us.

I feel as though I'm on my way to some kind of high-altitude spiritual spa for the 1990s. Not that I'm thinking of taking the plunge, but my journey is certainly changing. Since Petra, in Jordan, and my meeting with Dot, it feels as though it's become much more of a personal voyage and not just an opportunity to retrace my steps and make a film about the travellers of today. There's something special about India, too. A catalytic quality that's hard to define. A sense of spirituality, perhaps, that has nothing necessarily to do with being Hindu, Buddhist or the follower of an obscure guru. I think it's more about being in an environment that allows you time to pause and think and be yourself. Maybe I'm just learning to listen again.

It's very easy for all this to sound obvious or clichéd, but perhaps journeys are about helping to restate the obvious when all too often the obvious has been forgotten. Maybe they are also about relearning the value and truth of simple, uncluttered feelings and emotions that all too easily get dismissed as being hackneyed or buried under the confusion of choice and analysis. We must also live by instinct and allow those special moments of destiny to bear fruit.

At the Tushita Centre it's 'good karma', as the hippies used to say. Certainly that's what Claire found. She first came out from England in 1990 and is a follower of Lama Yeshi, a Tibetan spiritual master and the founder of Tushita. She's been helping run the place ever since.

The trees here are hung with fluttering lines of fading, coloured prayer flags and the main house, is a long, low, cool single-storey wooden building, is set back among the pines and surrounded by white-painted stupas. Above the house there are several huts where disciples and students can go into silent retreat. It looks and feels like a peaceful place to be. It is the Dalai Lama, the spiritual leader of Tibet, who is the main attraction in Dharmsala. There's certainly not much here for tourists. Claire admits that the number of Westerners at Tushita, and in general in Dharmsala, tends to rise and fall according to the popularity or, more accurately, the public profile of the Dalai Lama, the 'God King' as he is called.

'When he won the Nobel Peace Prize,' Claire explains, giggling a bit self-consciously, 'a lot of people came here because he was famous. It was like meeting somebody who's been on TV - you know, on *Wogan* or something.

'But some people are also experimenting. They are not sure what they want. It's a bit like being in a supermarket and going round trying Hinduism, Jainism, Buddhism, waiting to see what clicks most strongly. A lot of people finally settle on Buddhism because they think it's unconfrontational and because it doesn't embrace the idea of a god. Many who come here have been disillusioned by Christianity, Catholicism, Judaism or something like that. Others come just because they know that meditation is a really helpful way of being able to control and transport their mind.'

Tibetan schoolchildren and the Tushita Meditation Centre in Dharmsala

Claire has obviously found the best way - for her anyway. She has now taken the order, shaved her head and donned the burgundy robes of a Buddhist nun. This is her commitment to the future, and she sounds and feels delightfully happy with her choice.

Looking for answers in Dharmsala

Patricia, another Englishwoman, has also 'discovered the right way' to live her life. She came out to India in the late sixties, 'not with the intent of finding myself' but with an underlying sense that something was missing from her life back in Britain. 'I was here for seven years before I found Tibetan Buddhism, held here by what I felt was the mysticism of India. I'm not so sure about that any more, but there's definitely something in India that's not in the West, apart from the chaos and the dirt. There's definitely something below the surface here. I can't really say what it is but it is something spiritual, something very important.' Patricia too now lives and works at Tushita, and will probably do so for many years to come.

Dharmsala is the new Kathmandu, a place where the living is easy and the smokes are cheap. Every traveller here seems to be on some kind of pilgrimage, from those who came shopping for answers and stayed to others eternally passing through - probably searching for the next joint! It's a town of only a few thousand inhabitants, mainly Tibetans now, and dozens of wooden and stone-built cafés and restaurants, guest houses and hotels with names like Rising Moon, Om, Green, Aroma and Shangri-La. It's a sort of nineties New Age freak centre perched on the edge of some breathtakingly steep mountain slopes and dominated by the distant snow-peaked Himalayas. The streets are impossibly narrow and impossibly muddy in the winter. And it can get very cold at night. There are prayer wheels and prayer flags, and when they're not chanting or wandering, travellers and pilgrims alike still seem to play a lot of Dylan in small, candle-lit cafés. It's all a bit hairy and smoky and there are times, if I half-close my eyes, that I can imagine being back on the sixties hippie trail.

In the tree-shaded courtyard of the Namgyal monastery a group of young monks sit in a circle shouting at each other at the tops of their voices, threatening and almost coming to blows. It is an exercise in debating - in the expression of opinion and the argument of a point. It is one of the many disciplines that a Buddhist monk must master.

Only a few yards away, in a cold, unheated, wooden-floored classroom, other young monks sit in rows cross-legged on the floor, rocking backwards and forwards, reciting out loud from complex Buddhist texts - many thousands of them - and trying to memorize them. It will take most of these monks at least six years to attain a level where they can pass this extraordinary test of memory.

On the terrace of the monastery an old Tibetan woman falls to her knees, dropping her forehead on to a small wooden board and pushing herself out into a prostrate position of prayer, flat out on the ground. Then she pulls herself up again, before repeating the process. She will do a hundred thousand of these prostrations before she feels she has made an appropriate gesture of commitment to her faith.

Dharmsala is dominated by the presence of the Dalai Lama, secured away behind the gates and guards of the Namgyal monastery and surrounded by a staff of highly organized monks with Stateside accents, digital watches and Apple Mac desk-top computers. But he is careful to maintain his public profile, travelling abroad a great deal and holding regular public audiences when he's here.

I don't know how to react when it's my turn to shake his hand. I can't help feeling warmly towards somebody who smiles so readily and seems, if only for a moment, to give me all his attention. But it's not until I see him talking encouragingly and passionately to a group of very frightened Tibetans who have to return to life under the Chinese in Lhasa that I get a real sense of his spirituality and strength. Later, when we are talking privately, he holds my right hand and rubs my knuckles, firmly, round and round with his thumb.

'You must remember,' he says, 'that not all the Westerners who come here find answers. Some of them leave even more confused than when they arrived.'

I'm not confused, but I feel as though I have learnt something since I've been here. If nothing else, I've gained insight into how other people have managed to find a focus in their lives. I've learnt just from being here and listening with an open mind. And the red-silk prayer string that the Dalai Lama tied round my right wrist is still there. Well, I'm superstitious!

It's very dark, the moon half hidden behind the thick cluster of pines overhead and a night sky of gathering clouds. It's another scramble up another mountain along another rocky path following another Buddhist monk. I'm still in search of answers. Or *the* answer perhaps. The man I'm being taken to meet is close to the Dalai Lama, and one of the few Indian monks in Dharmsala. He's been

The Dalai Lama talks with Tibetan refugees

living in retreat in a small wooden hut, perched high among the trees, for nine years now. Clearly Tenzin Choedak wants his spartan life of solitude to stay undisturbed. But as he settles himself on the floor, laughing in his brown habit like a friendly, beaming Buddha, he seems as ready to talk as I am, once again, prepared to listen.

'I think people [Westerners travelling to India] coming here can benefit most by taking away something of ethics, of morality, of values which are lacking in the scientific culture of the West, but are much more readily found in the spiritual culture of the East. You see, the main difference between science and religion is that science has no ethical values that it inculcates. But I can say it was only when I went to the West that I really learnt what it was to be an Indian. I began to understand that there is a profound spiritual and religious culture here that has been the basis of everything Indian for thousands of years. I found none of this in the West. I found it completely lacking, absent, totally.'

At several points in the conversation Tenzin Choedak chuckles quietly to himself, rolling his head back on his shoulders.

'You know, if you look at all the great civilizations which were contemporaneous with India, say three or four thousand years ago, like China, Egypt and Greece, their ancient cultures have died out completely. For example, if you go to Greece you don't find anybody worshipping Zeus or Aphrodite, whereas in India the traditions that were here five thousand or so years ago are still here. A continuous, unbroken chain going on.'

But, given the rapid growth of materialism in India today doesn't it seem as though the chain might, in the end, be broken or at least reversed? Perhaps one day, in a hundred years or so, the spirituality of India will begin to diminish and Indians might, in fact, start going to the West in search of enlightenment and answers.

'True, true. Not only a hundred years - what are you talking about? It's happening now. In fact the truth came to me not in Hindi or in Sanskrit, it came to me in English, translated by Western people - and I'm an Indian!' And Tenzin Choedak leans back against the cushions and laughs again, and again.

'*Rade, rade, rade, rade, rade, rade....*' These are the chants of a thousand people shuffling and dancing in the heady, steaming, incensed and flowered night of a dimly lit tent on the banks of the River Yamuna. Six hundred kilometres south-east of the mountain meditations of the followers of the Dalai Lama and Tibetan Buddhism and I am in the land of Krishna worship, the god-philosopher at the heart of the Hindu faith. One of the largest ashrams in the medieval religious town of Vrindavan is in a state of orange-robed excitement. There's been **Michael and Robyn beside the River** a miracle: a bee has appeared in the middle of a **Yamuna - a long way from the pub**

religious ceremony and at an already sanctified spot in the ashram. The bee is believed to be a reincarnation of the Lord Krishna himself.

I am accepted into the crush of people without comment and feel myself swept along by the spirit of the event and the rhythm of the music that is helping to drive the chanting and dancing. Letting go, I feel as though anything could happen. But still, I don't expect to run into a London commercials producer, barefoot and prematurely silver-haired, video camera held above his head, struggling in the midst of all the heat and drama to film the celebration.

Michael Duffy takes my sudden arrival in his stride and has no problem talking about some of the reasons why he and his partner, Robyn Beeche, an Australian photographer, were drawn to this ashram and have now moved here to start a new life. 'In one way it's very much the drama and theatre here in Vrindavan which is attractive. For us, coming from that world of visuals and lights, the packaging is excellent.'

But it all seems so alien to anything that we, as Westerners, might be able to understand, let alone give everything up for and move to India. Michael takes me to meet Robyn in the comfortably furnished rooms that they share in the ashram. She is editing photographs for a new book on Indian handicrafts

'We haven't actually given anything up - nothing of any real value,' explains Michael. 'We've given up a property in the middle of London and sold it so we could put money in the bank to help us live here. We've given up a car, we've given up stress, we've given up negative things.'

But what have they replaced those things with? Isn't this all a bit like pagan mumbo-jumbo, or is it really a faith in which they can find something to believe?

'Life here,' explains Robyn, 'is continually a theatrical performance because it is a life of idol worship. Every day the deity, the image of Lord Krishna, is woken up, fed, entertained and put to bed again. Part of being here,' she adds, 'is learning to accept things as they happen and learning to feel about ourselves in a different way.'

Michael and Robyn walk with me round the town with its narrow cobbled streets, its ancient temples, its bustling religious life, its shops full of Krishna images and trinkets. There are many Westerners here, most with the shaven heads and orange robes of the Krishna Consciousness movement. The principal Hare Krishna temple in India is in Vrindavan. Michael and Robyn keep their distance. They have little time for the 'Harrys', as Michael calls them - not without a slight twitch. I can't quite make out the difference myself. Must be something to do with High and Low Church!

Later that night Michael takes me to the cow pen, one of the special corners of the ashram. Krishna was the son of a herdsman, and legend has it that he played his flute by the river here and made love with the many milkmaids who fell at his feet. This is where Michael comes most evenings, to spend time with Karen Singh, his

friend who tends the ashram's cow herd. We sit together beneath the banyan tree in the middle of the yard with some incense, a candle glowing in the dark and the shuffling and snorting of the cattle all round us. Karen Singh, a small, dark nugget of a man in a dirty white dhoti and a tattered vest, draws gently on a hand-rolled tobacco leaf.

'Karen Singh doesn't speak a word of English, unfortunately, or I swear he'd have a lot to tell us about cows and Krishna.' Michael laughs. He's obviously very much into the whole idea of spending time under a banyan tree with a cow-keeper. 'I'm not sure what they would say back in the pub in South Kensington, but there again I'm surprising myself.

'I guess we're soulmates in a way. I like animals, he likes animals and that's how we became friends - through these cows. We write together. I write one to ten, he writes it in Hindi, I write it phonetically, and slowly - and so we pick up a few of each other's words.

'He's never asked me for anything, ever. I don't know what he'd like. I think he'd like his stepmother's health to be a bit better, things like that, rather than a colour TV or anything. I suppose it's all to do with karma and what you are meant to have in this life.

'It's probably difficult for you and me to understand all this - knowing one's place and not being able to improve it - because our lives are full of ambition, full of greed to a certain extent. Well, mine was. Greedy in that I wanted more jobs, more commission, more profitability, everything. I'm now thirty-seven and have been through all that.

'All this is about trying to be a better person. That's the goal really. It's not to come here and all of a sudden see God. I think it's to do with beating back my sexual desires, alcohol, cigarettes - these practical things I want to get on top of. This lack of consideration I had in my other life in London - at times I was a person I didn't like being. It doesn't happen here. I can control myself now, be more the person I think I want to be, more the person I am, which makes me feel happier.'

Karen Singh calls to the cows. Michael leans against the banyan tree and smiles. It certainly is a long way from the pub in London.

CHINA

INDIA

Delhi

NEPAL

Kathmandu

Vrindavan

CHAPTER 16

Christmas in Kathmandu

A welcome break in the capital of Nepal

No longer red, but still going like hell, *Wah Wah*'s taking the Himalayan foothills in her stride and for the first time in a long time there seems to be an end in sight. Not that the journey is over - or even that we want it to be - but there's new life in the accelerator and a fresh spring in our step, more than anything else because we know that there's some time off ahead. In a way, the dust is as thick and engrained on us as it is on the Jeep and the Land Rover. Ron is definitely looking like a veteran from the Camel Corps, and Sean and Dan as though they've just discovered the joys of cross-dressing - increasingly ethnic if nothing else. Headbands and pouches, strings and silver round the wrists, necklaces and shades! And me, well I'm suddenly finding myself very focused. The road ahead goes to only one place and I've had my hair cut and started exercising! Incredible. I'm actually thinking of other things. No messing around this time: Nepal holds the promise of the start of another, more personal journey. I'm intrigued, puzzled even, but fired to see Dot again. She's flying out from London. We haven't been together since we said goodbye in Petra, Jordan, more than two months ago. We are both hungry and excited to know more about each other.

Christmas in Kathmandu is also going to be a gathering point for many of the travellers we met *en route* from the UK - as well as Audrey, Ron's partner of twenty years, and Sean's girlfriend Kylie. And don't feel sorry for Dan: since Pakistan he and Michelle have become our first (and last, given the make-up of the team!) on-board lovers. It's the small things that are giving the game away. I'm sure we're looking in the driving mirrors more often (Dan certainly is - endlessly squeezing what seem to be imaginary zits!) and there is an increasing number of energetically hand-washed tee-shirts around. We're all a bit easier to get on with, too.

It's hard work sometimes keeping it all together as a group, travelling and filming without a break for nearly four months and 23 000 long, hard kilometres. Nobody's asking for the sympathy vote, but to put it quite simply, we're all rather worn out and weary. It's been particularly hard on Ron, humping the camera day in and day out as well as having to put up with me being so demanding, and undoubtedly difficult too. But for **Only 110 kilometres to Christmas**

Sean and Dan too, even just the physical effort involved in driving and dealing with the logistics of the journey is beginning to grind them down. Michelle ('Lahore' - the boys' nickname, not ours) must also be feeling the pressure. Even though she's already in front of a log fire somewhere in Kathmandu, Christmas has got to be just right. We're very pushy when it comes to our pleasures.

We are certainly all suffering from a bit of sensory overload. Experienced out, you might say. Maybe it's just that we have to fit too much in too quickly. But that's the filming not the nature of the journey. Brain blow-up time, as Sean put it. The Jeep and the Land Rover are part of our bodies now, the seats moulded and battered around our bums and our backs, our hands blistered and hardened by all those hundreds of hours at the wheel. And it's other things too. Just how many different types of food can we get through without becoming gastronomically ruined? And if any of us see another plate of dal (lentils) and subji (vegetables) we will probably decide just to go hungry! And just how many more languages can we absorb without getting confused and run the risk of saying completely the wrong things? The edges are easily blurred between Arabic, Farsi, Urdu and Hindi and I keep finding myself counting in Turkish. Every now and then even a bit of Thai starts creeping in. Still, remarkably, people seem to understand.

If nothing else, I suppose we've got communicating down to a fine art, waving hands and arms, rolling eyes, tossing heads and trying a bit of everything all at the same time. Even the old 'shouting loud in English' trick seems to work. Really, though, it's because we are trying, pushing to be understood, wanting to talk instead of just mouthing. I love it! And we're not afraid, embarrassed or self-conscious any more. If that crowd of onlookers by the roadside insists on staring at us for any longer there is a solution: stand up and shout, act demented, roll in the dust even - and everybody will laugh nervously and soon go home!

But Sean, please don't growl in XXXX-speak - thanks to 'globalization' that's one word everybody seems to know these days. You can't be too careful. Strange but true: in the early 1960s, as the American military build-up in Vietnam got underway, the shoe-shine boys on the streets of Saigon used to run up to us Westerners first thing in the morning, smiling and laughing and shouting, very sweetly even: 'Fuck you! Fuck you!' - or 'Good fuck! Good fuck!' A couple of GIs had gone to a lot of trouble to teach them that this was the way to greet foreigners. God knows how many UN aid programmes and child welfare consultants (with World Bank funding, no doubt) it took to unteach them and get them to say 'Good morning' correctly, which they did eventually. It didn't, however, stop them trying to sell you their sisters or stealing your watch.

On this trip we are at least making our best efforts. But just how many more

customs can we learn to respect? How many more times do we have to check whether we should be using the left hand or the right or learn the most polite way to say no without causing upset or starting an Islamic jihad?

The people, the landscapes, the strange and wonderful worlds constantly revealing themselves to us round sharp mountain bends or across vast desert horizons: they're becoming almost too much to absorb. Everything has become the biggest, the highest, the hottest, the coldest, the wildest, the most beautiful, dangerous and exotic. Fakenham really cannot ever be the same again! Nor can London, for that matter. I remember on a previous overland trip Adam Peacock, the photographer, who had never travelled in Asia, just stopped taking pictures. He had already shot about four thousand and, as he put it, his eye couldn't focus on the images any more. I think the girlfriend back home had something to do with it too, but it's an aspect of travel that does, sooner or later, catch up with us all. Time to pause for a while. Believe me, it doesn't take long to feel good again.

We are climbing steadily up across the cool green slopes of the Himalayas, leaving behind the heat and dust of heartland India; the religious mayhem of the towns and cities that line the Rivers Yamuna and Ganges; and the increasing poverty of some of the northern states, like Bihar. Despite everything, I have grown to love India all over again during the past few weeks - to revel afresh in the variety of its textures and in its wonderful tumult: in its clashing colours; in the richness of its smells; in its daily assaults on my imagination - and my sanity.

And now Nepal, following the old single track road over a mountain pass that climbs to 2500 metres and presents, for the first time, a distant glimpse of the highest Himalayan points: Mount Everest and Annapurna. The air is colder now, the people fewer, the faces more lined, the backs bent from long walks up impossibly steep paths carrying impossibly heavy loads. Suddenly India seems a long way away and the faces are from China and Tibet. This is the Tribhuvan Highway, the first road to link the Kathmandu Valley with the outside world, completed in 1956. With the shimmering plains of India dropping away behind us, we enter a series of deep shadowed valleys before meandering slowly up into the sunlit hills and through magnificent forests of pine and rhododendron.

There might not be any snow around, but suddenly it does feel that Christmas is close. Dan and I are travelling together and talking perhaps as we have never talked before, family or not. We both feel the exhilaration of the journey behind us - and the rest yet to come. We feel the changes in ourselves, too. Getting some distance from all those old moulds helps. It's 16 December 1994, exactly 112 days since we left London. We are behaving like sightseers, stopping **Overleaf: Sunrise over Annapurna** to take snaps rather than film, posing with Himalayan **in the Himalayas**

backgrounds at every opportunity, talking about hot baths, food, drink - and lots of sleep in big beds.

Even I, so completely absorbed in what I do - driven in my journeying, in my hunger for experience, in my endless fascination with people and places - even I can't wait to close the door for a few days.

Meeting Dot in Jordan has been more to do with it than anything else. For an endless wanderer like me, for somebody who's reported from so many front lines, for a rootless one who's spent his whole life on the move, relating to somebody else in such a brief and brilliant way and being so completely inspired has got to mean there's much more to find out and discover. And judging by the letters, faxes and calls that have marked the last few thousand miles, the feeling's obviously mutual. What better time than now - wherever that may be? And why not here, high among the snow-clad Himalayas, on the roof of the world, to meet again? What better way for two people to continue a journey? We have the chance to be the keeper of so few dreams in our lives.

HIPPIE DHARMA

Captain
F.D. Colaabavala

An uncensored, eye-opening revelation of
the hippies and the hippiedom along its
mystic God--LSD--free love trail
WITH REAL-LIFE PHOTOGRAPHS

The great Bengali poet Rabindranath Tagore tells a story about the man who wandered the back roads of India in search of the touchstone. For years he looked, picking rocks from the road as he went, rubbing them against the buckle on his belt to see if they would turn it to gold. One day, in the blazing midday heat, he entered a small village. His eyes were no longer really seeing, his mind no longer really believing. Ahead, a great mountain soared into the sky. Suddenly around him, a crowd of children were pulling at his sleeve, pointing excitedly at his belt. Looking down, the buckle flashed and sparkled in the sun, as gold as gold can ever be. Somewhere, somehow, he had found the touchstone and thrown it away again without ever knowing he had had it.

Captain F. D. Colaabavala was in the Indian Army and Navy for eleven years before he obviously went through a mid-life crisis or some kind of great upheaval and wandered off to write *The Adventures*

of an Indian Tramp. Not so long afterwards, in 1974, he came out with *Hippie Dharma.* By this time he seemed to have slipped completely off the rails, upbringing and bearing gone by the board. 'There is a bizarre world infested with drugs, sex, nudity and wanderlust,' the captain writes eagerly in *Hippie Dharma.* 'Yet they preach altruism and mysticism, honesty, joy and non-violence. Social drop-outs and habitual dope addicts, they still swear by Buddha and Gandhi, and claim to conquer the world by love....' This is obviously a world that Captain Colaabavala considered well worth investigating. Undercover, of course! *Hippie Dharma* is one of those little obscure paperback books ('UNCENSORED - WITH REAL-LIFE PHOTOGRAPHS') that can be found in dusty piles, hidden away on the back shelves of bookshops throughout Nepal and India. The readership must be there, after all, Kathmandu and Goa have been the final overland destination since the 1960s.

> *'Standing like a magnet at the end of the hippie trail, there is a filthy little café called 'The Cabin' in Kathmandu, the 4500-foot [1300-metre]-high capital of Nepal. Here Kishore Rana serves Chinese, Indian, Tibetan and Western food to the pounding music of the Rolling Stones and the Beatles, bhajans and what-have-you. But the infamous specialties of the house are "charas" cakes and "joints". The one freshly baked, the other rolled into reefers - and both guaranteed "to turn you on in the lap of the gods".*
>
> *There is no legal restriction, no interference from the police, no fear of being caught or raided or busted. That is the attraction of Nepal for the hippies, hobos, freaks, flower children, the white sadhus and the longhairs of the world.'*

Nobody seems to know what's happened to Captain Colaabavala, and the only clue in his book is on the last page where 'with blood pressure soaring, heart pounding' he runs away with his sarong falling off. He had woken up to find a naked French-Moroccan 'high priestess' balancing upside down on her head with her 'double-breasted breasts - almost the size of footballs - an inch from my eyes'. Poor Captain Colaabavala! Did he survive the hippie experience? Is he wandering the back roads and beaches of India still? Can his life ever be the same again?

Only a few days back, when the Yamuna River was still in my sights, I had met a brain surgeon from Dallas. Yes, strange but true again, I had run into a real live neurologist, even if he was an ex-neurologist! 'Ray' has been wandering the back roads of India for more than twenty years. He went to a conference on neuro-surgery in London way back somewhere in the ganja-filled corridors of his brain. Someone had suggested a few days on a beach in Goa might make a good stop-over on the way home. And that was it. He's been in India ever since. He's a sadhu now, an Indian

holy man, bearded and barefoot, dreadlocked and almost naked, who refers to himself only in terms of the royal 'we'. As a man of the gods, he is traditionally fed and looked after by the people he meets on his endless pilgrimage around the promised land. Had he seen Captain Colaabavala? Or even heard of him? His answer is as obscure as it is delightfully mad: 'We are writing a book,' he laughs, 'but we don't think we will ever finish it!'

The Shiva Parvati Temple, Kathmandu

Kathmandu seems so far away when you are in a hurry to get there: almost as far, perhaps, as Dallas must be to Ray. So, by the time I push *Wah Wah* over the last ridge before the Nepalese capital, I'm feeling a bit like a kid on a school outing. 'Are we there yet?'

The city is a polluted sprawl across the floor of the Kathmandu valley, its suburbs edging up into the surrounding hills. In the distance is a backdrop of some of the great Himalayan peaks, now almost lost behind a grey screen of fumes. This is the price being paid by Nepal for the huge success of the tourist industry that has grown out of the hippie invasion of the 1960s. Nepal is now one of the world's greatest trekking and mountain-climbing centres - Kathmandu the starting point for it all. This is where you buy your gear and book your trails; this is where you rest up before you set off or after you've arrived. This is where most of the overland trucks end their journeys; where the hitchers finally run out of rides. This is where you gorge yourself sick and can find all those little things you thought you had forgotten (like Marmite and custard!). This is where you can still smoke a joint and not feel too nervous about the law. This is where they have real live pubs serving real ale - and where nobody stirs much before midday.

Even so, the city still looks like the capital of a great mountain kingdom, with its age-long Buddhist and Hindu traditions and its extravagantly royal history. The streets are lined with a crazy jumble of buildings whose carved wooden balconies lean in on each other above rows of tiny shops, spilling into squares packed with temples and monuments, and markets bright with stalls selling mounds of fruit and vegetables. Royal palaces with high walls and great curling roofs break the skyline, surrounded by parks where soldiers parade and politicians pronounce. In some ways the centuries still seem undisturbed, but in others you know that everything has changed - or is about to do so.

But 'The Cabin' is no longer there and 'Freak Street', where the drugs used to flow

as easy as a long, sweet glass of fresh lassi, is little more than a name on a tourist map. The long-haired, flared-trousered drop-outs are now just fading black and white pictures on the walls, or characters in books like *Hippie Dharma*. In many ways the narrow, winding alleys of the old part of Kathmandu have more the feel of a Western ski resort than that of a hippie mecca. Despite the fact that the foreigners who crowd these streets are continually pestered to buy souvenir Gurkha knives, Tibetan bells or Nepalese flutes (and, more coyly, 'Psst, you want joint, ganja, hashish?') it's all very clean-cut and respectable - and incredibly cheap.

Hubert sighs a bit like a romantic Greek ferry captain, leaning back in a chair, his stomach stretching comfortably against his tightly fitting shirt, his eyes passing with pleasure across the roofs of his adopted city. This man is a perfect example of the changing times. Eminently proper now, he's an ex-hippie in his forties who runs a roof-top restaurant that serves nothing but the best German food - and a bar that mixes the most brutal cocktails in town. The best time to catch Hubert is as the sun sinks and the air is just a little chilled - chill enough for a drink to be needed to warm the heart

and encourage a bit of story-telling. Hubert first came to Nepal in the early seventies when 'the city was a less crowded, less polluted' place and those who knew the scene divided their time between Kathmandu and the beaches of Goa. 'Nobody bothered you in those days, nobody asked you what you did, nobody cared. You just relaxed, smoked ganja and lived in this sort of timeless state. This was my greatest experience. It made living back in Europe seem so pointless, so mad. It made my life so much better.'

Trekking country in Nepal

It was much the same for D'Arcy, a Canadian hippie who kept returning and now runs a successful clothing and jewellery business here. 'I haven't been back to Canada in thirteen years this time,' he laughs, looking and sounding as comfortable as Hubert. 'I don't need to and I don't want to. This is my home now. I've fallen in love with the country and its people, and I've married one of them. When I first came to Nepal I stayed about four years. Sometimes I used to sit and smoke and look out over the mountains and watch them grow. I'm sure they did.' He laughs. 'I suppose this was my answer to getting away from it all. But, like I would anywhere, I sometimes wonder why I'm here. The most important thing though is that I still am.'

There are some, of course, who wish they weren't. The Nepalese law still might be pretty lenient and one-eyed, but it does at least function. Most days, Hope goes to see those who got caught. The young Dutch student, statuesque and pale-skinned,

dresses in her best, closest-fitting sarees for her visits to the jail. The prisoners, a hand-ful of European and American drug offenders, are allowed into the visiting room, with its central divide of rusting bars, once or twice a day. Usually there are no visitors except Hope. Today, as on most days, she sits on one of the hard wooden benches that line the walls and talks with them, or sometimes just sits silently and watches with her huge brown eyes, a strangely surreal figure in a faraway land staring at the anxious, haggard faces of men waiting to be sentenced or set free, their hands and bodies pressing against the bars.

It seems especially hard if you know just how close the mountains are, and how real is that sense of freedom outside your door. Nepal is a land that invites long walks across vast, empty landscapes towards endless horizons. And somehow, of all the people of all the countries along the road east, the Nepalese are the least judgemental and the most accepting.

Karna Sakya should know about that. As owner of several hotels and guest houses, including the Kathmandu Guest House, the oldest and most famous of them all, he is perhaps the man who did the most to open the door to tourism in Nepal. He believes that the hippies were the best thing that happened to his country, not the worst.

'When I was very young,' he recounts, 'only forty or so years ago, I had never seen a white man. I remember asking my uncle what they were like and why they were white. He had never seen one either, but he told me that legend had it that they came from another world, an underground world, and that they all had tails like monkeys. "They are white," he told me, "because they are so rich they only drink milk, not water." And you know, for many years after they started coming here in the late 1950s, I still believed that all foreigners were English and were very wealthy and could do no wrong. We all believed that.

'It was the hippies who helped us to understand that the children of white men can cheat and lie too, and can be poor and ill, and that they are not all supermen. The hip-pies came here barefoot and with long hair, they slept on the streets and they smoked drugs, just like us Nepalese used to do, and they opened the door to our future. And now some of them, like me, are getting older and have become businessmen and Members of Congress and MPs.'

I like Karna Sakya. He made me feel very normal and healthy. And so did the 'Cock Man'. Well, that's what some of the travellers call him. Actually, he rather likes the name. Cross-legged and seemingly at peace with himself and the world around him, he sits with his buddies, a gaggle of gurus, under a banyan tree and stirs the embers of a small fire. It's taken him fifteen years to get his form of yoga right. I can only admire his dedication. Maybe it's the smell of the burning bodies in the funeral pyres which line the river below his holy perch that gives him his strength.

He's small and wiry, his hard, brown body muscled and slim, naked except for the hang of an old loincloth. He pulls it to one side to show me how he performs his particular brand of yoga. His penis looks rather limp, dull and unhappy. Not surprising, really. He seizes it and manipulates it vigorously, coating it in ash, twisting and turning it between his fingers, softening and pulling it, stretching it until it looks as though he has tied it in knots. I'm cringing already, but Ron's staying as steady as they come, with his hand on the zoom. Then he repeats the process by stretching his penis again, this time round an iron bar, and twisting it some more.

Next come the weights, which he can't even lift with his hands. It's a sling full of rocks weighing about 70 kilos. I almost fall over trying (and failing) to pick it up. I can't believe what happens next. But it does. Pulling his foreskin out to an amazing length he loops it through the sling and, with a quick intake of breath but barely a wince, proceeds to lift the 70 kilos off the ground and swing it quite casually from the end of his penis. It's all on film if you don't believe me!

Cock Man's sex life must be either wonderful or non-existent. I'm inclined to think the latter. 'I lost my energy a long time ago,' he smiles rue-fully. 'I live my life for the power of my spirit.' But he does get a lot of mail. It seems he has friends and admirers all over the world. And like everybody else he gets his letters from a Poste Restante box at the Kathmandu Post Office.

On 24 December the room is probably at its most crowded, with eager faces queuing for a last chance letter from home and a taste of a Christmas that can only be imagined. We are all here too, all about to scatter to our different

Christmas mail for Sumela, Stuart, Chiara and me

hotels and guest houses, to meet again for Christmas lunch but then to go our different ways - at least until it's time to get back on the road again. There are a lot of dewy eyes in this room tonight, even among the most hardened travellers, and a lot of letters being shared - from distant mums and dads, sisters, brothers, friends, and once and would-be lovers.

Dot is here - at last. It seems like it's been a lifetime - but then I realize the world is so much smaller than I ever thought, so much easier to move about in and to share than I ever imagined. We talk for hours, of many things - and plan midnight runs up into the mountains to spend candle-lit nights in remote Tibetan lodges under huge, feather-filled quilts and to huddle in the chill blue light of many dawns to watch slow Himalayan sunrises. And then we close the door.

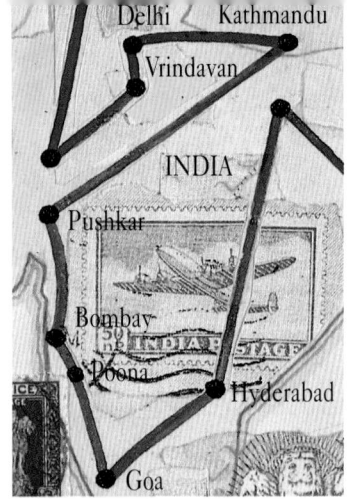

CHAPTER 17

Gods, Grass and Techno Roll

Chilling out on the beaches of Goa and Southern India

Dawn is a cloud-streaked salmon-pink sky opening slowly over a small market town on the edge of a night-time desert. Pushkar is a warren of narrow, winding streets, burrowed whitewashed houses and temples clinging to the edge of the flat, black waters of a holy lake. We are travelling south again, our course set for 1400 kilometres across India; driving along the sand-baked fringes of Rajasthan and the steamy, tropical landscapes of the Indian Ocean coast; past the soaring downtown skyline of the busy, cosmopolitan port of Bombay, the gateway to India; and further, to the distant palm-fringed beaches of Goa.

Kathmandu seems far away already. Ron has stayed behind in Nepal for a few days to trek with his partner Audrey. Sean and Dan are travelling with Michelle in the Land Rover. Dot is with me in *Wah Wah* - probably the only way I could ever have been persuaded to leave our room back in the mountains! It seems so strange to look across the increasingly cluttered Jeep, with its garlands of flowers, beads and precious things, to see the face of the woman I first met and loved on a mountain in Jordan. To see her beside me. It's all beginning to feel like Scottie's beaming me up somewhere. I've gone ahead and got in the spaceship. Certainly India has never been like this - less India, perhaps, more an experience in together travelling, something I have never done before. I love it, difficult as it is occasionally.

The town of Pushkar is a well-earned point of rest *en route*, a travellers' gathering-place where the grass is mellower, the gods are still Hindu and, as one of the great places of pilgrimage in India, there's no meat and not a beer in sight. It's also the place where they hold what must be the world's largest camel fair. Try fifty thousand at a time - camels, that is. And the human population of Pushkar swells from eleven thousand to more than a quarter of a million, the streets full of tribesmen, merchants, pilgrims and Western travellers from all over the subcontinent. And then there are the five-star tourists in their carefully groomed, air-conditioned tents, with garden surrounds and three meals a day - *en suite*. In India?

But mostly Pushkar's a trendy place to hang out and go shopping. Yes, travellers do go shopping. Far more than they would probably like to admit - and still manage to keep their road cred intact.

The Anjuna beach market, every Wednesday in Goa

They wear most of the gear that they buy and in India, in Pushkar in particular, start looking the part in bright-dyed cloths, leather belts and thongs, and the glitter of bangles and beads. New age hippies, really.

Nearly twenty-five years after leaving Venice, Marco Polo passed through this area on his way back from China. He described how he found 'good cotton and handsome works of scarlet leather in the markets, embossed with birds and beasts and stitched with gold and silver of very fine workmanship, exquisite to behold'. Not much has changed in seven hundred years, except that most of the market wear is now being mass produced, which probably means a lot more hands being employed, very cheaply. Like Alexander the Great, Marco Polo did eventually succumb to local fashions. His dress sense would never be the same again: a lot of long flowing robes, fine velvets and silks, elaborate beading and jewel trims.

Larry Brown is a stocky, dark American taking a break from his banking job in Geneva. It all seems wonderfully unlikely given that he laughs so much, wears layers of rings on his fingers and his toes, and paints his nails - all of them. I take a bet he's lying. He looks as though he should be in music management or maybe even advertizing. Anyway, he's hanging out with Elaine Dougherty. Tall, perfectly tall and voluptuously rangy; and freckled with a huge smile that lights up her whole body. Her eyes are sometimes green, sometimes blue. It doesn't really matter - they just seem to change all the time. She touches you when she talks, and plays to the camera with sideways glances. Elaine is an actress, but this is undoubtedly her real-life role, this year's fiction.

After so long on the road the last thing I want to have to do is work hard. Talking with Larry and Elaine is a video dream. An evening out with these two is like joining an Indian wedding procession, a glittering passage through a night-time bazaar, a blur of cascading colours and flickering lights, shuffling feet with shouts, laughter and song. Elaine is so good at playing the role I'm sure she must be out of work, and I only wish Larry was my bank manager. Like everybody else, these two are heading south towards Goa, their last stop in India before taking their laughter with them back to Europe. They have both become Buddhists and are very much 'into meditation'. Goa will be a last chance to sit and chill out their brains. We agree to meet on a beach somewhere. That's what it's like on the road - nothing cast in stone, but somehow you know you will.

Patrick Sweeney is pale and much more serious; poetic, almost. A tall, dark-haired Irishman whom you might expect to find sitting alone on a single bed in a sparse back-street hotel room, the remnants of a meal on the floor beside him, hand-scrawled papers scattered on a table in the corner. In real life I meet Patrick drinking sweet

lassi in a tropical garden on the edge of the Pushkar lake. He's talking with his sister, Siobhan, who's flown out to India for two weeks to visit him. But I have a good imagination. In any case, being alone in a strange hotel room a million miles from Dublin is much closer to the true image of this man.

Patrick is travelling to learn and to talk. This country is his perfect place. 'India's bubbling,' he says, 'you know, overflowing with life. Love it or hate it, and you go through both of these emotions and everything in between at least twenty times a day, it keeps you alert and alive. Interaction is forced on you.'

He laughs. 'You know, I sometimes think I must be some kind of a deviant. What the hell am I doing? I've left my job behind, and friends, and I've travelled for four years - and now I'm in India! I think a lot of the time though I'm like a voyeur, scratching at the surface of other people's culture, knocking but not getting in. I might be playing football with some kids and thinking as though I'm really communicating, but I still feel a sense of apartness.

'Now I'm really looking forward to getting back to my family and friends, to the culture I come from. To my stereo and the movies and all those things, because that's actually who I am. It's just basic to the human condition that we want to establish relationships and continue with them. I think it's practical too. We need all that. For our heads and our hearts we definitely need it.... But I will always want to travel again too.' And he laughs. Patrick never told me what he did. No doubt one day we will meet again and I will remember to ask.

There is an Indian couple in Pushkar, wandering minstrels, with a small baby son, who sing love songs together every night as the sun sets, sitting by the side of the lake and looking out towards the distant desert hills. They are travellers too. They carry their home and their possessions with them: a brightly dyed bedroll; three small cooking pots; some modest but neatly folded clothes wrapped in a white cotton sheet; a picture of the Lord Krishna in a silvered tin frame; a well-frayed notebook; and a sarangi, a small, wooden, stringed instrument. In the morning I sit with Ramphal and Shita as they pray together, making a small offering to the gods beneath the tree where they sleep. And they sing again too, religious songs in praise of Krishna, with Ramphal picking out the finest notes from his sarangi and raising his voice in counterpoint with Shita's. They hope their son, Ramnivas, will learn to sing and play the sarangi too.

Shita is like a goddess in miniature, her jet-black hair cascading around her face and down her back, her bright yellow saree wrapped tight around her tiny body, her toes glittering with cheap village rings, and silver bangles climbing up her arms. She raises her face to the sky, closes her eyes and has the sweetest, purest voice. She

A cow jam

likes to feed Ramnivas when she sings, lifting the front of her blouse and pressing her small, soft breast to his mouth. In this way, she believes, he will inherit the music in her.

Ramphal, who is forty, smiles proudly by her side and says there will be more sons, and daughters too, he hopes - though not too many, as girls must have the finest clothes if they are to marry well and he doesn't know if he will be able to afford such things. He and Shita, who is fifteen years younger, also hope to earn enough money from their singing in Pushkar to go and visit Ramphal's sister. He hasn't seen her for twenty-five years. She lives more than 1000 kilometres from here. They are ready to walk, but would prefer to take the bus because of Ramnivas.

I offer to pay for their tickets, but in the most roundabout way, not wanting to insult them. It would cost no more than five pounds. Ramphal looks very serious for a moment and then declines. They couldn't possibly accept, he says. 'You are my friend now, and I know that it would take a long time for us to repay such a debt.' There is nothing more to say, but before I leave I buy Ramnivas a small wooden flute and Shita a fine, bright-beaded cotton scarf to tie in her hair. Ramphal and I go and drink tea together and talk of other things.

A thousand kilometres from here could be many places, but to the south a cock crows and the rising sun stirs a gentle swell along a sweeping shore. A children's choir can be heard coming from a little whitewashed Catholic church, half hidden by the gently swaying palms that line the beach. It's another day, and another religion in the former Portuguese territory of Goa.

Skirts outnumber sarees in this place and there's an altogether different attitude among Goanese - in the way they talk and the way they behave. The people of Goa, predominantly Catholic, are much more liberal and easy-going than their Hindu or Muslim neighbours. One thing that immediately struck me is the directness of the women, a fact that's reflected in the laws of Goa, which ensure that a woman is entitled to 50 per cent of a couple's estate.

Old Portuguese colonial buildings nestle among the hills and down narrow streets in quiet towns surrounded by stretches of lush green paddies and clumps of coconut palms. Crumbling forts, their walls green with damp and moss, guard rocky capes and river estuaries. But it's the miles of beaches that hold the mind. Goa's the one place that has always been there as far as the travellers are concerned. It's now one of India's premier tourist attractions, thanks to the sixties hippies who once crowded its sands - naked or not so naked, but nearly always stoned. Today it's the club scene, packaged raves direct from London for all-night freak-outs on full-moon beaches and in clubs that could just as well be somewhere else, except for the bullfrogs desperately trying to hold their own against the onrush of the noise and the vibration of seamless, endless techno-beat. For many, it's great to smoke a joint, or possibly even pop a tab under a palm tree far from home - but let there be no illusion that this is anything to do with India.

For the traveller, arriving here overland from Europe and the Middle East, or even after several months on the road around India, Goa is a chance to kick back and rest up for a few weeks, get a tan and eat reasonable food - or do a little business perhaps, buying and selling. 'This nice belt, nice belt, take this, take this - cheap price! Little business, yes? Little business?' The local

Dot and me - still smiling after all these miles

Indian traders, most of them Rajasthani women down from the deserts with jewellery and cloth, are very persistent. Physical even, pulling at my sleeve, prodding my back. Anything can be made into a little business at Anjuna, the liveliest beach market in Goa, where bright-splashed sarees and sarongs sparkle in the sea breeze, and beautifully wrought silver jewellery lies next to tattered second-hand paperbacks.

Mandy - 'Top London Stylist' goes native

Goa is where many travellers gather over the winter months, spreading out their wares at Anjuna every Wednesday, like any other trader Marco Polo might have met - probably selling much the same kind of things, too. It could just as well be Camden Market. Some are skilful artisans in their own right; others are just struggling to stay on the road, selling their possessions to get by. Yet others bake cakes, cook crumbles, weave hair wraps, hand-dye tee-shirts - anything to bring in a few rupees. There are music and jugglers; beggars and freaks; flute players and dancers. For twelve short hours the sands beneath the palms throb with colour and life and a babble of music and tongues.

And Steve and André are here. The stilts and the costumes have been packed away for a while, and *Starbug* has been turned into an outdoor café. Cushions have been spread beneath a bright coloured awning and swaying lines of fairy lights, and André is serving Steve's home-made crumble and custard. And plates of chips too. Business is brilliant.

Under a palm tree less than ten yards away Mandy Forster sparkles, all smiles beneath her sign offering: 'Hair-Cuts By Fully-Qualified Top London Stylist.' She's been travelling for four years, working her way through Greece and the Middle East, and she's still only twenty-four, a pale, delicate girl, drawn like a magnet to India and still not quite sure why.

'It's hard to explain, because I didn't know really what to prepare myself for - it's just something that's been in my head for as long as I could speak. I come from a town up north, and I've always said that as soon as I'm old enough I'm going to London and going to get to the top of my trade and then I'm going to India. But nothing can prepare you for what India's like - it's so special. I think the people are really special. Even when their houses are drowned in water they'll come outside and wave at you. They're all really poor - but they're so rich inside.'

But do people like Mandy ever go home? 'No, I don't think I will ever settle in England because I think it's too out of sync for me. The materialism and things, just the whole system. But maybe, if I do find inside myself what I'm searching for, it shouldn't matter what's going on outside. So maybe I will.'

Others never will. I can see them, a group here or there, ageing hippies with white hair and beards, joints always rolled, slightly suspicious of cameras and questions - on the run from the world in a world of their own.

Down the road in Calungute, Bob's is a bit of a hideaway - one of those bamboo-and-beer places you can stagger into to get out of the midday heat and suddenly find

it's midnight already. Paul Griffin is a regular. He's in his fifties now, one of the sixties' travellers who opened up the road to India and one of the earliest to reach Goa. A hippie perhaps, but with a clear idea in mind. This man's got himself organized.

'I went buying antiques in Afghanistan, bartering my way across the world. In those days, we had just finished with nylon shirts in England. Everybody had got them, nobody wanted to wear them. So I had two hundred or so laundered and packeted and took them on the road with me. For a nylon shirt then in Afghanistan or India you could get anything - literally anything.' He smiles with pleasure at the thought of all that profit.

Paul, grey-haired and with a thickening waist, now lives half the year in Goa and half back in England, where he sells jewellery. He's married to a Goanese woman and has a son. Tipping back in a chair, he explains: 'Look, what I pay for my heating bill over the winter in England will rent me a house here for six months. So what's the point? I'm here in the winter - every winter.'

Jungle Barry is always here - though 'here' is pushing it a bit. He's really off in another world. Fifty-four and scrawny now, with an unkempt beard down to his waist, he's having a reunion for the first time in twenty years with Kevin, out from Wigan to catch up with all those years in between. They travelled out overland together in the early seventies. One stayed; the other went home. Does either of them regret his decision? Looking at them in the half-light of the bar - Jungle with his tattered shoulder bag and his penny whistle, Kevin with his comfortable second wife; and the way Jungle's hand shakes as he lifts his glass of beer, and Kevin's fingers curl firmly round his wife's thigh - I know who I would rather be.

No, neither has regrets, except that Kevin says he misses the travelling. Jungle, who admits he looks like the victim of a famine, says he could never imagine living back in England - or ever wanting to. 'I'm here for keeps. It's such a free existence.' He's been variously chased - and occasionally jailed - for overstaying his Indian visa by ten years; for trying to smuggle six kilos of hash out to Denmark; and for being Lord Lucan. When he's together enough, he can scrape out a living doing odd jobs sent his way by friends. But not much else.

Jungle Barry and Kevin - still crazy after all these years; and overleaf: Oh no - not another sunset in Goa!

Goa makes me nervous. I want to leave soon. The beaches have worked their magic, the travellers have told their tales and the real end of my road is now only a matter of weeks away. And I'm celebrating my fiftieth birthday - or is it forty-nine?

Eleventh of January 1995. Dot organizes a beach party with Steve and André, a cake and lots of free-flowing rum. And everybody comes - well, the family, anyway. The best present is seeing my daughter Tanya, who has flown out from England with her boyfriend Jeremy; Kylie is here too, keeping Sean in line; Michelle's organizing Dan; and Ron is here, too. It's our first party since leaving London. We turn up the music, light a roaring wood fire on a stretch of sand under a black, starlit night and for a few hours nothing else matters. Turning fifty with Dot was no crisis that night.

Poona is only a day's drive away from Goa - but it could be another world. A short step to heaven, maybe? That's what the followers of the late Bhagwan Shree Rajneesh, or Osho as he is now called, would have us believe. Their commune in Poona is perhaps the best known in India, attracting as many as 85 000 visitors a year. It's almost a natural extension of a visit to Goa. Osho is perhaps the most controversial of all the Indian mystics since the sixties. He's labelled by many as 'the sex guru', and by his disciples as 'the most dangerous man since Jesus Christ', while his books and teachings have sold more than 15 million copies worldwide - making this a very wealthy commune too.

It's an 11-hectare dream world of smiles and flowing robes, of chanting and meditation. There is an impressive black-fronted complex of university faculty buildings, self-help centres, open-air restaurants, an Olympic-size swimming pool, tennis courts and cool lakeside walks - dominated by a huge marble-floored meditation hall with a sweeping roof and open-air, net-covered sides. It holds several thousand people at a time. No effort spared in this place. No wonder they call it Club Med-itation! It's a bit like a journey through a white, fluffy cloud. Whether you approve or not, the commune is beautifully laid out, lush and green, relaxing and refreshing. Everybody seems to be young, lovely and white. Well, between twenty-five and sixty anyway. Dot certainly thought the tennis coaches (all six-foot, blond Germans) made the grade! And Ron's filming seemed to be pointedly female-orientated.

If you visit the commune, you can work in the kitchen chopping veggies, be a gardener or a printer, says Anando, an Australian devotee. She trained as a lawyer but ended up becoming one of Osho's longest-serving helpmates and is now one of the leaders of the commune. 'It doesn't matter what work you choose to do - if you work at all. The whole point is to come here and look at yourself,' she says. 'You don't have so much time for this back in the West, especially if you're working nine to five. Here it's a whole different approach.'

Before they'll let us in we all have to have AIDS tests. We could walk and film round the commune without them, but to don the flowing maroon or white robes and take

part in the evening discourses and meditations we have to have the tests. Nobody likes the idea. You never know - or at least we are naturally nervous about knowing. But we do - and we all pass. Believe me, heaven had better be good after this!

'I thought when I left London, "Ah, great, I'm going to have this instant change and revelation" - and that, of course, doesn't happen. You take yourself wherever you go.' Sheila is an Englishwoman in her early forties with a successful printing and publishing business. She felt the need to get more in touch with herself and sort out what was basically a professionally rich but personally poor life. 'So coming to Poona I was able to get a chance to look at things and recognize that the reason why I am not changing is because I'm trying to take an old pattern and change it from the outside. I have to relax and just let it be.'

John is a stockbroker in his late fifties, a regular city gent up to his eyes in profit-and-loss and high-stress living. He's now been to Poona twice - and plans to make it a regular event, taking time out to meditate and 'be there for myself for a few weeks in my life every year'.

Amrito, who was Osho's personal physician, has made it a regular part of his for the last twenty years - full-time. He's a tall, biblically handsome man with a thick, full, black-grey beard and wavy shoulder-length hair to match. 'I had absolutely no interest in anything spiritual or religious when I first came out to India,' he explains, sitting in a quiet corner of Osho's private garden. 'I always felt it was complete mumbo-jumbo. Then I came for a visit to the commune and went to one of Osho's lectures. But I got the date wrong and it was in Hindi, so I didn't understand a word. Even so, I found him a beautiful person to watch. It was a kind of dance of energy - and you know, there I was, a GP from Lewisham, filing past Osho at the end of the lecture. And as I got in front of him it suddenly seemed so natural just to bow down and kiss his feet. And this was somebody I'd never met before! Anyway it's not common practice in Lewisham.' Right!

My last view of Amrito was in his white robes, with his hands flung high in the air, his head thrown back, his body arching outwards and upwards, shouting 'Osho, Osho' - along with several thousand other followers - dancing in front of Osho's empty chair. 'The whole existence sings with you, dances with you,' Osho had told them from beyond the grave, in a big-screen video of one of his discourses, 'and when someone becomes enlightened the whole existence celebrates it because we are not separate, we are one cosmic whole.'

Kushwant Singh is one of India's best-known modern writers and certainly one of its most outspoken and controversial. He is eighty now and has been to Poona several times. He believes that Osho is one of India's greatest original thinkers, but he decries the whole culture of the Indian guru as little more than a money-making scheme.

'We have lots of stories about how easy it is to become a god-man or god-woman and start attracting foreign followers,' Kushwant explains 'I mean, even a person like me. If I donned a saffron robe, kept my beard and started spouting platitudes about religion, I'm sure I would soon get a lot of elderly ladies as disciples - then probably a lot of young ones too. The problem with India is that we spend far too much time in ritual and prayer - going to the temple, lighting candles and mumbling prayers. I don't think it makes us better human beings. It is, in fact, as Marx described, nothing more than an opium for the masses. But if you are faced with the human being's worst enemy - the ego, the "I am" - and if you can beat it and become a better person, and help make the society in which you live a better society, and you can do that by sitting in front of Osho's empty chair or going to a Krishna temple or a Buddhist pagoda, or even lying on a beach in Goa, then why not?'

India seems to bring out the spiritual from within most travellers, or at least a feeling that something might be missing from their lives. A continuity of thousands of years of ritual and religion has certainly left a deeply imbedded sense of spirituality in the culture and lives of Indians themselves. If this encourages travellers to undertake a different kind of journey and to look for something that works for them in a positive and fulfilling way, or just fills a gap in their lives, then indeed, why not? What's wrong with a bit of opium, anyway?

Red hot and chilling out!

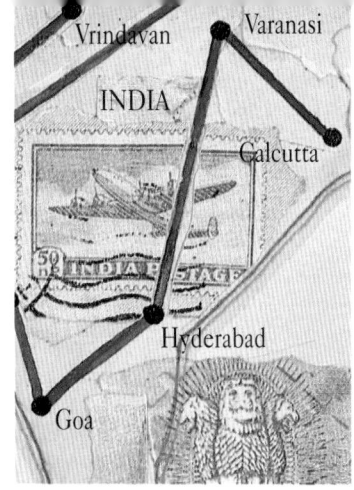

CHAPTER 18

The End of the Road

Calcutta - and it's time to go home!

The rains have come early, breaking without warning, just before midnight. The road ahead is a treacherous, potholed black ribbon, glistening like a silvered snake caught in my headlights, winding its way across a wild and empty landscape of huge boulders. At times the downpour is so heavy I can only see a few metres ahead - great sheets of red mud and water spraying up around the Jeep. I am heading across the centre of India again before swinging north for the last time and driving up through the heart of this vast country. It's about three more days to go before Calcutta, and I've decided to press on and try and get some miles on the clock.

It's hard to believe that my journey is almost over. It's going to be difficult not getting up in the morning, loading *Wah Wah*, reading the map and driving off towards yet another new horizon. But it *has* been nearly six months and almost 30 000 kilometres. It feels like it's time to go home. Sean and Ron are way up ahead somewhere in the Land Rover; Dan and Michelle have taken the train and are already in Calcutta; Dot is asleep across the front seat, her head on my lap, my hand resting on the side of her face and her neck.

The night is a blanket of darkness around us, broken only by the flickering, distant lightning, throwing up the shapes of the rocks as huge black shadows against a threatening purple sky, the rain slashing against the windscreen in sudden, angry gusts. The nearest town is still 60 kilometres or so away, Calcutta many hundreds more. India is passing in a blur of time and space and there is no longer any sense of distance, only an image of Dot and me, cocooned and alone, warm and secure, travelling across an endless, thunderous landscape.

I remember another storm like this in 1962. It blew up and swept down the River Yamuna without warning, driving the home-made bamboo raft I was punting on to a sandbank and sweeping all my cigarettes into the water. It was a freak storm that came and went in a matter of minutes - just one in a number of accidents that plagued my attempt to sail the raft from Agra, the home of the Taj Mahal, to Calcutta. Don't ask me why - it just seemed like the right thing to do at the time and it was more fun than hitch-hiking! I had written to my parents - but only after the event, and as usual had kept the story reasonably sanitized.

'A great deal has happened since I left Delhi, things that made it impossible for me to write. Arthur [with whom I had travelled on and off since Iraq], two other Englishmen and I decided we would try something different.

We decided to build a raft and sail...down the River Yamuna [from Agra] to Allahabad. Then down the River Ganges to Calcutta, a total of 800 miles [1300 kilometres]. The raft was 15 ft by 10 ft [4.5 m by 3 m], and consisted of 6 oil drums, 6 biscuit tins, a four-sectioned frame and a flooring of bamboo. There was a sail, two paddles, punting poles and a rudder.... The people of Agra gave us a great many things free, including provisions for the journey. The papers got on to us and made a big thing of it.'

We must have been out of our minds, of course, but it seemed like fun. It took us several attempts even to get the thing to float, and we had to keep cadging more biscuit tins to get the balance right. But at least our departure was spectacular.

The Taj Mahal is undoubtedly one of the great wonders of the world, breathtakingly beautiful, especially at midnight on a full moon - when its great white marble dome becomes almost translucent, hovering in the sky over the river like a huge planet. But it catches the light at dusk too and becomes a shimmering pink sun, a true monument to one man's great love for a woman.

We left Agra in the late afternoon, seen off by several hundred curious 'Agrarian people', clearly convinced that we were indeed crazy. But they had been very kind and generous to us, and in return we decided to make a small gesture of thanks. Standing on the banks of the river, on a huge flat expanse of sand, the crowd gathered around as we gave an ensemble demonstration of the twist with Arthur humming the tune of 'Come On, Let's Twist Again'; I sang 'Jerusalem' in my best choirboy voice; and then we all stood in a line and recited dirty limericks. Or was it Shelley!

The crowd was duly impressed and pleased by this great cultural event and cheered loudly as we pushed off, rather nervously, into the swirling current. I shall never forget punting past the Taj as the sun set that night and seeing the curious faces of the tourists peering down at us as we drifted by - each of us glued to a corner of the raft in case it capsized. Our adventure didn't last very long.

'We made about 100 miles [160 km] before we gave up. By river we had to cover 20 miles [30 km] to every 10 miles [16 km] by road. The river winds back on itself all the time. We spent half the day in the water carrying it over sandbanks (it's the dry season). We had a lot of our gear stolen including the sail and three of the oil drums. It was winter and the weather turned cold, wet and windy, two people fell ill with severe dysentery (not me). So we gave up.'

I also left a few things out. The main reason we gave up, apart from the fact that it took us three weeks to cover those 160 kilometres and Arthur got a bad case of piles, was that we were arrested - well, briefly.

Imagine: India is on the edge of war with China, and the papers and the national radio are warning that the Chinese might invade any day. It's dusk, and a villager is squatting, minding his own business, watering his cattle on the banks of the River Yamuna, when round the corner come four half-naked white men punting a bamboo raft. If you are that villager you are, of course, going to run for it. He obviously thought the invasion had begun. We beached the raft at the village only to find that everybody - all three hundred of them - had fled, leaving, quite literally, their dal on their plates and their chapattis in the fire!

An Indian Army unit arrived shortly afterwards and took us away for questioning. When they returned us to the village in order to explain that we were not Chinese, just mad Englishmen, we found that the villagers - doing their patriotic bit - had broken the raft up and, presumably, distributed it amongst themselves. I suppose they regarded it as legitimate war booty.

This is the great thing about India: you can do anything, really, and mostly people will let you get on with it. Gilles has lived in a tree for more than twenty-five years. He's seventy now and has forgotten almost everything he ever knew about Switzerland. He's happy enough living where he's living and doing what he's doing, as long as he has his dachshunds (twelve at the last count), his geese (three at the last count), ample supplies of Pepsi and vitamin C, and lots of opera cassettes.

Gilles' tree is on the banks of a spectacular, slow-moving river near Khajuraho, the site of India's most famous erotic temples. His British wife, Betty, lives a few miles away on their small farm and runs a café and restaurant in Khajuraho. Their children have grown up and left 'home' some years ago. For many years they all lived together - Gilles in the tree, the family in a house below. Then he moved trees.

His tree house is at present being rebuilt. It was badly damaged and partially swept away in a particularly bad storm last rainy season. But this is no ordinary tree house. It consists of a 15-metre-long open wooden platform and bar, on top of which are two more storeys, one for a bedroom, the other a kind of tree-top sitting room from which to view life going by. There is a shower and a loo and plenty of room for the dogs - both up the tree and below it.

'I get claustrophobia in a house,' Gilles explains. 'Up here my bed is at the same level as the rest of the world, so in the morning the birds and the monkeys can look at me and say to themselves, "Who is this strange animal?" Even in Switzerland, when I was a young boy, I used to build tree houses. Now I can never imagine not living in a tree. You must understand that if I didn't live in a tree then I would never have met so many interesting people. My marriage probably wouldn't have lasted as long, either.'

Gilles, white-haired and slightly stooped, came out to India to work in the 1950s and has been here ever since. He met Betty, the daughter of an Anglo-Indian trader, in Calcutta and together they bought the small farm where she now lives with her sister.

'I could never afford to live like this in Europe,' he says. 'That's one reason why I have stayed so long. Apart from that I don't think there is any country in the world, except India, where I'd be able to live as myself. I have found peace here. In Europe I only existed.'

And every night the great voices of opera, Maria Callas, Luciano Pavarotti and many others ring out across India.

Dawn on the banks of the River Ganges at Varanasi reveals itself in the same measured way as it does over Gilles' river. Slowly, a great ball of yellow and orange fire rises up through the early morning mist, drenching India's most holy city in a glowing, rust-red light. Already hundreds of worshippers, sadhus and priests are down by the water's edge, bathing and praying and welcoming the new day. They immerse themselves in the cold black waters, floating out into the current offerings of candles and flowers in small banana-leaf cups.

Dot and I drift in a small boat along with the candles down towards the ghats, where the dead are brought in solemn procession throughout the day and burnt. Other bodies are wrapped in cloth and covered with flowers and left to float away on the water. There is nothing to say. We float with the current too, draped in shawls against the damp and the cold, silently. The body of an old man, a crow sitting on his face, pecking at his eyes, most of the flesh from his skull already gone, drifts by - past the bathers, past the

Taj Mahal, Agra - at dusk

ghats, past the tourists in their boats, past us and away down the Ganges to gradually decompose and disappear forever.

It all feels strangely normal, accepted in the same way that the coming of a new day and the passing of another are so totally accepted and unremarked upon. This is India too.

Calcutta station is a vast echoing cavern swarming with red-coated porters balancing impossibly high piles of baggage on their heads, fighting their way through what feels like the whole of India on the move. Groups of Western travellers are poised ready for the scramble to get themselves places on the Delhi Express. I can tell by their look that it's the end of their trip and they are off on the long haul home, everybody comfortable now with their grubby sandalled feet and crumpled clothes, their packs knackered and stained, bulging with bright dyed wraps, souvenirs and gifts.

Sandy, from London, expresses a view that many must share with her: 'I feel as though I have discovered so many new things about who I am and just how many more choices and options there can be in my life. I won't ever again be afraid of challenging myself.'

Mark, on his way back home to Australia, explains: 'After a long journey like mine I think I've begun to be more introspective. In some ways it's almost a journey in the mind rather than a journey in the world. It's almost as though the outer journey is in some ways superficial compared with the things that you are learning about yourself while you are travelling. I don't know what it is but whenever I go to leave India, no matter how fed up I am with the place I always tell myself that I've got to come back one more time.'

Caroline, from Devon, has found something here even if she can't quite put her finger on it: 'It's while you are here that you think, "Oh, my God, the Indians are so annoying and the buses are always so late and why does it take sixteen hours just to get to the next village?" and all this kind of stuff. But when you leave you say, "Oh, India, wonderful." So there must be something nice about it.'

David, from Dublin, has learnt to see things through others' eyes: 'The Indian people, some of them are very taxing but some are very beautiful. In the villages, some of the old men, their smile is really radiant, you know they've got a real twinkle in their eyes. When you are in that space with those people, you learn the things that they see.'

For me too it will be the memories of people that remain uppermost in my mind, moments shared with so many over the six months of my journey. There's an energy and optimism that I've discovered all along the road East, especially in

India, that is completely at odds with the conditions of most people's lives. And it's infectious. Indians in particular always seem to be able to make something out of nothing, to have a good attitude.

Only a few days ago, where the old steam trains drop down out of the Himalayas towards Calcutta, I came across Inspector Samir Maitra, a young customs officer, posted to what must be the Indian equivalent of Siberia. Immaculately turned out in fresh pressed khaki, moustache trimmed, hair oiled, he had placed his bench in the middle of a dusty village road, perhaps in the hope that there might be at least one car that day. I stopped to share a cup of tea with him and ask him about his life, about how he spends his time in such an isolated place.

'Actually, after my day's work, whenever possible,' he explains in clipped, crisply formal Indian English, 'when the sun is setting in the western horizon I listen to a wee bit of Beethoven or Schubert or Tchaikovsky, or a little bit of Wagner. Then I listen to Indian classical music also, indeed I practise Indian classical music as well. And thereafter I read the books. Of late I have decided to write a story about the background of this particular place, where I find people a motley crowd rather.'

But doesn't somebody so immersed in books and thoughts of another world ever get frustrated, living in such a remote place with so little opportunity and so little money to travel? Doesn't he wish he had the advantages of some of the foreigners he must meet?

'Well, the thing is that one has to accept reality in its crudest form. I quite well remember one of the poems by Alfred Tennyson that "I will drink life to the least of it, to pause is to die." It seems at times that I am pausing here and that that pause seems to be eternal. I really get tired of my shadow. But of course I don't find myself jealous of the foreigners. I am not a learned man to such a degree where I can suffer from despair or frustration. I must try to create a world within me where I can be the monarch of all I survey, I must try to create something new. And that endeavour makes me ebullient with hope and joy and ecstasy all the time.'

So here I am, exactly where I ended thirty-three years ago, back among the chaos and the crush of downtown Calcutta. The traffic hurtling around me, the air thick with pollution, the noise almost unbearable. And I love it. The energy and optimism of it all. As for most of the travellers I have met, it has been a kind of pilgrimage, a chance to break all the old moulds, leaving me free to explore new options. But to be quite honest I never expected that it would change me to any great degree. I have not been in need, but I suppose I have always been searching. I feel driven by the same sense of curiosity and excitement that I had when I first ran away from home all those years ago. I am still

Overleaf: Life goes on along the banks of the River Ganges

thrilled by what I find, by what I learn, by what I experience - and by the people I meet. I can't imagine ever not feeling free to climb that hill, or follow that path. It's just that I never expected to find Dot. My work and my travels, or the combination of the two, have always enhanced my life and moved it along in different ways. But nothing has ever inspired and enriched me as much as meeting another person with whom I instinctively felt I could share my life and whose life I wanted to share. Only the freedom of a journey like this could have given me the chance to discover the touchstone in my world. And now, it's time to go home. My journey is complete.

'Calcutta, December 11, 1962

Dear M and D,

Well, here we are again, a bit overdue though, I'm afraid. I gather from your last letter that you are both well, and that things are fairly normal back in Fakenham. I am fit again and on the move.

There is one thing I must tell you though: don't keep saying 'hope to see you soon'. I'm not being nasty. I miss you very much and would love to be home again, especially for Christmas, but I've set my heart on this world trip and I can't turn back now. There is still, after this, Aussie, the Americas, Canada, Africa to see yet, and the months I have to work and travel soon add up to years. It will not be more than five at the outside though. That's only if I don't get sick of travel though. As soon as I have found out what I am looking for, learnt what I want to learn, filled my desire for knowledge, I'm coming straight home, no worry ...

...Well I will start winding up. I will write again before Christmas, but just in case, keep smiling, fit and the animals well fed, the garden tidy, but don't overwork either of you.

Most important though don't worry about me, just think about me when you are eating your turkey and Christmas pud, or drawing your next pint. I intend to go to communion on Christmas day, then, I don't know what.

Love to all, hope to hear from you all soon. God bless you all and have a VERY HAPPY CHRISTMAS, and don't worry or fret about me.

Love from <u>your</u> son

SIMON
xxxxxxx'

EPILOGUE

'I shall be telling this with a sigh
Somewhere ages and ages hence:
Two roads diverged in a wood, and I -
I took the one less travelled by,
And that has made all the difference.'

Robert Frost (1875-1963) 'The Road Not Taken'

One month to go and pick grapes in the South of France had turned into six and taken me halfway round the world to India. While my parents seemed to have made a real effort to get used to the idea of my great global adventure, they were clearly not very happy that their sixteen-year-old son was abroad and on the loose. My letters had been infrequent and, although they had been colourful and informative enough, there wasn't much that might have given them the chance to track me down. That was, of course, the way I wanted to leave it. I had run away and at the back of my mind there was always the thought they might try and get me home and have my passport taken away because I was under age.

After my father's death in 1991 I discovered my letters in his safe, alongside several he had received from the Foreign Office and various British Embassies and High Commissions along my route east. The British High Commission in India, in a reply to an inquiry from my father dated October 1962, said I had been sighted in Dehli, was well, obviously capable of looking after myself and had plans 'to go further'. Passing reference was also made to the fact that I

apparently wanted to punt a raft across India to Calcutta - 'which we advised strongly against'.

It was the fear of losing my passport that helped me decide about the next step of my journey. By December 1962, I had arrived in Calcutta along with the three other English travellers who had been on the raft. India's wildest city was almost too much to take after all those weeks spent messing around on the river - but it soon made us forget the raft. Apart from that, there were only twenty-one shopping days (that's every day in India) left to Christmas. But the reality was that we had no money and the prospect of Christmas in Calcutta was actually neither white nor nice. After so long on the road, all of us were feeling homesick.

I was the baby of the bunch, the others in their early to mid-twenties, but somehow age didn't seem to be relevant when it came to being hungry, dirty or despondent. To be quite honest I just wanted to move on. I felt as though I had not yet made anything out of my journey and now I found myself being swamped by the collective down of us four ex-rafters. Mass hysteria was setting in. They all wanted turkey, steamed pud and presents for Christmas far more than I did!

The British Consul was eager to do business and get us off the streets. All we had to do, he told us from behind his ridiculously large and empty desk, was hand over our passports and sign a form saying we were penniless and wanted to be repatriated to the UK. Our parents would then be contacted and various other lives signed away guaranteeing that until all costs, like air tickets (and free lunches and stamp duties, no doubt), were repaid our passports would remain in the sticky hands of Her Majesty's Government. I couldn't believe it when the others decided to do it. It all seemed so humiliating and defeatist. I hadn't run away - and put my parents through all this drama - in order to slink back home on the coat-tails of the Foreign Office. And just to have Christmas lunch!

What else is there to say really? I didn't go near the consul again and swore the others to secrecy as to which Sikh temple we

were in. They thought I was mad. What was I going to do? Where was I going to go? With Burma closed to overland traffic, Calcutta was, in effect, the end of the road. But I had learnt to read a map by now and, while I still might have had only two O levels, I knew there was plenty of world left to see - and plenty of opportunities to find work and move on. I just had to go for it, and word was out that Bangkok was a good place to try.

I remember going with the other three to Calcutta airport. I forget the exact date, but it was some time towards the end of the second week in December. It was a wonderful starlit night, chilly even, and they were really excited about the thought of going home. I was feeling a bit small and alone - nervous, to be quite honest. I had got used to having some 'big boys' around - and friends too. I can see it now, as clear as I must have done then: the BOAC Comet taking off and arching its back, the pilot pulling the stick and easing the plane west, a dark shadow disappearing into the night, the pinprick lights of its windows finally fading. I remember waving. I might have even cried. But I tried not to think about it all too much: there were things to do and places to go.

Of course luck always has a part to play. And it was luck that helped me leap the next hurdle. It was the following morning that I found a job. With little more than a pound to my name I had been wandering down Chowringhee, the road that runs through the centre of downtown Calcutta, quite close to the Grand Hotel, and this man invited me into his shop for a cup of tea. I am ashamed to say I can't remember his name. I only remember his kindness: it was a week's work helping to paint his souvenir and jewellery shop and the

room above, which he wanted to use as an art gallery. He offered me a place to sleep on the floor and enough money to buy a one-way student ticket on Burma Airways to Bangkok. Christmas had come to Calcutta - and this was the best present I could ever have wished for.

I arrived in Bangkok on Christmas Eve, 1962. It was a new and startling world for me, and also bloody hot! I decided to get to the centre of the city, find a park and take stock. Of the twenty-two shirts my mother had packed for me, there was only one left - and I had only one pair of trousers too. I opted to save my last 50p for Christmas lunch, found a quiet bush, rolled out my mattress cover and settled down to eat the sandwiches I'd nicked off Burma Airways. Christmas was a sparse affair - but it was a great day to make friends.

I had heard from some travellers in Delhi that the Thai Song Greet Hotel near the station in Bangkok was the place to go for good noodles and a chance to find work. It took me less than twenty-four hours to get myself some fee-paying students (from a local veterinary college) who wanted to learn English. From teaching English to vets I went on to proofread for a local newspaper, the *Bangkok World*, until its American editor taught me how to write and I became a sort of baby freelance journalist. Inspired and increasingly excited by journalism and the doors it opened, I moved to Laos, where in 1963 I started reporting for the *Daily Mail*, Reuters and, almost by mistake, for the venerable *New York Times*. In 1964, Reuters, thinking I was much older (my lie, not their mistake) sent me to Vietnam. I covered the war there for them for nearly two years.

The road to India had been my rite of passage, Thailand my school, Laos my college, Vietnam my university - and I had learnt hard, fast and well. I returned home in 1966 to find two very proud parents. When I saw them standing together rather awkwardly on the doorstep waiting to welcome me back after more than four years on the road, I knew it had all been worthwhile.

Thirty years or more later I started all over again. And that's the story you've just read.

Overleaf: I wonder if there's an airport near here?

INDEX

Bold page numbers refer to illustrations

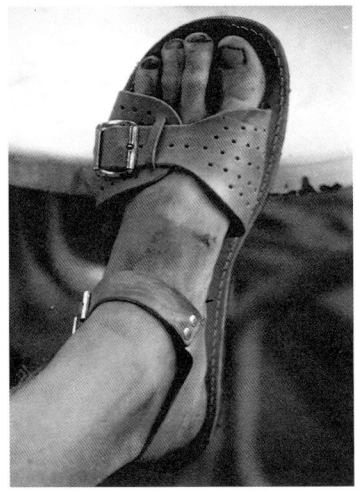